IN MEMORY
OF BREAD

In Memory
of Bread

A Memoir

Paul Graham

RC596.G73 2016
Graham, Paul, 1976-
In memory of bread : a
memoir
New York : Clarkson
Potter/Publishers, [2016]

Clarkson Potter/Publishers

New York

crownpublishing.com
clarksonpotter.com

CLARKSON POTTER is a trademark and POTTER with colophon
is a registered trademark of Penguin Random House LLC.

Library of Congress Cataloging-in-Publication Data
Names: Graham, Paul, 1976–
Title: In memory of bread : a memoir / Paul Graham.
Description: First edition. | New York : Clarkson Potter/
Publishers, [2016] | Includes bibliographical references and index.
Identifiers: LCCN 2015038555 | ISBN 9780804186872
(hardcover) | ISBN 9780804186896 (pbk.) |
ISBN 9780804186889 (ebook)
Subjects: LCSH: Food allergy. | Wheat-free diet.
Classification: LCC RC596 .G73 2016 | DDC 616.97/5—dc23
LC record available at http://lccn.loc.gov/2015038555

ISBN 978-0-8041-8687-2
eBook ISBN 978-0-8041-8688-9

Printed in the United States of America

Book design: Ian Dingman
Jacket design: Ian Dingman
Jacket photography: Mark Platt/Offset

10 9 8 7 6 5 4 3 2 1
First Edition

FOR BEC

I think it could be plausibly argued that changes of diet are more important than changes of dynasty or even of religion.

—George Orwell, The Road to Wigan Pier

Contents

INTRODUCTION

When I was thirty-six, I suddenly became a drastically differ-ent kind of eater. A genetic predisposition caused my immune system to stop responding to wheat and other glutenous grains as it always had. Instead of sustenance, they were poisons.

For a while I did not perceive any difference. Then severe illness jolted me out of my routine. When I recovered, I found myself in a strange place. It was as if a sinkhole had opened beneath an impor-tant part of my life and irretrievably consumed it. I had been an avid home cook and amateur beer brewer; these were the leisure activities that helped me define my place in the world, the things that I enjoyed most with my wife and close friends.

Overnight, I ceased to be someone who could enjoy bread, pizza, beer, and many other foods of cultural and personal importance—at least in the ways I had always experienced them. In a sense, I was no longer the same person. I was like an amateur athlete who tears up her knee and will never be the same runner, or an equestrian who de-velops an allergy to horses, or a proud homeowner sickened by some substance in his house. I was not, thankfully, making my living in food, but I had long equated good food with good living.

Few if any human activities are as natural and habitual as eating. In fact, it is precisely because cooking and eating food are essential to our survival that we lose sight of how much of our identity we ex-press at the table. We sit down three times a day, if we are fortunate, to eat what tastes good to us, what we can afford, and what we were taught to cook. Our meals focus on satiety, or so it seems. But the core of who we are, where we came from, and what we believe is often (if not always) on the plate in some way, whether dinner came out of the freezer section or the garden.

The changes in my daily routine were predictable, but I could not have anticipated the social or emotional changes, nor the differences in how I would relate to both my own past and, more broadly, human history. And I did not foresee my resilience, or the way longing—the poor cousin of necessity—can be a path to inspiration.

Eventually, I did learn these things. Changing how I cooked and ate altered how I saw myself in the world. And so, once again, the table seemed almost—if not completely—full.

LAST MEALS

A winter several years ago will forever be the time when I discovered the intense yet simple pleasures of great homemade bread.

As with most transformative experiences, the timing was everything. My wife started baking in January, after one of our friends introduced her to *Artisan Bread in Five Minutes a Day*. Its basic recipe, as *Artisan* devotees know, makes baking bread with a chewy crumb and shattering crust tantalizingly easy: you mix up a mess of dough, let it age in the fridge, and pull out handfuls to shape, let rise, and bake whenever the urge for a fresh loaf strikes. I often stepped inside—from walking the dog or carrying firewood, leaving behind a blanched sky and snow that literally blew sideways—to hot bread waiting on the wire rack. The windows were steamed over; the whole house bloomed with heat. What I felt was beyond anticipation or joy—it was a sense of wealth and gratitude that humans have known for a long, long time. I couldn't have contrived this feeling if I tried, and it had everything to do with the smell and taste of baked grains against northern New York's cold, sparse background.

As she explored the cookbook, Bec made whole-wheat loaves, white loaves, cheddar cheese bread, dinner rolls, cinnamon buns, and my favorite, limpa, a Swedish rye seasoned with orange peel, star anise, cumin, and sugar. At first she baked one or two a week. I tore off chunks while they still steamed from the oven. In the afternoons, I made a cup of tea with toast and chose a jar from "The Vault," a hutch in our dining room stacked with homemade preserves like brandied melon jam and crab-apple jelly. Every summer and into the fall, Bec puts up seasonal fruits and vegetables she gets from the market and our farm share, and (in the case of the crab apples, anyway) that we forage on the college campus where I teach English. By most estimates, you only have a year or two to eat that stuff. I was doing my part in the race against spoilage.

Sometimes, I ate a loaf in a day.

Once or twice, I may have eaten almost *two* loaves in a day—most of ours, and then most of our friends' when we went over to their place for dinner, where the talk, which always turned to food, inevitably gravitated to our helplessness around this bread.

Geography was a factor in our raptures. We live in a rural place, and at the time the sole good nearby bakery was attached to our local food co-op. We had been enjoying the co-op's loaves for years, but the *Artisan* bread was even better, and more fun. We loved the ingenious substitution for the steam jets in professional ovens, which involved pouring a cup of boiling water into a preheated sauté pan, creating a dramatic hiss. When we took the bread out and it hit the cooler air, we bent close to the counter and listened as the crust tightened with a series of crackles. But most of all, we loved the sweet, comforting smell of bread baking away as the temperature dropped and we turned local root vegetables into soups and stews.

If we and our friends were conscious of the symbolism of "breaking bread" at these meals, nobody ever mentioned it. And yet, I think if you'd asked any of us whether the experience would have been diminished without my friend David's triumphant soda bread, or without my friends Sarah and Mere's perfect airy, white loaves, or without whatever fifty-times-better-than-supermarket bread anyone else had made, we would have said, *Yes, of course.* Now I know that to be the truth. You can have fellowship over any meal, but sharing bread seems to deliver an especially high emotional return for a simple food. Bread has always inspired such excitement, even reverence, in those who have so much as stood near a fresh loaf.

In those days I had no reason to feel guilty or wary about my bread consumption. I did not obsess over calories or carbs, preferring to believe that if you're eating good food, whole food, and frequently moving your body, the math all works out in the end. I'll immediately add, however, that until genetics came calling, I had been one of those annoying types who never had to think about what they ate—or did not eat. In retrospect I see that I was consuming a ton of gluten. But I didn't know then that gluten could be a problem for me. I didn't think that gluten could be a problem for anyone, actually, until one day when I heard someone, a student of mine or a colleague, mention her dietary restrictions. I registered this person's pain distantly. (As a friend would later say to me, "All I know is that I'm glad I don't have what you've got.") I certainly did not yet understand that those who cannot tolerate wheat struggle against a tradition so long and so deep that some anthropologists believe that by now, the desire for grain in general, and bread in particular, is all but "hardwired" into people of European and Middle Eastern ancestry.

Bec registered the staggering speed at which I was consuming her bread. It took her time to make, she said, and it'd be nice if now and then a loaf could hang around the house longer than a day and a half. In response, I might have pointed out that ancient Egyptian temple officials, instead of being paid in cash, received a share of 900 fine wheat breads, 36,000 flatbreads roasted in coals, and 900 jugs of beer *per year,* if the archaeological records are to be believed. (That's 3,000 flatbreads a month, and you haven't even drunk the beer yet.) Surely these officials were feeding their huge families, servants, and slaves. But they still had a few flatbreads left over for themselves. Against such impressive consumption, my own looked modest, even pitiful.

.   .   .

Speaking of 900 jugs of beer: At about the same time as the *Artisan Bread* discoveries, my friend David and I began brewing beer. In this way, our homes were not unlike those of the ancients, who baked their bread and brewed their beer in adjacent rooms, often using the yeast in the beer scum (known in some places as "barm") to inoculate their bread dough.

That's not how our beer project came about, though. David is a volcanologist, schooled in the geology of small-scale environmental apocalypses, and thus concerned with living in a way that is as gentle on the environment as possible. He believed that home-brewed beer could be as good as most commercial brews, and also more ecologically sound: less gasoline used in transport, less refrigeration at the store, less packaging in the recycling bin. We set out to start our own school of sustainability—green hedonism. Our goal was to become completely self-sufficient in the beer department. The challenge was that David could drink a lot of beer. I had a lower tolerance but still put in a respectable effort.

We started in March by putting up five gallons of American-style amber ale from a kit. We boiled the wort and added hops, cooled it, pitched our yeast, and left our beer to ferment in a sterile and air-locked five-gallon bucket. After a week we added two ounces of Cascade hops, a common American varietal, and let it continue to ferment. Then we bottled our ale and waited for it to age. Finally, in May, we sat on David's "deck"—the flat roof of the porch below his second-story duplex, which we accessed by climbing through a window—and watched the sun set over the trees as we emptied the bottles over two or three weekends. Quite often we accompanied our beer with some cheese and, naturally, a fresh loaf of bread.

By midsummer, we had twenty-five gallons of beer—a couple hundred bottles—in some stage of the brewing process. The five-gallon carboys burped and fizzed with a new pale ale in fermentation, while bottles of stout and porter hibernated like black bears in the back of my walk-in pantry. We felt giddy with beer-wealth. The ATF had probably begun watching us. We could see the day coming when we would possess a mix of seasonally appropriate beers that we'd need only to go into the cellar or the pantry or the garage or the upstairs closet to retrieve.

Any home brewer will tell you that it's tradition, and good karma, to drink beer while you make beer. For us, it was also a practical necessity; every time we bottled a batch, we needed to empty some bottles. Ordering additional bottles from the home brew company, we thought, would just be stupid. Carbon would be generated in shipping them to us, killing the ethos of our project. If we were short six bottles for the new beer, we drank beer until we had the room. If one twenty-two-ounce tallboy would get the job done, we split it. It was important to check up on the previous batches, too, measure their progress, see how much longer they had to age.

When I woke up one morning in September following one of these brew-fests feeling a little off—not hungover exactly, but slightly food-poisoned—I first thought, *We didn't sanitize those bottles right.* It can get tricky, brewing when you're a little crocked. But David's good health suggested that the beer was not the problem. I did not know it yet, but I'd been paying attention to ABV (alcohol by volume) and IBUs (international bitterness units) when I should have been paying attention to PPM (parts per million)—of gluten.

I was in the early stages of a massive flare-up of celiac disease, an inherited autoimmune syndrome that leads the body's innate immune response to destroy healthy tissue in the small intestine when the person ingests gluten protein (which is technically two proteins, gliadin and glutenin). We most commonly consume gluten in the form of wheat and barley, though rye and spelt also contain gluten, as can oats, via cross-contamination in processing. The bread and the beer, though delicious, constituted a carpet-bombing of my gastrointestinal tract. Estimating my gluten consumption around that time is difficult, but some days I was probably taking in 50,000 PPM. A person with celiac disease should preferably have an intake of zero PPM gluten, though the definition of "gluten-free" has for a long time been 20 PPM because that was the lowest concentration the available technology could measure. More sensitive tests now exist, but 20 PPM remains the threshold of toxicity in the FDA's 2014 ruling on the definition of "gluten-free foods." Recent studies have found that level to be safe for people with celiac disease.

My GI symptoms—the bloating, gurgling, and diarrhea—came and went without any pattern until Thanksgiving, when they came to stay, and became uncontrollable. I felt as if something were rotting inside me, just below my navel. I was grateful that the university was on Thanksgiving break so I could focus on recuperating from what I thought was a stomach flu. I was feverish, my temples throbbed, and at times my blood pressure seemed to be so high that I could hear a whirring in my ears. One day I remembered that I had experienced the same symptoms a few years earlier, and a course of antibiotics had cleared it up. My doctor couldn't see me until after Thanksgiving, though. Until then, I would try to stay hydrated, eat gentle foods like toast and saltines, scale back on my activities, and ride out the infection.

The Sunday after Thanksgiving, I ate what I now think of as the first of my last meals. It's probably more accurate to call them "meals of lasts," but that phrasing is awkward, and it undercuts what was to come—which, for a person who loves food, was a type of death.

With our family obligations for the holiday over, Bec, my co-brewer David, his wife Mere, and I sat down to a dinner of Thanksgiving leftovers and special cheese—Rogue Creamery's Caveman Blue—that David and Mere had brought back from a recent trip. I did not feel well at all, but the spread was too fabulous to pass up. Bec made a loaf of limpa, and there was a white loaf and table water crackers to go with the cheese, and plenty of homemade cranberry chutney, applesauce, turkey, dressing, roasted Brussels sprouts, and pumpkin pie. I also seem to remember some cinnamon rolls left over from breakfast. The best part of this feast was that we didn't eat in the traditional order. We just put all of the dishes in the middle of the table and took whatever we wanted as the Stones blared from the kitchen and the smell of wood smoke wafted from the stove in the living room. We accompanied it with some ales David and I had recently brewed. For me, this was the real Thanksgiving: a casual meal of good food with friends, no traditional holiday script or menu to follow, and no stress. My gut was enraged, but I tried to ignore it.

Later in the evening, David and I took down two tallboys of Irish stout. When we pulled the cap off, we received our first good sign, that *fsst* which means the priming sugar took and the beer isn't flat. I needed only one sniff to know we'd nailed the brewing and the aging. The body was rich and malty, the head looked creamy and thick, and there wasn't a trace of greenness in the finish. We passed the tallboys around and everyone poured a glass, admiring our greatest brewing triumph yet.

I struggled through half of mine, then pushed the glass aside.

"Stomach's a little farked," I said to David, borrowing one of his Australianisms.

The stout was the last I ever drank. The bread stuffing, the crackers, the salty, pungent blue cheese (which can contain gluten because the inoculation of bacteria comes from moldy bread that is grated into a fine powder and then sprinkled on or injected into the cheese)—these, too, were lasts.

I had one more crack at piecrust and bread a few days later, because our friends Sarah and Cory had been away from town and missed the feed; so we did Thanksgiving a third time, as brunch at Sarah's house. Even though by that point my body seemed to be in a full-scale revolt—I'd stopped running and working out, stopped cooking, and had to struggle through my work and chores—the food on Sarah's table forced me, once again, to rise to the occasion. I also didn't want anyone to think anything was seriously wrong, though two weeks of GI trouble were beginning to show on my face as a combination of pallor and a blank stare. I tried to enjoy the quiche Lorraine, frittata, crêpes filled with preserves and cheese, and what must have been about three pounds of bacon and sausage from our friends at 8 O'clock Ranch, who supplied our meat. I shared in the mimosas and coffee. I avoided the bacon and the sausage because I was wary of the meat on my delicate stomach. Instead, I ate more bread.

When I look back at those two meals now, I think, *At least I didn't blow it. Not bad for a farewell tour.* I ate the right foods in the right place with the right people—not mindlessly at a rest-stop along the road somewhere, or even in our own kitchen, by myself.

In between those two post-Thanksgiving meals, I had dragged myself to my doctor's small but busy practice. Most residents of the North Country, a region that stretches from Syracuse and Albany through the Adirondacks and north to the Canadian border, would agree that we lack stellar medical care. We have other things—farms and rivers and fishing, mountains and hiking trails and skiing, good universities, craftspeople, artists, and the tightest community I've known anywhere—but I had long felt that this is not the place a person wants to be during a serious health-related event. The nearest major hospital is two hours away. I had come to look at the medical situation a little naïvely, viewing it as one of the trade-offs that inevitably come with putting down roots in such a place. This was easy to do because Bec and I were young—both of us were thirty-six—and healthy, in large part thanks to her work as a personal trainer.

I left my doctor's office with a prescription for Cipro in hand, confident that in a few days I'd be back to eating spicy dishes, vegetables, and meat. It had cleared up my symptoms before. This time, though, the drug seemed to knock the infection back without clearing the symptoms up completely.

The longer the GI troubles dragged on, the more they affected everything, especially my love of cooking. I've always been an instinctual cook, more interested in preparing what shows up at the market—or, as I frequently put it, whatever the fridge wants me to cook—than working off of set recipes. For weeks I prepared simple, basic meals that I thought would be gentle: lots of pasta with olive oil, bland soup with saltines, and toasted bread with tea. In my mind, I was being good, making sacrifices; I wanted serrano chiles, roasted winter vegetables, chutneys over chicken and pork, coffee, whiskey, and wine. Our farm share piled up as I avoided using Brussels sprouts, cabbage, spinach, cranberries, and apple cider. I talked about a strange craving for a Reuben, which normally I did not want, because everything I ate was so bland.

The next time I saw my doctor, he was convinced that I was suffering from an especially virulent infection or a parasite: giardia, maybe, or *C. difficile*. He ordered more tests and put me on Flagyl, a more powerful antibiotic, which I took for two days while trying to ignore signs that I was allergic to it.

Finally Bec took me to the emergency room, where they hooked me up to monitors, gave me potassium and magnesium through a drip, and read the first of several scary blood panels. I was severely anemic, with a hemoglobin score of 7 (a healthy male's is around 15). My hematocrit and iron scores were low. My red blood cell data were poor. On paper I looked like a castaway who had been living on bark and berries for a month. The ER doctor wondered out loud how I could become so quickly depleted of iron reserves; well-fed Americans, he said, usually have enough to ride out a bad spell. Around midnight, they released me with iron supplements and another antibiotic, Bactrim.

I took the pills and ate the same gut-friendly foods, and continued to suffer and lose weight.

By now, the damage to my small intestine was approaching a state of decline known as complete villous atrophy. The tiny hairlike projections in the intestines (called microvilli) that absorb nutrients had been all but razed by the onslaught my immune system had made in the presence of gluten. I was digesting and absorbing almost nothing, and at night I was incontinent. The drop in weight sped up as I stubbornly clung to my routine, walking the dog despite my wife's objections, teaching classes, hauling wood. Neurological symptoms appeared next: twitches and tremors, irritability, an inability to think through complex questions and problems. I walked out of classes and meetings wondering what had just transpired; at home, I would sit nearly on top of our woodstove and still suffer chills.

I made one last trip to my regular doctor, who drew some blood, read results that were even worse than the last time, forced me to make eye contact, and told me he wanted to do a CT scan. He was worried about cancer. It took less than ten minutes for him to have a phone conversation with a doctor who represented the insurance company. This physician turned the CT scan down on the grounds that a case of the runs in a thirty-six-year-old with no previous medical history was not a good reason to blow a few thousand dollars on imaging. The best my doctor could do was make me an appointment with a gastroenterologist for the next week. Until then he wished me luck, and said that I should call back if my condition worsened.

2

The Perfect Immunological Trojan Horse

I eliminated many foods during that time, from coffee (which was painful) to spices, from cruciferous vegetables to acidic foods like tomato sauce. I eliminated alcohol and fats. But I never cut out bread, or pasta, or crackers. I told my doctor about my adjustments to my diet. I told friends and family. Nobody suggested that I stop consuming gluten. As awareness of gluten intolerance and celiac disease increases, some people who suffer from gastrointestinal symptoms are starting to suspect wheaten foods *first*, or at least they are including them on a list of usual suspects along with dairy, soy, legumes, and nuts. But I didn't have any suspects at all.

It turns out that I was repeating a mistake common throughout medical history, all stemming from what I have come to see as the culinary centrality, and the cultural symbolism, of wheat and bread in Western culture. There is evidence that for thousands of years, the loaf, the flatbread, and the bowl of porridge (or anything made of wheat, oats, barley, rye, and spelt) have been a huge pathological blind spot, and thus the perfect immunological (or, in the case of celiac disease, autoimmunological) Trojan horse.

By some estimates, the discovery, domestication, and cultivation of wheat and barley is the most profound event ever to have happened to humans, largely because it ushered in the practice of farming, which eventually led to population growth and presented the chance to diversify and specialize human activities. Gradually, after hunter-gatherers traded roaming for settlement, they began to make cities, pottery, and literature. (Our Neolithic-era ancestors found some unfortunate pastimes too, like making war.) Few foods can measure up to grain calorically, and its "bankability," or storage potential, allowed, for the first time, a single staple to support whole cities. In fact, the common agricultural practice since the start of farming has been for a group of people to select a few grains—like wheat and barley in the West, rice and millet in the East—and depend upon them, utterly, for the entirety of that society's history until something prompts a change.

Not surprisingly, the earliest wheat- and barley-based farming civilizations believed that these powerful grains were a gift from the gods. Ceres, the ancient Roman goddess of agriculture, provides the Latinate root of our word "cereal." Demeter (Greece) and Ninkasi (Sumeria) were worshipped for providing sustaining, sapid gifts to humankind, in particular bread and beer. Philosophers (Plato being the most famous example) argued about which kinds of grain and which preparations were best. And, until relatively recently, grain was rarely maligned. Throughout the Middle Ages and after, unscrupulous millers and bakers stretched flour and bread by adulterating it with ground bones, sawdust, and other inedible materials—but that was an ethical problem, not an epidemiological one. Widespread "panophobia" does not appear until the nineteenth century, though there were instances of it prior to then.[*]

---

[*] Among the proto-panophobes was one Simon-Nicolas-Henri Linguet, a public intellectual who—in response to the public outcry in *ancien régime* France over bread scarcity and inflated prices that helped to fuel the French Revolution—revealed in a letter to his physician the earliest first-person evidence of celiac disease, or at least gluten intolerance, that I've encountered: "I have observed from the time I was a child that bread has always disagreed with me; only [bread] in however little quantity I ingested it, always gave me acidity, genuine indigestions." On the basis of his own aversion, Linguet deduced that the French populace's obsession with bread scarcity was overblown. Gluten never had a chance to kill Linguet, however; he was guillotined in Paris in 1794.

One of the more striking examples of bread's privileged status can be found in the history of ergotism, an illness caused not by gluten, but by a toxic fungus that infests rye. Eaten primarily by the poor in northern Europe and Russia, rye was consumed more widely when famine struck and other staples were scarce. As with celiac disease, ergotism symptoms varied from person to person (and even by region). In Limoges in 857, Gauls who ate ergotic rye bread and porridge suffered from a burning sensation in their limbs, which then turned gangrenous and rotted off before they died. (The ancient Romans had known about ergot, but their knowledge seems to have been lost.) The disease was thought to be caused by malicious supernatural beings, not bad bread. When the healthy people who hadn't ingested the mycotoxins burned a nonconformist or three without stopping the spread of the disease, they turned to the Church for help; St. Anthony's Fire, as the disease came to be known, took its name from the monks of that order, who had some success with cures. Suspicion of demonic possession as the cause of sickness and weird behaviors persisted through the Dark Ages and into the Enlightenment, where spikes in witch trials correlate to years of poor climatic, harvest, and economic conditions—all of which would have led people to eat ergotic bread. A combination of scientific understanding and the increasing stability of food supplies—brought about by the spreading popularity of potatoes and corn, and better grain yields—gradually reduced the incidence of ergotism. By the twentieth century, ergot had been eradicated from the bread supply everywhere except Russia, where symptoms persisted as late as the 1930s.

Wheat took longer to be connected to illness than rye, in part because gluten toxins, unlike mycotoxins, do not cause a person (thankfully) to bark like a dog, bang his head against a wall, or behave as if he has been dabbling in witchcraft. The first known description of celiac disease comes from the ancient Greek physician Aretaeus of Cappadocia, who was believed to have lived in the first century AD.

Other physicians of his era may also have observed the sudden onset of gastrointestinal distress, lethargy, and malabsorption, but Aretaeus gets the credit for naming the disease after the Greek word for "belly" (*koiliá*). We know that he was most likely seeing celiac disease instead of some other condition in his patients because of the specific type of diarrhea they presented: fatty and foul-smelling, which is consistent with malabsorption. The leavings of such patients would have undergone a characteristic process of putrefaction and fermentation in the gut, instead of digestion.

Aretaeus also appears to have noted the disease's cyclical nature: "[Celiac affection] is a very protracted and intractable illness; for even when it would seem to have ceased, it relapses without any obvious cause, and comes back even upon a slight mistake." This is a pretty accurate description of what I experienced around Thanksgiving, when I coasted for half a day on rice and bananas, and then, depressed, pissed-off, and hungry by late afternoon, treated myself with a slice of toasted white bread with butter, cinnamon, and raw sugar. Almost immediately, the symptoms returned with a ferocity that made me whimper. Though his observations were astute, Aretaeus missed the cause, blaming, instead of wheat or barley, a reduction of "heat" in the intestines, which he believed could be caused by something as simple as a "copious drink of cold water."

Aretaeus's writings appeared to have been lost until a nineteenth-century London pediatrician named Samuel Gee, who could read Greek, came across them while researching treatments for children with chronic (and similarly putrefied) diarrhea. Gee has been credited as the first to observe that diet was the most important factor in maintaining the children's health. However, Gee could not pinpoint the exact dietary cause of malabsorption. He eliminated milk when he noticed that the children could not tolerate it (which is typical of those with compromised GI tracts, as casein proteins can be difficult to break down), and prescribed raw meat, but he allowed them slices of toasted bread. He paid close attention to a child who improved "upon [eating] a quart of the best Dutch mussels daily," yet failed to figure out why the child's health declined when mussel season ended. (Gee had hoped to observe the child again the next year during mussel season, and was dismayed to find that the boy "could not be prevailed upon" to repeat the diet.) Notably, physicians in many places, including the United States, were struggling with the same questions at about the same time. Another pediatrician, Sidney Haas, famously observed the positive effects of a banana diet, one of many specialized diets prescribed in the early twentieth century.

The most commonly circulated—and apparently inaccurate— story about the discovery of wheat's ability to be harmful takes place during the *Hongerwinter* (Hunger Winter), or Dutch Famine, in the Netherlands in 1944, when a German blockade cut off supplies to cities in the western part of the country. An unusually harsh winter and a devastated infrastructure of roads, bridges, rail lines, and docks worsened conditions. It is estimated that 4.5 million people were affected by the winter food shortages, and 22,000 perished, many of them in the isolated highlands. Those caught in the famine were forced to supplement their meager rations with ingredients their poor ancestors had eaten whenever the wheat crops had crashed centuries earlier: chestnuts, acorns, and dried beans and peas.

Bread was especially hard to come by. Periodically the Allies managed to get supplies through, including flour from Sweden, which led to stories of bread being dropped from airplanes. It's a compelling image—hungry people standing in the frozen fields, faces and arms uplifted to packages descending from parachutes in a blue sky smeared with oily exhaust. Even the name of the endeavor, Operation Manna, conjures "manna from heaven." However, the people received flour, not baked bread, and it reached them in slower, more mundane ways.

According to the popular account, whenever bread did reach a certain group of Dutch children and their families, a Dutch pediatrician,

Dr. Willem-Karel Dicke, took notice. Dicke observed that the recurrence of GI symptoms and mortality rate among his patients was tied to the ebb and flow of bread consumption—essentially, to the resumption and cessation of a forced elimination diet. When flour arrived and bread could be made, the well-meaning parents offered it to their children instead of eating it themselves. The affected (intolerant) children got sick, and then improved when the rations were once again exhausted. However, other sources, including Dicke's wife, claim that he had suspected bread and wheat as the cause of malabsorption in his pediatric patients since at least 1932, and had experimented with wheat-free diets between 1934 and 1936, nearly a decade before the famine. Instead of providing a breakthrough, the conditions of the *Hongerwinter* allowed Dicke to further probe his hypothesis. Following the conclusion of the war, Dicke published his theory that wheat appeared to be the cause of the digestive maladies in these children. In the second half of the twentieth century, his hypothesis was confirmed by advances in medical technology—especially serology, imaging, and biopsy.

I didn't have to wait long to find out what would happen after my insurance company denied me a look at what was happening in my gut. Later that same day, I developed a GI bleed. The sight of blood in the toilet was alarming, and I returned to the ER. The attending physician was almost chipper when I recounted my full story, especially the part about the rejected CT scan.

"Well, now they'll *have* to pay for it," he told me, "because you came through the ER."

Bec and I anxiously awaited the CT results, which showed no signs of tumors. Instead, my entire abdomen was swollen with fluid. It was as if my gut had completely crashed, and what little I had eaten and the great quantity of water I'd drunk in an attempt to stay hydrated were just sitting stalled in the pipeline. Past this, though, nobody seemed to have any idea what was wrong with me.

The doctor told me I wasn't going home, and I didn't resist. I let them wheel me up to a room, weigh me—I'd dropped twenty-five pounds—and hook me up to IVs. If I had not been so fogged, exhausted, and ill, I would have been exasperated at my inexplicable physical breakdown, but I'd reached the point that every sick person eventually reaches, where I only wanted answers. The gastroenterologist took one look at me the next morning and said he suspected several conditions, from celiac disease to colitis or Crohn's. He needed to do a colonoscopy and an upper endoscopy to diagnose me (the first of many times I heard this joke, apparently an industry standard: "Don't worry, we use different scopes!"). Before he was willing to do those tests, though, I needed two blood transfusions and time for my body to respond to them. They weren't comfortable putting me under in my current state.

With nothing more to do but let the fluids run into me and listen to music, I often found my thoughts turning to food during the three days I was hospitalized. I'd once joked to my wife that hospital offerings would finish me off before whatever malady had landed me there. Now death-by-bad-food seemed a legitimate possibility. Every day at seven in the morning, noon, and five, the Chuckwagon, as I called it, banged through the hallway and its driver, the Chucklady, dropped off a brown tray with plastic dishes that looked almost as uninviting as what they contained: Jell-O, a broth so funky I couldn't tell whether it was vegetable, beef, chicken, or none or all of those, and weak coffee. I couldn't bring myself to taste the broth, which was a good thing: I later learned that some commercial bouillon cubes and packets, including the cheaper, institutional-grade bouillon, contain gluten in the form of wheat starch or soy sauce. This was one of many examples of how gluten is ubiquitous, able to fly under the radar, so to speak, and sicken people in a stealthy way. I was in a hospital; I was a

GI patient; the doctor suspected celiac disease; and still, in the broth, gluten might have lurked. I sipped the bitter coffee black and traded up for ginger ale. I poked at the Jell-O. Then I set them all aside.

My second night there, our friends Sarah and Cory snuck in some homemade beef broth. It was the first time in almost a month that I tasted and enjoyed food, and wanted more. I had actually asked Sarah for it, a request that still bothers me a little, now, because broth is not at all a simple gift to bring a sick person, not if you're making it the right way. And Sarah had indeed done it the right way, using aromatics, root vegetables, and marrow bones from Cory's mother's cow. I did not ask how long it took her to make; I opened the flask and gulped it down, ignoring everyone's requests to pace myself. The broth was deep and meaty, and Sarah had remembered to be generous with the salt. It remains one of the most satisfying meals I've ever had. The fact that I could see a Thermos of beef stock as a meal, that my body and my mind responded to it, was one of the first murky signs that I was going to be okay.

After the bags of blood and electrolytes paved the way for the dual scopes; after all the tests; after boredom and fatigue gave way to a feeling of imprisonment that led me to attempt to get myself thrown out of the hospital—by wandering my floor when Bec wasn't there, incoherently shooting the shit with anyone who would listen to me, making unsuccessful breaks for fresh air via the elevator, and running in place until the nurses finally relented and removed my monitors— after all this, the Chucklady surprised me with a full lunch of solid food. Beneath the covered dishes was a bacon-turkey whole-wheat wrap with mayonnaise and greens, a bag of chips, some fruit, and a chocolate pudding topped with the same nitrogen-propelled faux whipped cream that my brother and I used to shoot directly into our mouths when we were kids (and into each other's: "Here! You do me!"). The Chucklady set the tray down with a triumphant smile and a little ceremony. She thought this spread signified progress, convalescence, and hope.

The nurse, who was kind but tired of my insistence that I was not the pathetic fool I seemed to be, came in on the Chucklady's heels.

"The doctor says that if your system can tolerate this, you can go home."

I thanked her, waited for her to leave, took a bite of the sandwich, and immediately got a bad feeling. It was the first time my body, completely detoxified of gluten by the *gallon* of laxatives I'd had to drink for the scoping, sensed something poisonous. I hadn't been diagnosed, and I did not know yet to avoid gluten, but I knew an aversion when I felt one. I also knew that moving from a diet of clear liquids right to processed meat was stupid. But the doctor making rounds that morning was dangling freedom on the other end of lunch.

I called Bec, who was taking care of some things at the house. I told her what had happened. There was a long pause, which I knew took the place of an expletive.

"He *what?*"

"I can go home if I eat it," I repeated. "The thing is, I don't want it."

"He sent you *bacon?*"

"And turkey. Mayo, too. And chips." I was thoroughly pleased to be throwing this guy to the wolves. He was the hospitalist on duty, and he'd made me his enemy that morning when he repeatedly asked, with more insistence each time, whether I'd been tested for HIV.

"Well, whatever you do," Bec said, "don't eat any of it. I'll bring you something."

"I kind of already ate some. Because I want to go home."

She told me to sit tight. She'd be there in a little while with food that wouldn't kill me. Did I flush the sandwich to make it appear that I'd eaten it? I seem to remember doing this, but I cannot be sure.

The meal was one of the most questionable decisions made by my physicians in several weeks of them, especially given the range of possible diagnoses. Nobody in the hospital appeared to be communicating clearly except for my wife and me. There are days when I still bristle at that doctor's judgment, though in the end I've come to see all of those who examined me as contemporary variants of Samuel Gee, or Aretaeus, or even Willem-Karel Dicke before the Nazis starved the Dutch into eating chestnuts and beans, thus proving that bread can be very bad for some people (truly an odd legacy of the German Occupation). Although I admittedly lack a medical degree, I too was assiduously searching for answers online—and I didn't do any better than they did.

I'm not certain a doctor someplace else would have immediately diagnosed me accurately, either. Celiac misdiagnoses are common. Some estimates put the average time from first presentation of symptoms to final diagnosis at four to ten years in the United States—which is a long time to be suffering. Most physicians and researchers working on the disease will quickly argue that the medical community has only recently learned to screen for it. Complicating the process is the idiosyncrasy with which the disease can present itself; more than three hundred symptoms have been associated with celiac disease, the most common clustering around gastrointestinal distress and malabsorption. Getting it wrong isn't cheap, either; misdiagnoses can lead to medical expenses that average around four thousand dollars, between insurance payouts and premiums, over a period of four years. I hit the jackpot with a $24,000 bill, most of which was, fortunately, covered by insurance.

I left the hospital that afternoon twenty-five pounds lighter than I'd been at Thanksgiving three weeks prior, with edema in my legs from the massive amounts of fluids I had received, and still no answers. My discharge papers did not list celiac disease; they listed a GI bleed and recommended a diet of clear liquids to which I could add as (or if) I showed progress. Nobody sent me home with instructions to eliminate wheat, barley, or gluten. I think everyone, especially Dr. Sandwich, expected to see me back at the ER in a few days.

It nearly happened. Over the weekend, in order to bring a little cheer into an otherwise dreadful month, Bec hosted her annual Christmas cookie exchange. I heartily endorsed it. My system was totally cleansed, and even though I wasn't physically hungry, in an emotional sense I was *hungry*. All of the women who attend this annual event can bake, and not just a little. They're tempering chocolate, fearlessly blending sweet and savory, making strange and wonderful confections from the countries they've traveled to or lived in. I ate a few cookies, and then a few more, and quickly felt the familiar despair return. Something about my mental state, probably a diminished capacity to think owing to exhaustion and malnutrition, once again kept me from connecting my discomfort to wheat. It seems so obvious now.

I was so out of it when my follow-up with the gastroenterologist arrived a few days later that I could barely get myself seated on the exam table. And yet, Dr. Song seemed oddly pleased to see me.

"So I have good news and bad news for you," he said, the delivery sounding, as did the endoscopy joke, like another industry cliché. "Your condition is entirely curable. But you're not going to like the cure."

The test results revealed celiac disease with "99-percent certainty." The biopsies of my intestinal tissue put the damage to the microvilli between Marsh III and Marsh IIIb (the Marsh scale is a staging rubric for the histopathology of celiac disease), a state that looks flattened, like a city that has been firebombed. The blood tests taken in the hospital showed high levels of gluten antibodies even though I'd eaten very little gluten then.

The cure sounded ridiculously simple. All I had to do, he said, was stop eating gluten. If I cut out wheat, rye, barley, spelt, and oats, I would recover. (Oats, while they don't contain gluten, are often processed at plants that also handle barley and wheat; even gluten-free oats, however, can cue an immune response in some people with celiac disease because of similarities between the avenin protein in oats and the gliadin and glutenin proteins in wheat. I turned out to be one of those who cannot have oats at all.) Notably, Dr. Song did not name actual *foods*. He did not say, "Sir, brace yourself. You will never have a slice of real bread ever again, nor will you have a bottle of real beer, a real cookie, or a real pizza." Rather, if I avoided those *ingredients*, those *agricultural commodities*, I would most likely see a full recovery. He stressed that the dietary change was the only treatment available to me. If I followed it, I would improve in time. If I didn't follow it, more serious complications, like lymphoma, could ensue. Full recovery and healing usually take a few years; it would depend upon the damage and how "compliant," as he put it, I was with the gluten-free diet. In the meantime, Dr. Song sent me home with a prescription for iron supplements and a handout on celiac disease. He pointed out that there was a celiac support group in town; if I'd been capable of listening closely, I would have understood that this fact augured darkness on the horizon.

In the car, on the way home, I said something like, "Well, shit."

"Of course," Bec said, "I will do this with you."

She meant the gluten-free diet. She was not answering a question but preemptively declaring a truth, as if it were plainly written in the snowy fields. She loved me; she sensed that it would be hard; she believed that we were in this together. I can't remember what I said in reply, but nothing, then or now, seems a fitting answer to such generosity.

Neither of us, however, truly understood at the time what this diagnosis would mean. We were not giving up milk, or meat, or even coffee. We were stepping out of Western civilization's most important culinary and agricultural tradition. We were about to go back in time as eaters, to a period before the invention of leavened bread; when, technically speaking, "bread" could be made out of anything that a cook might grind, mix with water, and griddle into a hotcake. We were about to visit the sad and squalid pockets of eating history, getting by, or attempting to, with what have been described as "breads of poverty." Along the way we would make discoveries both disastrous and delicious as we battled—against withdrawal first, and then absence—with ingenuity, innovation, and a shit-ton of rice.

3

WHEAT EXILE

I know the very last gluten-based food I ever ate—by which I mean intentionally, not by accident or by "getting glutened" (celiac-speak for poisoned) at the hands of an unknowing or careless person, or even a well-meaning friend. This was my third last meal, the last stop on my farewell tour-du-wheat.

I remember it well because the same day Dr. Song stamped my celiac passport, I drove to our health-food store, Nature's Storehouse. I was filling a basket with yogurt, coconut, aloe vera juice, slippery elm powder, and some other natural remedies that the owner had recommended for ravaged GI tracts,* when the idea occurred to me. I texted Bec and told her I'd be just a little longer. Keeping in touch was part of the deal, in exchange for letting me get back behind the wheel. We both knew I shouldn't have been driving, but she didn't have the heart to clip my wings, and the store was less than a mile from home.

She should have grounded me, because after my shopping I drove

---

* Did these natural remedies work? It's tough to say for sure, but only the yogurt, which I couldn't tolerate yet, seemed to hurt me. I had entered into a mental space I never thought I'd go, one where scientifically unproven treatments seemed completely legitimate, and no potential cure sounded too strange or unpalatable: a breakfast of rice grits with powdered marshmallow root and slippery elm powder, washed down with a glass of watery cactus pulp (that'd be the aloe juice), for example. It was the meanest, most desperate eating I've ever done.

across town to the pub in the Best Western hotel. I walked in and or-dered a Reuben sandwich and fries to go. Then I sat down and waited in the lobby while the order was being prepared. As I reclined by the gas fireplace, my head light and buzzing, I considered, distantly and vaguely, what I was about to do to myself.

Well? Why the hell not? What was one more day? How much worse could my gut get?

I had kept craving a Reuben for the several weeks I'd been sick. At odd moments of the day, apropos of nothing, I kept bursting out with "You know what I could really go for? A Reuben!" Bec always looked at me doubtfully; I didn't seem like a man who could handle a child's portion of applesauce. I behaved myself, holding to my bland diet of tea, rice, and toast. But in the midst of the Taste Desert, I had never forgotten about getting salt, fat, sour, and cream, all in one bite.

I should have just eaten the sandwich like I wanted to back in Novem-ber, I thought. *I should have eaten ten of them.* What had I gained by trying to placate my gut? Nothing.

When the order was ready, I paid and took it to the car. I unzipped my parka, opened the clamshell packaging, and ate the whole thing. I was breaking all the rules I usually worked so hard to honor; the ingredients of this last supper, if that's what it could be called, were processed and from no place that I could even pretend was local. God only knew where the corned beef came from, and how it had come to be "corned." I now also know that the industrial bread had been sta-bilized with vital wheat gluten, and there was likely additional gluten in the Russian dressing.

I ate without any mindfulness. I ate mechanically. Anyone glanc-ing inside the car would have seen a man whose face was utterly blank except for a few stray crumbs. And very white and sickly-looking, too. I was, I now realize, stress-eating. I'd never done anything like this before, but I was so out of my mind that I didn't even register the strangeness.

And yet, eating the sandwich also felt a little like getting even. A kamikaze valediction. I was going out on my own terms, in a blaze of gluten, not crawling away like some pathetic creature that had been beaten into submission without stealing one last bite. I felt like a badass—until remorse arrived. That took all of fifteen minutes. It was as if I'd swallowed a live grenade.

Though a little crippled, I still had enough foresight to take care of the evidence. I tossed the container into a public trash bin before I pulled away. I drove home with the windows open to disperse the smell of grease and rye toast even though it was twenty degrees and snowing. Thinking about it now, my final encounter with the Reuben even *sounds* shabby, like a food tryst, right down to the meet-up at the hotel bar. I told myself I had no regrets.

But I *did* have regrets. I should have ordered extra rye bread and a beer. Two beers.

I suffered through one more day of GI agony while Bec wondered over the cause. I should have told her, but I kept my secret because, by now, I was ashamed: of my stupidity, of my weakness, of the fact that I couldn't handle what I had just been told by my doctor, *and it wasn't even that bad.* I didn't have cancer; I didn't have Crohn's; nobody was going to have to snip away a piece of my colon. It was just an intolerance to gluten.

And had I enjoyed my Reuben?

Years later, I can't even remember what the sandwich tasted like. All I know is that it's impossible to get enough joy from one meal to sustain one's imagination for years. I had eaten takeout, that was all—and middle-of-the-road takeout at that. There are so many better foods that I might have chosen, but I didn't have immediate access to them, and anyway I don't think that desperately stuffing my face with a crusty baguette and brie, or homemade ravioli, or a slice of pie would have been any more sustaining.

In the coming years, I would ask almost everyone I know, *You're about to lose everything made of wheat, rye, barley, and oats—all of it, forever. What is the last food you eat?* Everyone has an answer. Everyone thinks it's a good one. Everyone is wrong.

Within a few days of that emotional train wreck, the most obvious symptoms of celiac disease abated just as Dr. Song had said they would. I had doubted whether I could really recover even a semblance of well-being simply by cutting out things made of wheat. I hadn't believed these foods could be harmful because nobody else seemed to think they were, and because wheat and gluten surrounded us, and I didn't see other people keeling over.

When I accompanied Bec to the grocery store for the first time since coming home from the hospital, I perceived that not just a few aisles, but complete zones of the food world, had suddenly ceased to apply to us. We walked past the bakery section, with its glass cases full of doughnuts and cakes, its faux–French market display of wicker baskets tipped on their sides, spilling heaps of not-very-good bread (but bread nonetheless), rolls, and muffins. We skipped the aisle with the rows and rows of snack bags stuffed with chips, pretzels, wafers, and puffs; bypassed the mosaic of cereal boxes with colorful panels of inane cartoon toucans, tigers, dinosaurs, cavemen, and bandits; avoided the granola and energy bars, crackers, the wall of pasta in every shape imaginable, prepackaged seasonings and soups, prepared meals, and the endless cookies and snack cakes that contained, collectively, enough sugary energy to propel a rocket into low orbit. And I couldn't even bring myself to look in the beer cooler. Our store had a gluten-free corner—it would be an exaggeration to call it an aisle—but we didn't investigate its offerings yet. I was still subsisting on clear broth.

None of these foods were, as I would learn to think of it, *for me.* Some of the international aisle still applied, as did the produce and dairy departments, but I estimated that well over half the grocery store was lost. And while most of it was processed junk that our great-grandparents would not recognize as food, let alone a Mesopotamian farmer grinding wheat flour millennia ago, many of them had formed the tastes of our childhoods: Oreos, Trix cereal, cookie-dough ice cream. They also comprised a garish world of convenience foods and guilty pleasures in the present. The more I thought about it, the more I felt as if I had been suddenly exiled from American food culture. Meanwhile my wife was expatriating herself, willingly turning in her passport to an entire world of food just to come along with me.

In fact, we had rarely eaten most of these processed foods, and hadn't brought them home in a long time. Doritos, SunChips, pre-packaged doughnuts, Mallomars: we'd nearly forgotten they existed. Same thing with imitation crabmeat (which contains gluten, believe it or not), Cheez-Its, and ramen. Not long after Barbara Kingsolver published *Animal, Vegetable, Miracle,* Bec and I became invested in community agriculture, shopping mainly at the farmers' market and living off our farm shares. Kingsolver's book, which was so inspirational to many people but tricky to imitate for a variety of reasons—including, most important, access to time and money—nonetheless awakened us to the joys of the agriculture community in our backyard. We were already ripe for conversion because of a cluster of books and authors we read at that time, including Michael Pollan and Wendell Berry. We extended our roots further into the North Country soil, and slowly transitioned to a heavily local diet. The "locavore movement" has its share of doubters with valid criticisms, but despite the long winters, local eating is easier in the North Country than in most places, provided you're fortunate enough to have the resources (money, knowledge, and time) it requires.

In the grocery store, though, I felt keenly that a locavore diet was different from an elimination diet. Philosophical inclination was different from medical mandate. As a locavore, I knew I could at least have a Dorito, or a handful of Nilla wafers, if I wanted to. Did a GF Nilla wafer exist? Did I even want to know?

When I finally began to absorb nutrients, I found that I could think more clearly. Questions started forming: Where the hell had this come from? Why had it come for me? And why *now*?

As far as I knew, I was the first person in my family to be diagnosed with celiac disease. Double-win: I was also the first in my circle of friends. When Bec and I went to visit our families in Maryland for Christmas, I sat at the kitchen table with my parents over a dinner of gluten-free lasagna (the Tinkyada noodles, which are made of brown rice and do the job credibly), and we struggled to recall anyone in the family who might have had celiac disease. None of us excels at genealogy or family history; those who did have passed on, taking with them stories and information that have only recently piqued my curiosity. I had always known that we were generally a healthy and long-lived group on both sides. The majority of my relatives suffered from the typical physical deterioration that comes with old age. Unclaimed by cancers or cardiac events or infectious diseases in their sixties and seventies, they went out peacefully in their eighties and nineties. Some had died of pneumonia or heart failure. There was not a confirmed celiac among them.

Nor could my parents remember hearing about a family member who had suffered from anything *like* celiac disease back when it might have been misdiagnosed as a stomach infection, an allergy, or an irritable bowel. Both sides of the family were big gluten-eaters, because both sides were cheap. Bread, pasta, and dumplings figured prominently on the family tables. As my mother tells it, her family featured few if any accomplished cooks. My father's mother cooked well, albeit with as much red meat, butter, sour cream, sugar, and even lard as possible, accompanying all of it with gluten in some form. The

Grahams packed away the cold pasta salads and beef Stroganoff over egg noodles and breaded pork chops and cookies. They appear to have made a concerted effort to avoid nothing except alcohol and chiles. I did, however, recall a family joke about my paternal grandmother barking at my grandfather to "take a Tagamet!" whenever he felt uncomfortable, which must have been frequently enough for us to find fun in parroting her. That was my only clue, and it wasn't helpful.

"I wish it had been me, instead of you," my mother said to me, the implication here being that I still had half my eating life ahead of me, whereas she had eaten her fill. Of course this wasn't true.

I did not point out that there was still time for her to present celiac disease, if she was carrying the gene. Or for my father, God help his beer-loving soul. Three things must happen for a person to "get" celiac disease: they must have the genetic predisposition, in the form of the HLA (human leukocyte antigen)-DQ2 or -DQ8 immune-response gene; a trigger, possibly an environmental factor, has to activate the gene; and they have to be consuming gluten. The HLA-DQ2 and HLA-DQ8 immune-response genes are common: according to the University of Chicago Celiac Disease Center, about half the American population carries one of them. There is a one-in-twenty chance of developing celiac disease if a person has the DQ2 gene, and one-in-fifty in the event of DQ8. (This is why celiac disease is estimated to be the most common autoimmune disorder in the world.) What causes the gene to "turn on" remains a mystery. It might have to do with levels of gluten consumption, but just because I presented celiac disease at a time when I was eating so much bread and brewing so much beer doesn't necessarily mean that the baking and brewing *caused* celiac to occur, though some theories about causation say that my dietary habits might have been a key factor.

Dr. Song had told me in his office that diagnosis used to come most frequently in a person's fifties or sixties, often after a physical or emotional trauma (I had suffered neither). Recently, however, better testing and awareness have led people of all ages, including infants, to be diagnosed. The increased prevalence cannot simply be explained by improved screening, though. A recent study by the Mayo Clinic, which compared blood samples collected in the 1950s from young airmen to those of a contemporary cohort, suggests that the genetic predisposition for celiac disease is more widespread in the American population than previously thought, and that the incidence has climbed by fourfold in the last fifty to seventy years. For decades, Caucasians exclusively seemed to be prone to celiac disease (Swedes and Finns especially), but diagnosis rates have been increasing all over the world, including places where researchers once thought they'd encounter few if any cases, such as China.* Of all the statistics, perhaps the most alarming is the estimate that more than half (58 percent) of the people who have celiac disease are undiagnosed—sufferers of "silent" celiac who do not experience overwhelming symptoms as I did, but who nonetheless are suffering from intestinal damage. This means that people in my family could in fact have had the disease without knowing it.

Outside of my parents, my brother was the most likely to be a carrier of the genetic predisposition. The chances of a first-degree blood relative like a brother or sister having the gene if another sibling does is about one in twenty. (Other researchers have put the risk for first-degree relatives of celiacs as high as one in ten.) Like all genetic diseases and disorders, the emergence of celiac disease in a family can prompt some tough questions: Do the other family members get tested now, or later—if and when the symptoms start? Should a per-

---

* One particularly caustic article on the Web referred to celiac disease as the trendy condition for "rich white people"—a display of ignorance that underscores the need not simply for better awareness of the disease itself, but for better education in the latest research findings on the disease. While it's true that people of African and Latino descent are least likely to have the HLA-DQ2/8 markers, the disease affects far more groups than wealthy whites.

son like my brother go preventatively gluten-free, moderate a little, or eat and drink as much gluten as he can hold while his body can (apparently) still handle it? Should he take better care of himself in general, so as to minimize the stressors that may turn the gene on? Since that winter when my gut flamed out, no one else in my family has been tested. The genetic test involves only a mouth swab. And yet it seems, from conversations I've had with other celiacs, that many siblings do not want to know whether they have the genetic predisposition. They'd rather enjoy a full table until they present symptoms—if this ever happens.

I get that. I wouldn't have wanted to go preventatively gluten-free if a family member had been diagnosed, either. But unchecked, celiac disease can lead to an increased cancer risk; and those who go undiagnosed, or are "noncompliant" with the gluten-free diet, have by some estimates a 400-percent greater chance of mortality by age sixty-five. Other complications, such as hyposplenism, infertility, and high rates of miscarriage in female patients, have been linked (although some recent investigations into the effect on female fertility in particular have yielded no statistically significant data). In the wake of a diagnosis, specialists often order bone-density scans, since a person who isn't absorbing iron also isn't absorbing calcium or vitamin D, and so has a higher risk for fractures. Children suffering malabsorption from undiagnosed celiac disease can experience slower growth rates and slower cognitive development, and are at risk of developing other illnesses. The list of things that can go wrong when you're not getting nutrients is idiosyncratic—and long.

Among the many things my gastroenterologist could not tell me was how long it would take my body to detoxify from the gluten. Having uncontrolled (or recently-brought-under-control) celiac disease is a little like knowing a parasite lurks in your body, with the curious twist that your own body is manufacturing the parasite. My antibody results* sounded disturbingly high, though when I checked into the online celiac discussion boards where people flash their numbers like battle scars, I found scores two or even three times higher. I took some small comfort in this. I had a long way to go, but I was better off than some.

I was anxious to see progress not only because it would mean I was healthy again, but also because I would be able to return to real eating—albeit within my new limitations. After two weeks of broth, I transitioned to bland meat, rice, and vegetables. After a while on that fare, I would be able to add dairy and spices, and then foods that were more inflammatory, provided that everything was going well. I tried not to think about the low percentage of cases where a gluten-free diet doesn't work, though I sometimes worried that I would turn out to be one of those especially unfortunate souls cursed with "refractory" celiac disease, which calls for a more aggressive treatment plan with immunosuppressant drugs. The odds of having refractory celiac were not minuscule, but low: 90 percent of people with celiac disease respond to a GF diet and show recovery within two years. Most of the time, however, I wondered about more extreme scenarios, including far-fetched circumstances I wouldn't be able to control. For instance, what would happen in a national emergency, when the grocery stores all closed or were looted, and the National Guard rolled into town in their armored cars to distribute bottles of water and crates of food to sustain the community until life returned to normal? How much of those emergency supplies would I be able to eat? Would this be the moment when evolution caught up with me, and the Great Boot,

---

* The antibody results gastroenterologists and celiac patients pay attention to are tissue transglutaminase (tTG), immunoglobulin A (IgA), and deamidated gliadin peptide (DGP). Together, the tests are effective at ruling out false negatives and false positives. They can also be used to evaluate compliance with the GF diet and encounters with cross-contamination.

which had tried to kick me off the planet in December, finally landed squarely upon my ass? I imagined a smiling staff sergeant, feeling a little like Santa Claus, handing me Pop-Tarts, or those little sandwich crackers with the brittle layer of cheese in the middle, or packages of hermetically sealed Wheat Thins and Triscuits. And what would I do *then*? Ask for an apple? My only choice would be to head into the fields and woods, where I would begin foraging for berries, acorns, and wild leeks. I would try, without success, to kill a squirrel with a sling-shot. I'd be a good bet to poison myself with a mushroom I wanted to believe was a morel. It's the sort of thinking that turns a newly diagnosed celiac into a GF prepper who builds a bunker and stocks it with GF supplies.

I wouldn't have shared these musings with anyone, but people who are recovering from bad cases do sometimes need to be talked down. It's not unusual for GI doctors to assemble a team to respond to the first few months of recovery or even longer, including any specialists one may need to see because of complications (neurologist, rheumatologist, orthopedist, etc.) and a registered dietician to help address the nutritional deficiencies from malabsorption, as well as to help navigate the demands of a gluten-free diet. Between the chemical and emotional withdrawal, the sudden holes in their diet, and the inevitable encounters with sources of cross-contamination, many people are bewildered after cutting gluten. For as much as I knew about food and cooking, I could have benefited from a few conversations with a dietician, especially because recently diagnosed celiacs have intolerances to foods that *don't* contain gluten. In the forums online, I read lamentations from people who were "six months gluten-free" or longer about their inability to eat lactose, canola oil, soy, legumes, fish, cheese, and many other foods they had been consuming without discomfort only a year ago. I discovered "safe" and "not safe" lists all over the internet, and while there is agreement on the dangers posed by many foods (such as soy sauce, which clearly contains gluten), I also encountered fierce debates and outright misinformation: for a time I was glued to a discussion thread about whether the molecular similarities between the proteins in gluten and coffee, of all things, meant that a celiac needed to eliminate his morning cup. I was so horrified that I never plumbed the scientific basis for these claims. *No fucking way*, I thought. *I'll give up beer if I have to, but I won't give up coffee, too.*

Some of these lists are simply posting old news, are old themselves, or are plain wrong. Citric acid, a common ingredient in everything from store-bought condiments and homemade jam to Coke, was temporarily suspect, especially if it was manufactured in China (and how the hell would you determine that?). Now it's on the safe list. Caramel coloring is theoretically safe for celiacs but bad news for some, myself included, which was why for a while I couldn't drink Coke or eat many GF cereals—a few handfuls of GF Honey Nut Chex literally made me feel like I was high. Many people with gluten-related disorders have no problem with artificial colorings and dyes, but I was reminded of my own sensitivity—and the fact that farmed salmon can be dyed to look like Coho—when a fillet made me sick. For a while I couldn't tolerate yogurt, which was frustrating, because I knew that after a month on antibiotics, the flora in my gut were in a state of nuclear winter. And I never regained my ability to eat processed meats, fake dairy creamer, and just about anything else that has a long list of chemicals in it (no real loss there). Sadly, the only way of knowing where one's sensitivities lie for sure is to turn one's body into a laboratory, eat fearfully for a time, and document what happens. My own personal solution was to stop reading the blogs and just focus on what was happening in my own gut.

Many eaters with gluten-related disorders opt to go a step further, though, attempting to eliminate all potential for cross-contamination, intolerance, and other bad encounters by going on strict diets. One of the most popular has been the "Paleo diet," so called because it's meant to mirror the eating practices of pre–Neolithic revolution eaters who roamed the plains and forests before wheat evolved from a plant called goat grass and was domesticated. If the food doesn't walk, swim, fly, or sprout out of the ground, Paleo eaters don't eat it. A true Paleo dieter, as opposed to a modified one, also does not eat any cultivated fruits and vegetables—such as Brussels sprouts, which only appeared around the 1600s—instead relying solely on those that can be foraged, like asparagus, onions, and berries. By following such a diet, Paleo dieters also seek to avoid eating commodity, strategically bred, and GMO crops, which many of those afflicted with a digestive disorder believe to be a source of their illness.

I would never try the Paleo diet. Even in the darkest days of that first winter, when I wanted so badly to recover and was making less progress than I'd hoped to, I was never tempted. For one thing, I love food too much to regress to the eating and cooking practices of a hunter-gatherer with a tricked-out kitchen. A pre-Neolithic diet means going without many things that are, in my view, cornerstones of good eating. Wine, for instance. Butter. Olive oil. Ice cream. Chocolate. Cheese. I had already surrendered enough—too much, in fact. Why voluntarily take on more restrictions? Eventually, I would be able to eat almost everything I had been eating only a few months prior. Telling myself this might have been a form of denial, but it turned out to be true.

Yet in my more panicked moments I often thought, *Well, you won't let this celiac shit define you.*

That's a funny thing to remember myself thinking, because I believe the nineteenth-century French writer and gastronome Jean Anthelme Brillat-Savarin's famous saying: "Tell me what you eat, and I will tell you who you are." He was definitely not the first to think it and probably not the first to write it, but Savarin got the credit. And his words are true, to a large degree, both because of the way food functions as nonverbal communication, and because of the links between what we eat and the stories we tell about ourselves: who we are, where we came from, how we're connected to those who came before us and will be connected to those who come later, all because of what we set on the table. We do this constantly and unconsciously, as I began to see right after my diagnosis. It had been common, on those annual trips back to Maryland, to share a beer with my father, or to sit down for a light lunch of bread, fruit, and cheeses. I may have been paying too much attention, but there seemed to be a new unevenness at the table, a mild awkwardness, as we all wondered which items were ones we could all enjoy, and which were not. Eventually these feelings went away, as my mother greeted us with gluten-free pancakes in the morning, and Chianti, cheese, and GF crackers in the afternoon.

Savarin's words also worked just as well, I realized, the other way around: *Tell me what you do* not *eat, and I will tell you who you are.*

Or: *Tell me what you do not eat, and I will tell you who you are* not.

The negatives in those formulations seemed far more powerful to me than the positives.

Over the holidays, everyone we knew seemed to be having parties small and large at the rate of two or three a week. On New Year's Eve, Bec and I shared a light, gentle dinner of chicken and rice at home, and then we slowly walked to Sarah's house. We arrived to find that she had moved her kitchen table into the living room to serve as a buffet, and had covered it with several kinds of cheese, fruits, nuts, olives, and sausages. There were different kinds of bread, crackers, and wafers, hot dips, cold salads, and, on the end, leftover Christmas cookies and fancy desserts. Immediately, instinctually, Sarah pointed out what was safe for me and what was not. She had thought ahead and made sure to have some things I liked: Fontina, kalamata olives, pistachios. The kindness and gentle inclusion that I experienced in her house on this first night would remain a constant feature of the meals I ate there. It would turn out to be the same at the houses of many other friends as we redefined, as a community, our eating habits when we were together.

Guests kept arriving, bringing food and drink with them, and setting it on the table. The room ballooned with energy and noise as midnight drew nearer. I wandered from conversation to conversation, wasted on half a glass of wine (anemic people are cheap dates) and trying to keep to myself the story of what had recently happened to me. I introduced myself to people I didn't know so I wouldn't have to rehash the details. Near midnight, I returned to the table and looked at it with dismay. Sarah's careful order had come undone. Some of the people in the room were trashed by now, and so was the buffet. Bread and cracker crumbs mingled with the cheeses. Knives and serving forks and spoons had been used on several dishes. There were cookies near the olives, cake near the nuts. This was the first time I asked myself, in a social setting, *What here is safe?* Well, since it looked like raccoons had come through, theoretically nothing was safe. *Hell with it*, I thought, and I cut some cheese. Cory needed a beer, so I volunteered to get him one from the fridge. I chose a Great Lakes Edmund Fitzgerald Porter, the perfect match to a cold, snowy New Year's Eve. I put a few ounces into a plastic wine cup and downed it.

What the hell was wrong with me? The Reuben had been a kamikaze; this was not so much a sabotage as a desperate attempt to make the evening feel familiar and safe, to fit in as I always had. I wanted to be normal—but cheese, olives, nuts, and wine *were* normal. I wanted to be the old normal, then. Unchanged. I was sure that Bec did, too.

The New Year arrived. I noted the symbolism: new beginnings, fresh starts. I didn't make any resolutions to do better with my elimination diet, though, because a resolution is a choice. I didn't have a choice. I could only try harder. Figure this out. Swim against the tide. This new thing in my body, in my life, could do me serious harm in time, even kill me, but only if I let it.

4

CLEANING HOUSE

It was a sad, cold January day when we cleaned out the cabinets, refrigerator, pantry, and freezers of anything that would make me sick. We should have done this immediately after my diagnosis, but we had let things linger awhile because we weren't cooking much anyway. Bec gave pounds of flour away to Sarah and Mere, her *Artisan Bread* co-conspirators, though we held on to the cookbook itself, like a souvenir of a place we'd once been and enjoyed tremendously but to which we were unlikely to ever return.* Our friends accepted these displaced ingredients a little guiltily and only in the interest of not seeing quality flour go into the trash. *Starving people from just about anywhere, at any point in the last ten thousand years, would be happy to have that.*

We gave away boxes of pasta, crackers, bottles of soy sauce, teriyaki, and other suspicious-looking items to friends and the food pantry. We dumped other bottles down the drain and threw an entire container of bread dough into the trash. The process of elimination left the cabinets and pantry with conspicuous gaps. Just as I had never thought that wheat could make me sick, I had never imagined my kitchen without any wheat-based foods in it. I had abstained from

---

* Eventually, in 2015, the authors did release a GF version of this cookbook, but we found the results far inferior to what we thought of as the "real" version.

sugar, coffee, alcohol, red meat, and fish for extended periods of time before, but I had never banished crackers, and certainly not pasta or bread. I saw these foods differently—they were essential, not luxuries, and imbued with a purity that made them unnecessary to sacrifice.

Then we set about sanitizing. We cleansed the toaster, scrubbed the baking stone, scrutinized the pots and baking dishes, the cutting boards, the grill pan, the underside of the KitchenAid mixer's arm, the tongs, the sheet and loaf pans. Our goal, the necessity, was to have gluten gone literally without a trace, because even a trace— one-eighth of a teaspoon, according to researchers at Massachusetts General Hospital—could make me sick. It would have been easier to throw some of these kitchen items out and buy new ones, but it mattered to me to keep them. Some had been wedding gifts. Over the years of cooking with them, I'd come to feel as if I had developed relationships with them. I knew their quirks and tendencies, and they contained history, triumphs, failures, important meals.

In the pantry, I hesitated when I came to the pasta machine. What to do with this? It was the non-motorized, hand-crank type, shiny stainless steel, a gift from my in-laws. It weighed more than the cast-iron skillet (which also needed to be scrubbed down and then re-seasoned). The C-clamps never grabbed the countertop right, and so when I cranked the pasta through, I had to pin it down with one hand or my forearm, subduing it like an animal that wanted to slip away and plummet to the floor, where it would break my foot or kill the dog, who liked dozing at my feet despite having the whole kitchen at his disposal.

For all its inconveniences, I loved this gadget. I loved the process of making pasta, the way three simple ingredients, eggs and flour and salt, combined to make something so deeply satisfying and wonderfully more than the sum of their parts. I loved cracking the eggs into the well of flour and swirling them together on the counter, pulling and mixing, pulling and mixing. An afternoon making any type of fresh pasta, whether linguine or spaetzle, said *leisure* to me; when else did I feel up to the trouble, except for those stretches when life was good? The hand motions came to me naturally, as if through some form of muscle memory I had been born with: a connection to those earliest Middle Eastern and Chinese makers of humankind's first noodles, or to my own ancestors in Naples. I loved the golden color of the ball of dough, and the fact that no matter how many times I fed a sheet through the rollers, it never broke. That was what gluten got you—a magical tensile strength. (This was why the Chinese had come up with a far better neologism for gluten than the Romans, who drew on its "glue-like" qualities: *mien chin,* or "muscle of flour.") I made sheets of lasagna so thin I could see my hand through them; or, if I was feeling lazy, I kept the noodles thick, another type of treat. When I cut fettuccine with the machine, a frustrating process because the edges weren't sharp enough and failed to separate the noodles, leaving them in stuck-togther twos and threes, I separated and hung them from coat hangers in the dining room to dry.

It was with this machine, with homemade pasta, that I first discovered the pleasures of "cooking up" for guests. The year I received it—I think I was thirty—I threw Bec a birthday dinner party and stole the stage, I'm not overly sad to say, by cooking homemade ravioli stuffed with a mixture of a friend's goat cheese, puréed roasted butternut squash, roasted shallots, and sage. Shortly before the guests arrived I told Bec her job was to enjoy herself and keep me sharp. Then, for the first time, I let it rip: salad, seared lamb loin, brown butter sauce, toasted pine nuts, and the pillowy ravioli.

I knew I couldn't give the pasta maker away. There was, for one thing, the slimmest chance that the diagnosis was a mistake. And if nothing else, it could make for a weird but effective doorstop.

And then one afternoon, David came over and we transferred the carboys, wort chiller, sanitizer, bottle washers, and beer pot into the trunk of his car. We moved box upon box of home brew: stouts and porters, pale and red ales, IPAs and ESBs we'd cooked up while blasting classic rock on summer Saturday afternoons. I don't think he knew what to do with all that beer. Or, he *knew*—you drink it, stupid—but he objected that he didn't have room for all of it in his duplex, and that I had paid for half of it.

I didn't care about the money or the space. I just wanted the beer out of my house.

He'd take it, he told me, but he would buy out my share with gluten-free beer.

Sure, I said, thinking, *If gluten-free beer is even drinkable.*

After he drove off, I removed from the fridge a remaining six-pack of Lake Placid Ubu Ale. I'd kept it back intentionally, secretly. This beer was the last glutenous foodstuff in the house: a dark, hoppy, English-style strong ale that I still find myself craving, still dream about.

I put the beer under the counter, in the liquor cabinet. It would be good to have some beer on hand for a friend who dropped by. And there was always a chance that the zombies might indeed invade, as everyone from some of my students to the Centers for Disease Control and Prevention apparently believed. If *that* were to happen, it definitely would be good to have beer in the house. I would want to go out in the middle of my own street, with a .45 in one hand and a bottle of Ubu in the other. The gun was just to buy me time to drink my beer.

Except I don't own a gun, and the beer would be warm.

Gluten withdrawal set in right around this time. First I had to re-cleanse my body from New Year's Eve, and then I needed to stay gluten-free. This time, I did. Since I had been suffering from headaches, mood swings, body aches, lethargy, and just about everything that withdrawal brings for months already, I do not think I felt the full force. In fact, from a physical standpoint, I felt better as my body ceased to destroy itself and my overall health improved. My wife, on the other hand, had a harder time. For a long while—several months—Bec experienced headaches, sluggishness, and, ironically, gastrointestinal symptoms. We kept waiting for her head to clear, for her body to adjust to a life without gluten, but it took longer than either of us predicted, even though she was as rigorous about maintaining the diet as I was (even more so, considering she hadn't snuck any porter), and had gone into the change strong and healthy.

Instead of physical or chemical withdrawal symptoms, I felt in those first weeks an emotional void. There were, in truth, not that many empty spaces in the cabinets and the refrigerator, because we had always made most of what we ate from scratch, but the missing items bothered me. And yet, we still had plenty to eat. I wasn't even close to having a kitchen ravaged by hunger, which I knew was something that plenty of my North Country neighbors lived with every day. Instead, I was bereft. I felt bereft even when I discovered a hidden upside to iron-deficiency anemia: red meat, which we'd always consumed sparingly, had suddenly ascended to the status of health food. We live on top of some superb beef, pork, lamb, bison, and chicken farmers, and we love what they provide us, but I had never been in the habit of having a burger for lunch. During the weeks of recovery, though, I ate double bison patties with homemade bread-and-butter pickles and cheddar. "It's a pharmaceutical!" I exclaimed as I got the burger down with gusto. But where was the roll, toasted brown yet moist and flavorful from the juices? In the midst of so much good food, it was embarrassingly easy to focus on what was *not* there.

Although I didn't want to, I had begun a running tally of all the foods I had lost, whether I was in the habit of eating them regularly or not. That didn't matter; the fact that they were now unobtainable was what counted. The list began with bread, of course, in dozens of forms, from baguettes to limpa to whole-grain toast to croissants.

Then sandwiches: Montecristos, croques monsieur, cheesesteaks from a sidewalk cart in Philadelphia. The list meandered into the first-course offerings of crostini and bruschetta and croutons atop salads, and curled into the next morning's breakfast of French toast, English muffins with eggs Benedict, waffles, bagels, or scones. From there it zigzagged randomly and associatively: real chocolate chip cookies, egg pasta, a slice of pizza from the kind of dive joint one walks into precisely because the fact that it *is* a dive joint augurs good things.

At some point I added crab cakes—it didn't matter that I rarely ever wanted them, even though I'd been raised in Maryland. Next, a cold pint of Guinness, or even better, a black and tan like David and I made on St. Patrick's Day with a spoon I bent backward to a right angle so as to divert the stout gently onto the lager. We used this contraption until Mere bought David a real barman's turtle. True soy sauce with sushi instead of GF tamari didn't matter much, but plain old oatmeal did matter, especially with raisins and almonds and maple syrup on a January morning, when NPR murmured on the radio and, outside the kitchen windows, the yard was whitewashed. Fried chicken, New England clam chowder, Louisiana gumbo, béchamel made from a classic French roux; quiche Lorraine, real apple pie, spanakopita, napoleons. I would never again pick up a warm blueberry scone at the co-op's bakery and slide it into a wax paper sleeve for a midafternoon snack with tea. And why couldn't they have brought out their home-made pretzels a year sooner? I would never eat most kinds of Christmas cookies, including *lebkuchen,* a favorite on my father's side of the family—lard, cloves, icing, and all—and a Christmas tradition in our house until the year my mother grew suspicious of a dough so dense with saturated fat that she couldn't stir it herself, and finally put the kibosh on them.

Every time I thought I had reached the end of this list, had suffered through the inventory of foods that mattered, something else sprang to mind: beer-battered fish, haddock or cod, deep-fried. Traditional fish-and-chips with a bottle of pale ale. Yes, please. Just one more.

Perhaps the expansiveness was a testament to how greedy we have become as eaters, how our minds, once trained in a certain gastronomical direction—omnivorous, in my case—refuse to bend back the other way.

Twix bars. Ritz crackers. And Girl Scout cookies: Samoas! Tagalongs! I rarely ate these things, and I never craved them. Same for astronaut ice cream, which I tasted once at Cape Canaveral (utterly unmemorable), and which may contain gluten, as I discovered one day when I idly read the back of a package of freeze-dried Neapolitan ice cream while shopping at an outfitters store. "I'll be damned," I whispered, as I felt, illogically, a pang.

I could sometimes see the questions in the eyes of people who had never needed to make such a compromise in their diets and probably never would. *Okay. No more birthday cake from regular flour. I get it. But there are GF birthday cakes. No more whole-grain toast. But there is GF bread, there are GF buns for your lamb burgers with feta and wax pepper jam (furthermore, why should anyone lament, if he has lamb and feta and exotic jam?). Yes, you have to eat special food. But at the end of the day, so what? It's still food.*

It always seemed to me a stupid question, but okay, I would bite. Taste was only part of the loss, albeit a big part. But what about the relationship between food and memory? The most famous example of the intertwining of the two is Marcel Proust's "madeleine moment," when as an adult on a trip back to his childhood home in Combray, France, he ate a cookie and remembered, in vivid detail, entire segments of his childhood that he had completely forgotten. The reverie started with a morsel of madeleine soaked in tea, which brought back mornings when he was watched by his aunt (who used to like the tea-soaked cookies) while his mother entertained a male suitor, M. Swann, a personage who filled the young Proust with anxiety. This memory seemed to explain, or connect to, other mysteries in Proust's life, and what followed was a chain reaction of recollection, and a literary work that has been called a novel but is really a seven-volume magnum opus of a memoir. All from a lump of butter, sugar, and flour.

Here is the idea that haunted me as soon as I realized just how many foods I had lost: one of Proust's key observations is that forgotten pieces of our past can be reclaimed only randomly, through the senses, especially taste. The trigger for these recollections is in the chemicals in the food as much as in the actual taste. Such memory is completely involuntary; it's the difference between craving a meal that reminds you of your grandmother, and eating, at a friend's house or a restaurant, lasagna prepared exactly as your grandmother used to make it, and thinking, *Wow. It's like she's* here. And then things you had forgotten about her suddenly reappear: the slope of her shoulders as she stood at the counter; the quick, confident movements of her hands; the love in her eyes.

I believed in these kinds of food triggers. I had been unexpectedly catapulted into reverie by them before, first with maple walnut ice cream and then upon cutting a tangy, sulfurous-smelling honeybell orange, both of which placed me in my late grandfather's house in Florida. I had no way of knowing how many memories, how many encounters with my past, whether joyful, painful, or confounding— but always real, always significant—celiac disease would cost me. The fact that wheat and gluten were the basis of so many foods suggested that many memories were now irretrievably lost.

The bright side? I would never know what I was missing.

5

Guy Fieri and Me

In addition to our personal food memories, we also share a cultural eating history (or several of them, simultaneously), which is really a collective form of food-memory. It might be more accurate to call our history with wheat and bread a love affair, one that is around 10,000 to 12,000 years old and that began on the plains of the Fertile Crescent, which includes modern-day Iraq, Turkey, and Syria. The first cultivated wheat appeared there around 8,800 BC. Signs of wheat farming appeared in the Jordan Valley about a millennium later, in 7,800 BC. However, humans were harvesting wild wheat much earlier than that. Einkorn and emmer wheats in their wild form appear to have been first encountered around 10,000 to 12,000 BC (einkorn is now coming back after a long history primarily as animal fodder, and emmer has found prominence as farro). Several separate communities likely noticed and began collecting wild wheat grains at about the same time.

Our Neolithic ancestors would have quickly realized that wheat and barley grains were so easy to gather that the plants cried out for domestication. In a famous and telling 1960 experiment, the archaeologist J. R. Harlan re-created the Neolithic reaping process, and discovered that a single person could gather two pounds of grain, or around two thousand calories, in one hour. In three weeks of eight-hour days, a gatherer with the same tools could collect enough grain to feed a family of six one pound of wheat per person each day, for a year. That's a big insurance policy against starvation, especially after millennia at the mercy of roving herds and the fruiting of plants. When farmers began to domesticate the wild grains, they next would have observed that wheat germinates rapidly, pollinates itself, and responds well to dry (no irrigation) farming. Grain was, in many senses, the perfect crop.

The immediate culinary payoff, however, is a little harder to see. Even after domestication, the leavened bread that today is all but synonymous with wheat was still some 3,000 to 4,000 years in the future (it is a development credited to the Egyptians). And after the easy harvest, the rest of the processing was drudgery. Early gatherers and farmers freed the edible part of the wheat grains from the chaff, or the tough, indigestible casings, by pounding them: a knuckle-busting, finger-sanding, and sweaty process that makes any modern kitchen chore, from deveining shrimp to breaking down pomegranates, seem pleasant. After the grains were freed and sifted to separate chaff fragments, they still couldn't be eaten; raw wheat is not digestible. Some unlucky people must have first tried emmer, einkorn, and barley right from the plant and, an hour later, felt a little like a celiac feels after downing a bagel.

While the Chinese had been making clay vessels for several millennia by the time people in Mesopotamia were gathering wild grain, pottery was still a few thousand years away in the Near East. Thus there were few cooking options. One was to dig a pit and boil the grains by leveraging in rocks heated red-hot over a fire—an inefficient approach that some early European communities later used to make beer. Another process completed two steps at once by cooking the grains with hot coals where they were threshed. Threshing is the loosening of the grains from the chaff that surrounds them before the chaff is removed, or "winnowed." The hot coals split the shells and made separating the chaff easier once the wheat was cool. But a fire of this kind was uneven, scorching some grains, roasting others perfectly, and leaving others incompletely cooked. "Let not the perfect be the enemy of the edible" must have been the guiding philosophy of most early meals.

Roasting those grains created yet *another* problem. The coarse, dried groats, as they're called, were now digestible but too dry to eat. Popping a handful would be like eating dry couscous. The solution was to grind the cooked groats into a primitive flour on a saddle-shaped stone called a quern (more knuckle-busting, finger-sanding, and sweating), mix them with water in a gourd or skin to make a paste, and then eat the paste. You can call it mush, if you like. Thinned, it becomes gruel. Thinned even more, and left to be inoculated by wild yeasts, it becomes one of the earliest precursors to beer. Indeed, there is a debate as to which might have come first after these pastes: flatbread or beer. As unappetizing as "emmer paste" or "einkorn paste" sounds, this food, and not beer, likely provided the nutritional rationale for domesticating grains.

In a culinary (as opposed to caloric) sense, the bigger motivator for domestication was the invention of flatbreads, which an early cook made by slapping the paste on a rock heated screeching-hot in the fire—a primitive griddle—and cooking until golden and crusty. Behold the earliest Near East ancestor to the tortilla, the chapati, the crêpe, the pao ping. For those people who first smelled the browning, caramelizing dough, the payoff after all the work must have been more immense than even what we feel when bread is baking in our ovens. At the first whiff, they desired to have flatbread tomorrow, and the next day, and the day after that. I'm pretty sure that's how I would have felt.

Perhaps nothing speaks to the innate human response to wheat and barley more than the speed and completeness with which these grains spread across Eurasia. From its epicenter in Mesopotamia and Anatolia, wheat traveled to Greece, Cyprus, and India by 6,500 BC, and to Egypt by 6,000 BC. Around that time, the true magic and joy of gluten was discovered when bread became leavened. This second breakthrough might have come as early as 6,000 BC, but certainly no later than 4,000 BC. The first loaves of leavened bread were accidental creations, kitchen mistakes made glorious by a combination of time, atmospheric conditions, and the microorganisms (yeast, or a fungus named *saccharomyces cerevisiae*, technically) circulating in the ambient air. A cook set down a bowl of emmer or club-wheat dough—by this time, both varieties were preferred to einkorn—meant for the fire, and forgot about it. The wild yeast in the air was attracted to it like iron filings to a magnet. By the time the cook remembered it and returned, the dough had doubled in size.

Like the first taste of flatbread or sip of frothy, refreshing beer, the experience of eating an airy, risen loaf for the first time must have been powerful and inspirational. I find it a wonder that the discovery of leavened bread did not lead to a mythical story of yeast's arrival into the world. It seems fitting that such a thing came to human tables because, as with Prometheus's fire, someone absconded with yeast from the kitchen of the gods.

Few foods have shown leavened bread's power to completely rewire eaters' brains throughout an entire section of the globe. *We must have this. All the time.* Usually such foods have stimulating qualities that speak for themselves, like the caffeine in coffee and tea; or pungency and depth, as in the case of spices. Leavened bread is more mysterious in its capacity to hook humans because it is neither psychoactive nor especially exotic. Despite this simplicity—or because of it—leavened bread moved rapidly across the West, reordering societies socially, economically, and gastronomically, creating insiders and outsiders, contented eaters and those with their noses forever pressed to the proverbial bakeshop windows. Bread inspired greed and artistry. Monarchies toppled over the want of grain. In Europe especially, bread became equally a sustainer and, when the wheat and barley crops on which millions depended crashed, an executioner.

By the late Middle Ages, wheat had displaced all other flours as the grain of choice in Europe, except in rural communities that farmed for subsistence and could not trust their well-being to wheat, which could still be difficult to grow in northern climates. Wheat tasted better, cooked better, and was believed to be more digestible than other grains. In the countryside of Tuscany, millet apparently made a decent bread and was used until relatively late, but anyone who could afford to live above subsistence preferred wheat because it is delicious. Finely milled, wheat is sweeter, nuttier, smoother, and makes bread that is more beautiful to look at than any other grain. Not everyone was eating finely milled flour, of course, but wheaten bread in any form was valued enough to remain a form of currency. As late as the 1300s, the salary of a Sicilian worker remained 1.3 to 2.0 kilograms of wheat bread per day.

Well into the eighteenth century, Britons lived on two to four pounds of wheat bread daily, a figure that humbles my own pre-celiac consumption. By 1870, this figure had dropped to about a pound per person per day, and in 2002 it was 3.8 ounces. By that time, even the French averaged only 5.6 ounces of bread per day. Americans also eat less bread now than we used to, because of a monumental change in the mid-twentieth century: the cost of industrial meat production fell, making meat more accessible. However, wheat remains crucial. Through a combination of bread and other foods, Americans consume approximately 114 pounds of wheat per person per year—still more than any other grain, even corn.

This was the history I was up against.

And when Bec and I began testing commercial gluten-free products, we got an immediate education in why so many populations have always preferred to eat wheat. We bought GF brownie mixes and prepared cookies, GF cereals, GF prepared pastas and crackers and breads. Most of the store-bought items used mixtures of brown rice, cornstarch, and less-familiar things like tapioca and millet. While it seemed pretty hard to screw up a brownie, every other food we tried fell far short of its wheaten counterpart. The pastas may have been the least offensive, though the noodles made of beans and quinoa tended to turn mushy if you didn't watch them closely. Compared to wheaten pasta, almost all rice pasta tastes at least a little insipid. We tried co-conut macaroons that fell into dust; gritty chocolate chip cookies that left something astringent, a little metallic, on the palate; cornstarch-based pretzels with oily aftertastes; pizza crust that tasted like a paper plate; and "panko" that tasted about as flavorful as blender-blitzed packing peanuts. In a very short time, we compiled a list of disap-pointments that outnumbered the good (let alone great) experiences.

The "fresh" GF breads were the worst: soft and squishy yet dry, with a powerful yeasty scent, they became grainy in my mouth almost the moment I bit down. Given their shelf life—somehow, they're sta-ble at room temperature for *months*—I had no reason to be surprised that they tasted so bad. The frozen loaves (which were completely baked and ready to eat) were overly sweet, seemingly to cover the lack of bready flavor, body, and depth. I thought toasting slices of them might help, but that made them even worse: the grit sucked up the butter and made the bread, if it could still be called that, gummy and pasty. I considered finding out just how big a train wreck French toast would be, but decided to save my money.

In the midst of this inauspicious introduction to the GF world, my friend Margaret, who had recently been misdiagnosed with ce-liac disease (quite the reversal of alimentary fortune), brought me the leftovers she hadn't eaten from the "poor, sad freezer," as she called it, where the GF products lived at the health-food store. Thus we en-countered the calamity of our first gluten-free "baguette"—a roll of tapioca, rice flour, and oil so weirdly greasy that it seemed to come out of the oven pre-buttered. Bec and I each tried a slice and then threw the remainder away. We also pitched the brown-rice "tortillas" Margaret brought, and shoved a cookbook with a ghastly title—*The Bland Diet Cookbook*—into another desultory corner, where it belonged.

Why the hell were people eating these foods? I realized the answer after we, too, kept going back to the grocery store for products that we didn't even like: eating a GF signifier of a familiar real food can be more comforting, if not better-tasting, than eating a strange food nobody in your family grew up eating, and which therefore conveys no meaning at all. And to be fair, food producers are only leavening dough made of sorghum, or making cupcakes out of batters of cornstarch, cocoa powder, and coconut oil, because consumers are *asking* them to do it, both with their "likes" on social media and their dollars. There is so much money to be made that any large-scale producer would be foolish not to meet the demand. In 2014, the GF industry totaled sales of $10.5 billion, and 2016 sales are expected to top $15 billion. Furthermore, I am aware that the efforts of these companies are appreciated by many gluten-intolerant eaters, especially those who have been eating GF for decades and not a few brief years or months, as I have. They can remember the days when the options were even smaller in number, and tasted worse.

I might have found the commercially prepared GF foods less disappointing if they did not cost so much. It was offensive to pay five dollars a pop for snacks like pretzels or crackers that were shadows of their wheat-based counterparts. I knew that I gambled every time I tried a new product—a bottle of wine, cheese, a new type of sorbet—but the stakes seemed higher when I bought gluten-free. As of 2013, the prices for GF products were, on average, 252 percent higher than for their conventional counterparts. The numbers change as prices for ingredients and fuel fluctuate, but fixed costs include maintaining a dedicated GF facility to ensure no cross-contamination, and, in the case of some companies, testing to make sure the product is safe (though the FDA does not require food producers to test for the presence of gluten). The cost of GF bread, whether it's good or not, is especially high. The better flour blends tend to be proprietary mixes of rice, chickpea, tapioca, millet, or coconut. The cost of these ingredients on average is higher than for a commodity like wheat or corn, and that expense gets passed on to the consumer. For example, a package of California-based Pamela's bread mix—which is widely regarded as one of the best prepackaged bread mixes available (and I came to agree, despite an aftertaste one GF artisan baker once accurately described to me as "alkaline")—goes for nearly $6.00 for a one-loaf bag, compared to $1.29, and sometimes less, for a loaf of generic grocery-store white bread. You still have to add eggs and canola oil, and bake it yourself, so the cost is closer to $6.50 or $7.00. (You also need a stand mixer, or at least a hand mixer, if you're going to get the best-tasting loaf of bread out of your investment.) For sure, this GF bread can be an effective stage for homemade preserves, but it was still far from the real thing. Nonetheless, I kept baking and eating it anyway.

Almost everyone is going to feel the pinch of a 200-plus-percent increase to their grocery budget, but the cost of "going gluten-free" is a particular concern for those who must do so from near or below the poverty line. The IRS allows tax deductions for GF products because, for celiacs, they're a medical expense. But not everyone is going to itemize his deductions down to the GF cereal he eats for breakfast—I don't, though I've met people who do—and a tax deduction is not the same thing as a price break in the checkout line; it's actually a regressive tax policy, because most people who are struggling to buy groceries are not paying accountants or splurging on tax-prep software. When I asked my gastroenterologist about his worries for his poorer patients' abilities to comply with a gluten-free diet—St. Lawrence County is the second poorest in New York State, and celiac, like all diseases and conditions, does not discriminate—he became visibly frustrated.

"I know of many patients," he told me, "who simply cannot afford the foods. And so they don't buy them."

Those days would have been even darker if we hadn't had a winter farm share (CSA) with our friends and growers Dan and Megan Kent, and if we hadn't had good meat from our local ranchers, the Bartons. Winter vegetable farm shares are a rarity this far north. Even with insulated greenhouses and triple-lined high tunnels, a grower courts disaster when he tries to provide fresh greens in a place where the temperatures regularly drop to ten below. That is why the Kents and their workers harvested an abundance of storage crops and root vegetables in the summer and kept them in a cooler the size of our house. So in the depths of winter, we were well stocked in supplies of onions, garlic, winter squash of four or five varieties, celery root, cabbages red and green, beets, turnips, potatoes, radishes, shallots, carrots, and, as well, produce that Megan froze fresh out of the fields in their certified kitchen: peppers, corn, cauliflower, broccoli, cherry tomatoes, and beans. Subscribers received fifteen pounds of vegetables biweekly to mix and match. As Dan was fond of saying, there was always plenty to eat (notably, he never said, "You will get exactly what you *want* to eat"). We also received popcorn on the cob, frozen apple cider, cranberries, strawberry jam, maple syrup, and pickles. On top of this, they provided subscribers with every northern grower's holy grail for as long as it lasted: fresh greens in the form of spinach, kale, chard, and lettuce. If memory serves, they were helped by a milder winter that year.

Eating the foods grown in this place, by these people, raised my spirits. They kept me from falling over the edge into gloomy GF eating of the sort that can lead a person who goes on an elimination diet to experience even more problems, as the hole in his diet becomes a vacuum for fake food out of despair. Simply because the CSA kept coming, I was forced to transition back to real eating, to use great ingredients, no matter how humble, to make meals. The hope I felt stemmed from a belief I've long held that cooking and sitting down to eat, whether alone or with another person or a group, is the single most important and restorative thing we can do each day.

When I began cooking these ingredients for my breakfast or dinner, I felt as if I was finally back home again; my life resumed some of its normal rhythms, so many of which are based in the kitchen. For the entire month of December I had barely cooked. Now the knife once again felt familiar in my hand. The pots and pans again hissed with aromatics, or a hash of butternut squash, onions, celery root, and herbs. I turned the berries we'd frozen in the summer into crisps and crumbles, substituting ground nuts for oats. From the sweet corn, potatoes, and peppers, I made spicy chowders. I regularly raided The Vault for tomato sauce to make a ragout, Bolognese, chili, goulash. Eventually, as my health improved, I made soups, boeuf Bourguignon, chicken fricassée, poule au pot (my sister-in-law had given me *Mastering the Art of French Cooking* for Christmas that year), and plenty of gratins, sautés, and braises.

And yet, immediately after dinner was over and the dishes were washed, something strange often occurred.

I turned on the television and watched Guy Fieri—sometimes for *hours*—as he moved through the lurid, greasy world of mega-gluten-eaters on *Diners, Drive-Ins, and Dives*. Our basic cable service had recently added the Food Network, and for some reason Guy Fieri drove into our living room almost every night in one of the many red Camaros he purportedly keeps on reserve throughout the country, shouting over the wind as it zipped through his spiked, bleached hair. The only explanation I can offer for the amount of time I spent watching Guy in January and February is that if I had no energy in the middle of the day, I was totally drained by evening. My resistance was down. I was in a strange mood, caught somewhere between rage and resignation, withdrawal and recovery.*

I watched Guy hoark down burgers. I watched him tip his head back and drop in the noodles, the dumplings, the fritters. I watched him drink beer from a glass the size of a bucket.

I developed a refrain that I delivered aloud from the couch even as I helplessly kept watching: "Fuck you, Guy Fieri."

Guy hit up Blimpy Burger in Ann Arbor, Michigan, where we'd lived about a decade ago. I could still picture the obese polar bear slouched against the porch of that tumbledown diner on the corner of Packard Street, where the undergraduate dwellings clustered. There were couches on the roofs of rental houses, debris fields in the front yards, and more gluten per square mile than I will ever be around again. Guy ate a quadruple Blimpy. With crispy onion rings.

"Fuck you, Guy."

He found an Italian place in Syracuse that we could have driven to, if all this shit hadn't gone down, and then a seafood joint in Maryland. I believe Guy might have hit up Burlington, one of our favorite food-haunts. And Montreal: Joe Beef. I wrote the name of the place down, it looked so promising.

Of all the strange, counterintuitive things I did at this time, my extended voyeurism of Guy's eating habits might be the most extreme, given my loathing for television. And most of the dishes I watched him eat, since they were not from places that used local or regional ingredients (though some did), I wouldn't have allowed myself to consider eating in the first place.

---

* In the same helpless, drifting way, I also watched a lot of *Chopped*, and dreamed of taking revenge on the gluten-eating (and cooking) world by designing dastardly mystery baskets out of nothing but the worst GF substitutions on the market.

What the hell was I *doing*? Well, for one thing, my brain cells were starved for oxygen. I had the numbers to prove that. I think, though, that I was bidding farewell to a part of my future as an adventurous eater, a lover of food. I was making celiac disease real through a form of particularly irritating and punishing desensitization. And I was preparing myself for what was to come: the awkward social situations; the sight, in person, of the restaurants I would not be able to enter no matter how much I might want to; the dishes on the menus that I would order and eat only if I wanted to lose a week of my life; and the cravings that would come over me without hope of satiating them. I was inoculating myself, or attempting to, through a medium that has been described as "food porn."

I'm not sure that the gluten-voyeurism worked, though. Guy couldn't really help me with the longing. I had only hoped he could.

6.

In Memory of Beer

Shortly after my first foray into the GF offerings at the grocery store, I worked up the courage to have a GF beer tasting. I drove to the beer store in town and received a shock.

The place I'd been frequenting for all of the brews David and I purchased to supplement our cottage operation featured, at the time, three—yes, *three*—gluten-free beers. I had learned on the internet that there were more GF beers out in the world someplace, but I would never be able to find any of them within a hundred miles. The three offerings—Bard's, New Planet, and Redbridge—were tucked into *another* sad corner, way at the end of the shelves past the six-packs of Great Lakes, Middle Ages, Lake Placid, Saranac, Lagunitas, and all the others I used to drink. A pattern was emerging between taste and the location of GF items on the shelf or in the store; it did not augur good things. Still, I bought all three beers.

Later that night, I opened a bottle of each when David and Mere came over for dinner. Get it over with all at once, I thought. One of them had to be decent.

I sniffed the glass of Redbridge. There were no hops to speak of, which wasn't necessarily a bad thing; many of the better light lagers do not have discernible hops, either. But the Redbridge tasted like a brew I could not have been prevailed upon to drink in college. On the bright side, that might not be as damning as it sounds; I had come of age at the turn of the century, in the late dawn of microbrews and craft beers, and I transitioned almost immediately from iced tea at home to beer snobbery in my dorm. My favorites were strong and hoppy ales and brooding, dark stouts. The first beer I ever tasted was Labatt Blue. Not a craft beer, to be sure, but not too shabby, either—especially when my roommate and I paired the twelve-pack with an entire box of grocery-store doughnuts. I shudder to recall all of the gluten I consumed in those days.

The problem was the finish, which tasted of vegetal funk, like old lettuce. Malted sorghum, when not countered with a contrasting element like hops or other aromatics, has a tendency to get chewy. This is a painful discovery for someone who loves the burnished, even tarnished, bittersweet taste of malted barley, the basis of beer since long before the Beer Purity Laws. Enacted in Germany in 1487, this series of regulations declared that beer could only be made from barley, water, and hops; other countries have similar notions of beer purity, mostly because you can't make a good dark beer or even a mediocre light-bodied beer out of wheat or rye alone. The starches in wheat and rye do not convert to sugar as readily as the starches in barley do—a process known as saccharization—although wheat and rye can be, and are, used as flavoring ingredients. Sorghum does malt agreeably, but the taste is thicker, greener, and sweeter. And somehow also flatter, in my book.

"I don't know what this is, but it's not beer," I said to David.

He didn't want to agree with me, but I could see the pained look in his eyes. Bec, for her part, said she could imagine drinking Redbridge in the hot, hazy stillness of the summer, on the tailgate of someone's pickup. That might have been true, but I knew from experience that quality pale ales and IPAs went just as well with pickups, Johnny Cash, and that particular strain of Americana.

Next we tried the Bard's. The beer smelled, again, of funk, not toasted malt and hops. The body tasted a little fuller than the Redbridge, but there was a cloying saccharine taste on the back end that Bec accurately likened to Diet Coke, possibly owing to a heavier proportion of sorghum malt.

David screwed up his face. "It tastes like that Wee Heavy we drank back in October," he said, referring to a Scottish ale he brought back from Rochester that we drank around noon, if memory serves, while brewing up a double-IPA. This was not a compliment.

New Planet, another stalwart of the GF industry, makes a pale ale that tasted better to me because the sorghum was cut with brown rice and molasses. I finally found some hops in this bottle, though Bec pointed out that the beer was overcarbonated. She was right, but I ranked New Planet as the least of the three evils sitting on the table before me.

"You know what the solution is," David said, trying to be optimistic. "We get a Bard's clone from the brewing supply and we bomb it with hops."

It was an interesting idea. But I wasn't in a place to think about brewing right now. When dinner was ready, Dave asked me which of the beers I was going with. I told him I'd finish them later. I needed to raise my spirits with some wine first.

My next-door neighbor, Matt, also a professor at the college where I teach, must have predicted the paucity in the local offerings. We had brewed together several years back, too, and we shared a love for IPAs. One afternoon he showed up at my door with a box of assorted GF beers that he had picked up from a beer emporium in Rochester as a consolation. *Here you go, buddy,* he seemed to be saying. *Better you than me. Drink up and try not to lose your mind.*

Some of them I'd already tried, but a few were new: Estrella Daura Damm, a lager from Spain; Brewery Brunehaut's ale from Belgium; Green's Dubbel Dark Ale; and Dogfish Head's Strawberry

Tweason'ale. Since a dark beer in the winter is as good as hearty bread, I opened the Green's first (and saved what I anticipated to be a strawberry fiasco and a raspberry beer from New Planet for last, preferably for never). Green's is brewed in Belgium, from a mixture of sorghum, buckwheat, brown rice, and millet. The best-tasting GF beers, I would eventually learn, utilized a mix of malted grains as well as interesting flavorings, instead of expecting sorghum to be able to replace barley on its own, and the best of them did not use any sorghum at all. I thought that surely the *Belgians* couldn't screw up a GF beer, though it would have been telling, had I noted it at the time, that Germans, Czechs, and Irish did not appear to be attempting GF beers (yet the British were).

I poured the Green's that night in front of a hockey game. I liked the darkness of it in the glass immediately; it was reminiscent of a beer like Lake Placid's Ubu. Before I even tasted it, I proclaimed to my wife, "This is a beer I can drink and still feel like a man!"

But I was wrong.

I was only momentarily buoyed up by the novelty of the color. This beer disappointed too, precisely *because* of its promising color. Through the familiar sorghum sweetness I tasted the compost heap once again. The head looked like the brown, scummy foam that appears on the banks of the nearby Grasse River during the spring thaws.

The Brunehaut and Damm, when I tried them, I liked better, but I couldn't find them in our town, so there was no point in getting too excited about them. (No matter how hard I tried, every beer supplier would tell me they couldn't get the good GF beers from their distributors.) And like the bread, and the other GF products we tested, every beer I sampled that month was more expensive. Since no one is buying GF beer unless absolutely necessary,* the production volume is

---

* There's an exception, here, in more ways than one, with Omission Beer, about which I'll say more later.

lower and the cost of ingredients is higher. This meant that I got four GF beers for the price of six real ones. It was like being kicked when I was down.

So I renounced beer for a time. I turned to cider, which I enjoyed, though not as much. At first, all I could find was Woodchuck (fail) and Angry Orchard, which I drank until I got so sick of its one-note cloying sweetness that I took to calling it Bitchy Tree. I found Stella Artois Cidre to be significantly drier, more in keeping with the long history of hard ciders in America, and able to pull me through. Later on, I discovered craft and artisanal ciders, including a dry-hopped cider made in Vermont that was so wonderful I considered filling a carboy with local cider and dry-hopping my own version. But I was still more than a year away from those discoveries.

So I just started drinking straight whiskey when I went out with friends, which is safe for celiacs because the distillation process breaks down the glutenin and gliadin proteins. I have always enjoyed Scotches and bourbons, but drinking whiskey while my friends all drank beer meant that I was one cheap date, especially in the early days, when I was still anemic. It was like getting an ethanol IV. Not good.

Trying to bolster my spirits, a friend of mine who had literally filled his basement with wine through an internet wine retailer remarked that I was fortunate to love wine as much as I loved beer. And this was true; I did love wine, all varieties from all over the world. I loved learning about where they came from and enjoyed pairing dishes with them. Selecting a really good bottle, like a Châteauneuf-du-Pape or Barolo, and cooking up to it is one of my favorite things to do. But loving wine did not make losing beer any easier. There are different seasons, moods, meals, and social situations that are better matched to beer. And, as with bread, I sometimes wondered if the sharpness of the longing I felt for real beer, a strong ale or a porter like I used to drink, was not simply gluten-withdrawal but something deeper, the gravitational pull of history and tradition.

Humans, after all, have been enjoying beer for as long as bread, and by some counts for even longer. Even the wine drinkers among us who object, as the Greeks did, to the taste of beer (Aristophanes, being a true Greek and partial to wine, called beer a "dark purgative"), have beer running through their veins. The ancient beers made by the Egyptians, Babylonians, and Sumerians, all of whom were ambitious and skilled brewers, would be unrecognizable to us today; they were unfiltered, uncarbonated, and unhopped. Many of them, with an alcohol content between 1 and 2 percent, served as potable drinking water more than a festive libation, though the ancients also made stronger brews for hedonistic purposes. Beer spread just as rapidly throughout the ancient world as bread, and it, too, constituted a form of payment. Some views hold that writing and accounting were invented in response to bread and also beer, as a necessity for keeping track of their high-volume exchange. Beer supported workers in the fields, builders of houses and temples, and slaves. Our light, effervescent "lawnmower" beer is probably the closest brew in our time to what people drank to refresh themselves thousands of years ago.

Like bread, beer might have reached Europe around 5,000 BC (in Barcelona), and its reach extended to central Europe and north to the Hebrides between 4,000 and 2,000 BC. Consumption was not low, either. By the late Middle Ages (circa 1300), a normal allowance for a monk was a gallon each of strong and weak ale *per day*. In 1593, the British Crown purchased 600,000 gallons of ale and beer—about 3.2 million of today's twelve-ounce bottles. These were my people. And so I railed—to Bec, to David, to anyone who would listen—against losing this history along with bread. None of the replacements I found that winter seemed like anything those cheerful monks would have recognized as beer.

Technically speaking, though, "beer" is *any* alcoholic drink derived from "fermenting sugar-rich extracts of starchy plants." I still want to dismiss this definition as excessively forgiving, as would become immediately clear if one were to walk into any licensed seller in America, whether a gas station or grocery store, and ask where to find the beer made with fermented bananas or manioc. But these drinks (which do in fact exist) *are* beer, chemically speaking, and they're seen as beer by the people who drink them. That's apparently the key, if you can get your head around it: beer is whatever the drinker believes it to be. To begin drinking beers made of barley substitutes like sorghum, or millet, simply means you fall out of one brewing tradition and land in another that is just as long.

It can be comforting, to a tiny degree, to know that a gluten-free beer like the UK's Hambleton Ales' Toleration,* which my friend Cory brought back for me from Buffalo that winter and contains no malted grain at all (it's made only from fermented sugars), does in fact have a precedent somewhere: in east Africa, where palm sugar and dates were fermented and consumed by the lower classes throughout antiquity, and still are in some communities to this day. All over the world, people have chosen to ferment *something*, usually whatever was growing plentifully in their backyards. The Chinese may have brewed the world's first beer, known as *li*, from fermented rice and millet as early as 10,000 BC. The Amazonians brew a fermented drink from manioc root, called *chichi*. South Americans have long made beers from corn, which, like millet, sorghum, and rice, is becoming a common base for contemporary gluten-free beers, like Glutenberg's Blonde Ale.

Africa, though, is the ancestral homeland of most gluten-free beers

---

* In no other market have I found such a high density of punny product names. See also the Epic Glutenator Ale, Glutenberg, and New Grist. To this point, I've resisted calling in the artillery of beer-review websites, but in the case of Toleration I find it difficult to avoid doing so any longer: Toleration receives an average score of 64 out of 100 ("Poor") on BeerAdvocate.com, and garnered comments such as "a body so light I'm surprised I finished it" and "absolutely horrible." Toleration is, according to the brewery's website, the only Paleo-friendly beer on the market. The archaeological evidence suggests, however, that cavemen were most likely getting their buzz by drinking early precursors to mead: honey that had fermented in the holes of fallen trees after it had been rained on.

sold in America—at least in spirit, if not in an actual recipe. Sorghum is the essential African grain, supplying the bulk of calories consumed by rural eaters on most of the continent, often in the form of beer. I did not know until I was forced to leave barley and wheat behind that Africans were such huge beer drinkers. There are men in Cameroon and Burkina Faso, if the anthropological studies are to be believed, whose beer consumption of several liters a day would far surpass that of anyone I know. Like brews from the ancient Near East, sorghum beers from Africa would not look like "beer" to American drinkers; they're thick to the degree that one is said to "eat" beer instead of drink it, usually through a long straw.* The alcohol content of these African sorghum beers is often high, and there are special social traditions around the brewing and the drinking of them.

And even Europeans, who were the most dependent on barley beer, brewed with other ingredients as a last resort. In times of shortage, beer lovers in northern Europe, where grapes for wine did not grow, had a simple choice: make a beer out of whatever was available, or go without fermented drink. Not much thought was required, here; they threw whatever they had on hand into the beer pot. They fermented it. And then they drank the brew until they enjoyed themselves, which sounds like it could take quite a while sometimes.

An example of such a brew is Mumm, which was an unhopped "ale"—kind of—dating formally to at least 1492, though descriptions of it appear as early as 1350 to 1390. Mumm did not arise exclusively out of a shortage of barley, though it would have been attractive when

---

* Here, and also in the case of the Mesopotamians, I am reminded of my maternal grandfather, who believed one of life's grandest pleasures, in addition to fresh-squeezed orange juice, grilled onions and peppers, and German shepherds, was an evening spent on the porch sipping a can of Coors through a plastic flexible straw. My mother thought him ridiculous, but it appears that he was simply reclaiming a forgotten beer-drinking practice.

the barley crops failed, because of its flexible recipe. According to one document, Mumm was

> *a wholesome drink, brewed from wheat malt, boiled down to a third of its original quantity, to which were added oatmeal and ground beans, and after working, quite a number of herbs and other vegetable products, including the tops of fir and birch, a handful of burnet, betony, marjoram, avens, pennyroyal, wild thyme, and elderflowers, and a few ounces of cardamom seeds, and barberry.*

Other vegetable products? The crowns of resinous trees? Seriously? I've never seen so many brewing adjuncts in one recipe. Talk about a drink that requires a straw: it sounds more like fermented compost. However, Mumm does show how "beer" has long been viewed as a malleable product—if the drinker can only be convinced to imbibe it. And, in fact, Mumm was widely drunk into the 1600s in England, until its popularity finally waned in the eighteenth century. Don't knock it 'til you've tried it, would appear to be the lesson here.

For as much as I felt alone with my sorghum brews, some of which were laced with the strange, unappealing taste (in beer, at least) of raspberries, strawberries, and honey, in time I would come to appreciate Dogfish Head's Strawberry Tweason'ale—brewed from sorghum, buckwheat, honey, strawberries, and hops—as a distant relative of other cultures' beer. Understanding this intellectually and accepting it at the table, however, are two different things. History and culture are powerful forces that we respond to without much awareness until something jolts us loose from their hold; they make us adept at pointing out the real thing, whether a glass of ale or piece of cake, from the impostor. But the truth, as any historian could tell me, is that for most of human culinary history, a distinction between "real" and "fake" has been irrelevant. Shortage and famine have been the norm, not the exception, and they have always led people through a combination of ingenuity and willpower to find ways to satisfy themselves. With one part of my mind, I knew the only reason I was crying foul was that I had taken for granted that foods like barley beer and wheat bread would always be on my table, simply because I live in an age, and a place, where I had never before even contemplated going without them.

The other part of my mind didn't buy this for one second. It wanted the first part to just shut the hell up, stop intellectualizing, and find some food—and beer—that tasted like it was supposed to taste.

7

What's Wrong with
the Wheat?

E at enough fake bread, drink enough fake beer, and a person be-gins to ask, *Why?* I understood the genetic predisposition. I accepted the mystery over what causes a gene to flip to the "on" position. Lots of people have that question, from those who receive a cancer diagnosis to victims of Parkinson's disease, and they had much more to worry about than I did. The fact remained, though, that I had not, thankfully, come down with cancer or Parkinson's. I suffered from a sudden inexplicable intolerance to several grains. Why was this starting to happen to more and more people? And why *now?*

I'll admit that I immediately suspected the grain. I wasn't the only one. For the next two years, whenever I met someone with a gluten-related disorder—whether celiac disease, wheat allergy, or gluten sensitivity—I casually asked them where they put the blame, and often received the same answer: *Something is in the wheat.* It's a sign of our times, revealing of our tense and troubled relationship with food producers. We immediately suspect corporate agribusiness when people start getting sick: glyphosate (the generic name for the weed killer Roundup), genetically modified organisms (GMOs), plant breeding, and the unsanitary conditions at feedlots and slaughterhouses. Big agriculture, whether the producer is harvesting chickens or watermelons, is far from a blameless industry, and investigations of contemporary foodways have taught eaters how and why to mistrust. The suspicions are valid. And yet the world we move through is far more complex than the dinner on our plates, and how that dinner got there.

Are gluten-related disorders caused by something in the wheat? Has wheat changed significantly from the plant it used to be? Sometimes I wondered what would happen if I flew to a dig site in the Nile Valley, located an ancient king's tomb, and found viable seed in a ceramic vessel buried with him. I concocted a whole food/science fiction mash-up in which I stuffed the wheat grains into my pocket Indiana Jones–style and hastily departed, careful not to trip over the corner of the king's sarcophagus and hoping he'd had his fill of the wheat already, or that he was so far into his trip to the other side that it was impossible for him to reach out and curse me.

I returned home. I ground the grain into flour with the Cuisinart. Using emmer or einkorn flour, I proceeded to make a loaf of bread according to the *Artisan* recipe. Or I could go old-school and mix up a paste with water and salt like they used to do in Anatolia, back in the day, and slap it on a preheated brick in the middle of the Weber.

When the bread was done, I timidly put a piece of this truly ancestral food in my mouth while it still steamed. I chewed, savoring the nuttiness. Then I took a deep breath and swallowed. What now? Would my stomach bloat in gaseous rage at my stupidity? Would I rush to the bathroom? Would the neurological storm of headaches, brain fog, and mood swings arrive?

Or would I smile a few hours later, realizing that I felt completely fine, and proceed to make a Dagwood-style seven-layer monstrosity that I nearly had to unhinge my jaw to eat? Maybe a portion of French toast so monstrous that not even IHOP, that purveyor of glycemic excess, would put it on their menu?

And then, thus fortified, inspired, and returned to my proper place at history's table, I could begin the search for ancient barley with which to brew beer . . .

Besides the fact that such a plot is impossible to carry out, the problem—or one of them—is that the conversation about the causes of celiac disease (and other gluten-related illnesses) among doctors, researchers, and advocates is complicated. There are many studies and no shortage of opinions. One of the thornier issues is the multiple ways gluten and wheat can be reactive and harmful: there's autoimmunity (celiac, for which a person needs the genes and the trigger), wheat allergy (non-autoimmune, with typical signs of allergic reaction, like histamines), and gluten sensitivity (no antibodies, histamines, or genetic markers present, but well-being improves demonstrably when the individual cuts out gluten). Taken together, the three disorders appear to present a variety of negative effects gluten can have on some people, but they all potentially have different routes to pathogenesis. At times it seems as if the only statement those involved in the research seem to agree on is "We don't know for sure why this is happening." This is not what a person wants to hear, given the limitations of the "cure" for the foreseeable future.

Broadly speaking, there are three camps in the causation debate: There are those who believe that raiding an ancient king's tomb for wheat *would* result in my procuring safe grain, because something, though we don't know exactly what or why, is indeed making modern wheat more reactive. On the other side are those who believe that stealing ancestral wheat from a dig site would only lead to my getting glutened in a more elaborate, expensive, and entertaining way. This camp is interested in environmental factors, from modern hygienic practices to the way we raise infants so as to either bolster or compromise their immune systems. And then there are those who say the cause of celiac disease and possibly other gluten-related disorders is a combination of all those factors, a synergy between plant changes, alterations to our environment, and our habits. It's not hard to find this third position especially grim, because it suggests that the conditions of modern life have gotten so complex so quickly—our food, environment, and medical practices—that our bodies (especially our immune systems) cannot keep up with the pace of the changes. This complexity not only makes it challenging to identify a single cause of intolerance to gluten, but also suggests that gluten may turn out to be only one of many reactive foods.

Some basic immunology is required to understand the arguments about how and why modern wheat appears to be different from ancestral varieties, and thus harmful. Proteins like gluten contain components called peptides, or chains of amino acids. While some peptides are harmless, certain ones can, in people with the proper genetics (i.e., possessing the specific HLA markers for celiac), function as antigens—that is, they cue an immune response in the body. The surfaces of peptides have regions called epitopes, responsive areas that fit into the HLA proteins like a key into a keyhole, in order to bind with proteins on immune cells called T cells. T cells recognize gluten peptides, and with the appropriate additional trigger, they become activated as the main players in causing the damage in celiac disease. Usually this destruction gets visited on a foreign invader, not healthy tissue; autoimmunity is a case of misrecognition, when the immune system fails to recognize its constituent parts—like the walls of the small intestine—as belonging to itself. With celiac disease, a confluence of the correct genetic markers and other, poorly understood environmental triggers must occur before the immune system fires up. Stress, surgery, illness, pregnancy, or some other event could serve as a trigger to initiate the adverse reaction to gluten.

Most of the discussion about the differences between modern wheat and ancestral wheat (and barley, spelt, and rye) emphasizes a specific peptide present in modern gluten proteins called 33-mer gliadin. Since the early 2000s, this peptide has been identified in the celiac response to gluten, though research suggests there are likely other immunogenic compounds in gluten, as well. Numerous studies overlap in their assertions that ancestral wheat and barley, and even grains consumed by humans as late as the Middle Ages, contained less of this peptide, and so the wheat those people ate presented less of a challenge to their digestion and their immune systems. The 33-mer gliadin peptide might even have been absent from ancestral wheat strains entirely. Some researchers have also noted that even as celiac-causing peptides are expressed at higher levels in modern cereals, non-celiac-triggering epitopes—the safer peptides—seem to be expressed less.

Nobody knows for sure why this has happened. Possible factors include the industrialization of agriculture, the use of pesticides, and the hybridizing practices that produce new strains of wheat. New wheat hybrids have been presumed safe for human and animal consumption, and so they often come to market with virtually no testing. Furthermore, the time frame in which the changes from wheat breeding have occurred, relatively speaking, is short. While wheat has gone through thousands of hybridizations in ten thousand years—there are some 25,000 cultivars—the pace accelerated markedly between the 1940s and the late 1960s, during and after the Green Revolution, which revolutionized wheat hardiness and yields. Some views hold that the rapid alterations to a plant that provides up to 50 percent of the calories consumed in industrialized countries (and an average of 35 percent of caloric intake) have far outpaced the abilities of the human gut and immune system to keep up.

The handling of the wheat could also be a factor, and so industrialized bread-making has fallen under some suspicion (though it's important to remember that modern eaters consume gluten in many more forms than bread). Fermentation times in modern factory bakeries are shorter than those used before the late nineteenth century, when bread-making became automated. Less fermentation time might prevent detrimental peptides from breaking down; in some studies, slow fermentation with lactobacilli seems to result in sourdough breads that those with less severe (i.e., less sensitive) gluten-related disorders, including celiac disease, can tolerate. Meanwhile, other industrial food-processing practices have further modified the proteins in cereals, and it's been argued that the rising rates of celiac disease might be driven by the availability of large quantities of highly refined wheat with a high content of gluten, or reactive gluten fragments.

To add further complexity, it's also possible that other parts of the wheat plant beyond the glutenin and gliadin proteins are immunogenic. In a recent study, pest-resistance molecules in wheat have been observed to cause an innate immune response in people who carry the HLA genetic markers. Did these molecules naturally evolve, or were they bred into the plant? At this point, thousands of times removed from the earliest wheat cultivars, we're unlikely to find out.

Finally, the changes to wheat may be especially important since modern eaters consume high levels of gluten. At first such a claim appears to fly in the face of the historical data on bread consumption, which—the recent increased demand for artisanal bread and revival of small bakeries to the contrary—is at its lowest point in thousands of years (excluding times of famine, war, and natural disasters). But eaters who depend on processed and prepared foods because time, money, or both are short might in fact be consuming as much or even more gluten than a working-class eater in nineteenth-century England or France. It is a tough case to make numerically because the exact amounts are difficult to measure and are specific to each individual's diet. It is possible to estimate, though. The average slice of whole-wheat bread contains about 4.8 grams of gluten. In addition to the obvious wheat flour, most commercially produced breads (and breading, bread crumbs, etc.) contain vital wheat gluten, a concentration of the protein that increases the elasticity of industrially made loaves and improves shelf life. Slice for slice, mass-produced bread might pack more gluten than the bread our ancestors ate. A typical serving of pasta contains 6.1 grams of gluten. And so it becomes easy to see how Europeans consume, on average, 10 to 20 grams of gluten per day, with some people ingesting as much as 50 grams if they're following a Mediterranean or Middle Eastern diet (or drinking a lot of beer). Fifty grams might not *sound* like much, but that quantity would exceed my threshold for damage 2,500 times. According to the National Foundation for Celiac Awareness, 0.1 grams of gluten—the equivalent of 1/48th of a slice of bread—will do enough damage to a person with celiac disease to show up on a biopsy.

Vital wheat gluten, in particular, is an interesting consideration. It has contributed heavily to the increase in gluten consumption in the United States since the 1970s, which by some estimates has tripled. The increased usage of vital wheat gluten came when whole-wheat breads and other products began receiving praise for their positive health effects. Whole-grain breads presented a challenge for industrial-scale bakers, though: they stale and toughen up faster than breads made from highly refined flour. Vital wheat gluten was the solution. Even researchers who do not think wheat breeding itself has any causal role in celiac disease find the correlation between increased vital wheat gluten consumption and the rise in celiac disease interesting, and worth more exploration.

An eater can add up the gluten in his bread and pasta, but the rest he eats is likely to be hidden. Wheat goes into all kinds of pre-made sauces, from Asian condiments like ponzu and teriyaki to cheese sauces, salad dressings, and marinades. There is wheat and/or gluten in imitation crab, cream-based soups, sausages and hotdogs, and vegetarian "meat," some of which is nothing more than a brick of gluten. Malt extract from barley is in Rice Krispies (and in other non-wheat-based cereals, cookies, and prepared desserts), and most other breakfast cereals—whether in flake, granule, dinosaur, or animal shapes—are made of wheat. Anything hit with brewer's yeast or malt vinegar carries gluten. Licorice, Reese's Peanut Butter Cups, most processed desserts and snacks, and hard candies can all contain gluten, as do some protein shakes, nutritional drinks, smoothies, vitamins, supplements, and medications. A trace amount turned out to be in the Augmentin

I was once prescribed. In the midst of acute GI distress I called the manufacturer, who told me that the drug *tested* to be GF, but one of the inactive ingredients was derived from wheat.[*]

Finally, there are sources of wheat and gluten that are not in food, but which a person still might ingest: cosmetics, shampoos, Play-Doh, the glue on the flaps of envelopes. The most extreme case of gluten poisoning from an unlikely source that I have ever heard of occurred in 2012, when forums on celiac-disease websites lit up over the story of a girl whose GI symptoms persisted despite a strict elimination diet. Careful investigation eventually revealed that the polymers in her orthodontic retainer were derived from wheat, leaching into her saliva, and causing a reaction.

There are some problems with the modern wheat hypothesis, though. Anyone who believes that the ancient physician Aretaeus accurately diagnosed celiac disease around 100 AD must also accept that the triggers for celiac disease existed in the wheat and barley. They might have been less concentrated, though. The HLA immune-response genes may not have been as prevalent in the population then, either, meaning that fewer people reacted to the harmful peptides.

One thing we can say for sure: while hybridization may play a role, genetically modified (GM) wheat is *not* the cause of gluten-related disorders. Hybridization occurs via the crossing of plants; genetic modification requires a laboratory to alter the genome of a plant so that it expresses traits that are not inherent to it. As of 2015, in the United States, Canada, and the European Union, there is no GM wheat on the market. That doesn't mean that bioengineering corporations haven't

---

[*] I might also have been especially sensitive to that broad-spectrum antibiotic—which is not good. I was able to discontinue it, but what would I do if I needed one? I'm told an injection would bypass the gut and avoid causing an autoimmune reaction.

tried to introduce GM wheat, because they have, and it doesn't mean that they won't try to introduce it again, because they will. By some forecasts, GM wheat could enter into the regulatory process within the next five years.

In fact, the resistance to the bioengineering firm Monsanto's attempts to introduce GM wheat in Canada in the late 1990s and early 2000s highlights how wheat is still viewed as sacrosanct in contemporary culture. Monsanto's GM wheat strain was modified to tolerate Roundup, also known by its generic name, glyphosate. "Roundup Ready" or "RR" crops tolerate doses of this pesticide (technically, it's an antimicrobial) that are lethal to weeds, allowing for blanket treatments. It's an efficient means to reduce competition for soil nutrients and sunlight, and glyphosate has been regarded as safe by the Environmental Protection Agency for years, although recent scholarship has suggested that it may not be as benign as initially believed. In 2014, the herbicide turned up as a possible cause not only of celiac disease itself, but also of gluten sensitivity. It is an effective desiccant used for "drying down" crops to speed them into processing. A review article hypothesized that malabsorption in carnivorous fish had been caused by glyphosate because its antimicrobial properties also targeted bacteria resident in the gut; the same might be happening in humans who come in contact with glyphosate. The problem with the review, as the study's critics pointed out, was that the levels of glyphosate the fish were being dosed with were extremely high. Nonetheless, the World Health Organization's research program recently declared the herbicide a probable carcinogen, independent of the celiac-causation studies.

As the Canadian geographer Emily Eaton describes the reception of GM wheat in Canada, Roundup was only part of the issue. Rather, Canadian farmers, consumers, and environmentalists believed that it was important that the wheat and the bread they were eating remained the same as what their ancestors had eaten. Of course, the wheat wasn't the same, exactly, but they saw a significant difference between the breeding their forefathers had practiced on the prairie and the laboratory activities of a bioengineering corporation. The early settlers of the prairie provinces of Manitoba and Saskatchewan had carved out identities as wheat farmers, which in turn became part of the Canadian cultural and patriotic identity, especially in the west. (The same could be said of Americans with ties to the "bread basket" of the Central Plains.) In much the same way, religious communities throughout Canada expressed dismay at the thought of blessing and breaking GM bread and wafers for the Eucharist.* It hardly mattered that the bread would look and taste the same. The idea that the Host was not an unaltered, God-given food but an engineered one threatened to desecrate Christians' sense of living symbolism.

Proponents of bioengineering have suggested that, someday, it might be possible to genetically modify wheat to be celiac-safe. Much though I'd like to think I wouldn't eat GM wheat, a few years without gluten, and many struggles and disappointments in the kitchen, have shown me that the idea of "purity" at the heart of the resistance to GMOs looks different when your choice is between GM bread and beer, if it were to become available, and ersatz bread and beer. I feel that I'm on tricky ground here, close to hypocrisy, because if I can avoid it, I won't eat meat from industrial farms and feedlots that keep animals in cruel and filthy conditions, factory-farmed eggs where the hens never see the light of day, indiscriminately harvested fish, or produce from companies that exploit and dehumanize workers. If no harm were to come from celiac-safe wheat—a big "if," given the trouble that famously came to family farmers in the Midwest after GM corn pollinated their fields, putting them out of business—there

---

* The definition of purity in bread would appear to cut both ways, though. Many churches are loath to bless GF bread for communion rituals, and rely instead on "gluten-reduced" breads, which are not safe for all celiacs, though some can tolerate them.

would be no foul.* The point is that celiac disease has shown me another side of purity, one that has less to do with the genetics of the cultivar than with the experience of eating the same food as the other people around the table: inclusion, comfort, and pleasurable eating. And for me, at least, this other kind of purity sometimes seems significant enough to tip the scales.

I don't have to worry too much about solving that conundrum anytime soon. Skeptics believe that bioengineering celiac-safe wheat will be challenging, because while the 33-mer gliadin peptide has been identified as a smoking gun, researchers have admitted they do not know all of the genes in the plant responsible for creating autoimmune responses. The problematic sequences or fragments may not even be located in the same sites on the wheat genome, thus rendering them harder to identify. And it's possible that if all of the immunogenic compounds in wheat *were* neutralized, the baking properties of the grain would be altered. That would be a cruel turn indeed: now I would have flour I could eat, but I wouldn't be able to make a damned thing out of it.

On the other side of the celiac-causation debate is convincing scholarship suggesting that wheat breeding may have little or nothing to do with gluten intolerances. This camp finds statements about strategic breeding leading to increased protein content questionable for a simple reason: farmers were not able to systematically increase gluten content until a couple of hundred years ago, because there was no way to accurately measure the protein in wheat until then. That would not preclude coincidental increases in 33-mer gliadin peptides as a result

---

* Another possibility: a modification like non-immunogenic properties might be "stacked" on top of other, more desirable traits, such as pest- or drought-resistance, so as to increase the appeal of the GM seed.

of breeding for other qualities; nor would it account for the impact of the Green Revolution on hybridized wheat varieties. It's notable, however, that thousands of years ago, farmers were selecting for *lower* protein content in grain, not higher, because protein is inversely proportional to starch. Early farmers strategically bred for bigger grains because they were easier to harvest and thresh, and bigger grains are bigger because they have more starch. Once bakers started leavening dough around 5,000 BC, they would have noted that some types of wheat made better raised bread than other types—emmer and other bread wheats were preferable to durum, for example—but the growers would only have been able to increase the protein content from one generation of wheat plants to the next intuitively, not empirically.

It's not even desirable, from a miller's perspective, to constantly increase protein content. All cooks, but especially bakers and pastry chefs, share at least one goal with scientists: to have a reliable replication of the same chemical reaction every time. While durum semolina flour ideally contains about 7 to 11 percent protein, and bread flour 11 to 14 percent, the protein in unmilled, unblended grain fluctuates wildly, sometimes reaching values as high as 28 percent. What causes that? It's been argued that environmental factors have more influence than breeding practices—even more than pumping the soil full of fertilizers, a practice that became commonplace following World War II, when tons of nitrogen was repurposed from the munitions industry and found its way into the corn and wheat fields of the Central Plains. The most popular belief is that protein content is tied to climactic factors. The solution to the variation is to blend flours of different protein contents to assure year-to-year consistency: 7–11 percent or 11–16 percent, depending upon what the flour is for. This means that even if the protein content of unmilled grain itself has gone up, the amount of gluten an eater takes in would have remained relatively unchanged since the advent of reliable measurement. It also suggests that those who ate wheat and barley breads before the advent of protein measurement—and, as a result, the blending of flour for consistent ratios—might have seen their own gluten consumption vary wildly from year to year.

If the epidemiology of celiac disease does not always support wheat breeding and the quantity of gluten in the Western diet as causes, then what else could explain its rising prevalence? Recently, explorations of the human microbiome have become especially exciting. We are only just beginning to understand how the resident microecology, or assembly of bacteria in our guts, could have a key effect in many human immunological functions, including our tolerance for gluten— though it seems that several factors can influence microbial diversity in a person's gastrointestinal system. Breast-feeding, for instance, has been shown to increase resident lactobacilli and bifidobacteria in infants—an important observation in light of one study that found that a drop in lactobacilli precedes a celiac-disease diagnosis. Breast milk is rich in bacteria that compete with other bacteria such as native strains of E. coli, which have been shown in vitro to intensify gut inflammation, whereas strains of bifidobacteria appear to protect against gut inflammation. An individual's toleration of many foods, not just gluten, might then be linked to low populations of "good" bacteria. Among the most compelling evidence is a cultural turn away from breast-feeding in Sweden from 1984 to 1996, which correlates to a population of Swedes who turned out to be diagnosed with celiac disease at a rate three times the national average.

Overall municipal hygiene, and the role of hygienic practices in preventing exposure to microbes from other sources, also seems to have an effect on gut health. In 2013, the *New York Times* reported on the Russian territory of Karelia, which shares a border with Finland. Genetically, the Karelians share many similarities with the Finns, though there are a few key exceptions, among them that the Finns are diagnosed with celiac disease at much higher rates. While celiac-disease cases in Finland have doubled in the last twenty years, the Russian Karelians appear not to present it at the same rates even though statistically 30 to 50 percent of them are likely to be carrying the genetic predisposition. According to the hygiene theory, the most important difference between the Finns and the Russian Karelians might be the infrastructural and economic challenges that effectively stalled the Karelian territory in the early twentieth century. The lack of development has affected many aspects of life, including overall hygiene; Russian Karelians encounter more airborne and waterborne microbes than the Finns. However, the study had some limitations, including not tracking dietary factors such as the type and quantity of bread (and other glutenous grains and foods) consumed by the Karelians.

But the identification of celiac disease nearly two thousand years ago seems to complicate the hygiene theory as much as it does the wheat-breeding theory, since it predates many of the inventions, child-rearing practices, and environmental conditions that subscribers point to. Even relatively recent history is problematic to the hygiene theory: Samuel Gee, the nineteenth-century London physician who identified diet as the key factor, did not have an antibiotic at his disposal. The invention of penicillin was still more than half a century away. And London during the Industrial Revolution—or during any point up to the advent of indoor plumbing, sanitation, and disinfectants—was a dirty place, teeming with microbes that paradoxically both sickened and protected people. The animals in the food chain were not receiving subtherapeutic antibiotic treatments to help them gain weight, as so much industrially raised livestock does now (another potential cause of reduced gut flora in humans). Furthermore, Samuel Gee's patients at the Hospital for Sick Children had been breast-fed, as had Willem-Karel Dicke's pediatric patients decades later in the Netherlands. Despite all of these environmental differences, celiac disease existed in the ancient world, and potentially in greater numbers than anyone knew.

All of this research into the cleanliness of one's environment and its impact on gut health got me wondering. I called up my mother one day. I knew she had kept the house I grew up in extremely clean, which meant I had likely come in contact with fewer microbes. But for how long did she breast-feed me? How did I take to it? At what age did she put me on solid food, give me my first piece of bread, or Barnum's Animals Crackers? Was I three months old? That would be a good age to be introduced to gluten, according to the latest information, as it may help build a tolerance to immunogenic peptides, while six months would, by the same estimates, be too late. And what about antibiotics? When was the first time I needed them? I know my brother was always getting ear infections, but was I any hardier? I was hoping to hear about all kinds of assaults on my young microbiome—it would have at least suggested that one theory was more valid than another in my own case—but it turns out that I had a normal infancy. I liked breast milk for a while, and then I liked gluten even more. That only left the cleanliness of the house. Maybe my mother should have moved to Karelia for a few years, or taken me to play downwind from the city dump.

Put all of these factors together—the changes wheat has undergone over ten thousand years, especially in the last fifty or so; the changes to the human environment; and the changes an individual like me can kick-start in his own body without intending to—and it's easy to see how there are multiple pathways to the disease. The most cautious studies seem to emphasize the ongoing mystery of causation while acknowledging that any one hypothesis, whether hygiene or wheat breeding, is reductive. Celiac disease, and even other gluten-related disorders, could be the result of a perfect storm of factors. It's now common for researchers to talk about the "celiac iceberg" as a metaphor for the many considerations that rest below the apparent surface of the disease.

There is increasing urgency to uncover as much of the hidden part of the iceberg as possible. In the United States, there's been a fourfold increase in diagnosis in the last fifty years, with some blame falling on the grain-heavy "Western" and Mediterranean diets. For every one person who is diagnosed, it's estimated that there are five or six who have "silent" celiac disease and still carry all the risks of long-term exposure to gluten. Researchers are also seeing increased diagnoses in places where only a few decades ago they never expected to see celiac disease: Africa, Asia, and South America. In Asia in particular, the combination of increased fast-food consumption and the tendency to view wheat as a "preferred staple" as income levels rise and diets get Westernized—away from the traditional staples of rice and millet— means diagnosis rates will continue to increase.

There are rarely easy answers to such questions. And in the end, what difference would having a "return address" for my celiac diagnosis make? It might allow me to feel a little better intellectually, by filling in the holes in the story, but knowing the cause isn't going to fix anything at the table.

Pharmaceutical companies are at work on that, however. To date, the most advanced research is in drugs that wouldn't "cure" the disease so much as make it possible for a celiac to eat gluten once in a while, or to recover more quickly after getting glutened. The figures on the disease's rising prevalence have made therapies look more profitable, and thus many drugs, expensive drugs, will show up on the market in the next several years.

The more I emerged from withdrawal that winter, and the more I adjusted to the boundaries of my new diet and, as a result, my life, the more seriously I promised myself that I would not take any of the drugs when they came on the market. In my opinion, it sounds as if most of them are being designed as crutches, not cures. I would want to wait a good long time to see what the unintended side effects are. Learning about the epidemiology of the disease has given me respect for the intricacies of the human body. Ten years from the point of introduction seems like a safe if arbitrary length of time to keep some celiac canaries in the mine shaft ahead of me.

But set a sandwich in front of me. Put a pint of stout beside it. Then, see what I do.

8

STRANGE GRAINS

Like explorers in a strange territory, Bec and I purchased guides to help us acclimate. Every one of the cookbooks we acquired featured a cover photograph of a loaf of bread. There were pictures of other baked goods too, usually cookies and pies, sometimes a pizza. The bread, though, was the most hopeful-looking. It appeared to rival any loaf turned out by the finest bakery on its best day. Perfectly risen, browned, dusted with flour, and graced with airy crumbs like I remembered eating only months ago, these rice or sorghum or potato (or all three) breads stood as proof to eaters who had recently been exiled from the land of wheat and gluten that all was not in fact lost.

I clung to those images at first. Then I learned that they were lies. What else could explain how the loaves we so earnestly attempted in our own kitchen turned into such colossal disappointments? Actually, quite a lot, from the age of our oven to the chlorine in our village water supply to the strains of yeast and loaf pans we were using. Baking with wheaten flour is already an exacting process, but baking a dough made of the ten to twelve ingredients a GF recipe calls for adds more variability.

The first GF recipe Bec ever attempted was for a cinnamon-raisin bread from a popular GF cookbook. At the time, it was one of the standard-bearers in the genre. The recipe called for a blend of several different flours, which we went out and bought to the tune of about twenty dollars, plus a bag of xanthan gum for structure. It utilized a big dose of canola oil in an attempt to hide the grit. The spices, raisins, and sugar promised to help, as well.

Bec found the preparation stressful. The batter—it would be an exaggeration to call it dough—didn't want to come together in the bowl, as of course it wouldn't, lacking gluten. The mixture fell apart in her hands as she tried to shape it. For an hour we kept checking on the pan as the batter struggled to rise like a mortally wounded animal. It gained about half an inch before she gave up and shoved it in the oven anyway.

As the mixture baked, though, the kitchen filled with that familiar smell: the nuttiness of caramelizing grains, spices, and a hint of yeast. This aroma has probably deceived eaters of faux-bread since the first desperate people decided to make loaves of peas and chestnuts. Like me, they must have lingered near the oven, breathing in a promise that disappeared the moment they sliced the loaf and tasted it.

Which was exactly what happened with this bread.

After it had cooled for an hour, we cut it. The crumb fell apart in chunks, like pieces of a dried-out plaster wall.

It was a bad sign, but I remained optimistic. Okay, I didn't have to toast slices. I would eat the chunks as they fell off. I could try to brown them in a skillet. Hope was clearly the operative factor here, along with denial. That ended when I tasted the bread and got the sugar, the spices, a ton of grit, and little depth. I applauded Bec's efforts anyway. She was trying a form of alchemy in the kitchen, attempting to turn rice into wheat.

Every recipe we tried, no matter where it came from, turned out somewhere between disappointment and a complete flop. The breads failed to rise, or they failed to hold together, the grains tasted weird, and those loaves I could slice still left behind an oily, gritty paste in my mouth. Some were edible only with a tablespoon of butter and a quarter-inch layer of jam. The best loaf came from my sister-in-law, who greeted me on a trip to Maryland with a surprisingly good white bread she had made in a bread machine. I wasn't going to rush out and get a bread machine, though, at least not yet. And the low point came when Bec made an Irish soda bread from an online recipe. It was the most spectacular failure I've ever seen: sandy, sour, salty, and completely without structure—like a lump of baking powder, drywall, and water. We hovered over it like an accident scene for a few seconds, and then pitched it, still warm, into the trash.

I would remember this winter as the one when I thought about food all the time, and not in a good way. Late in the afternoon, as the dinner hour approached, I ran through the naturally GF foods I couldn't tolerate because my system was still trashed: fish, dairy, legumes, quinoa. I thought about the traditional dishes I didn't want to attempt as GF any longer, like pasta with olive oil, Parmigiano-Reggiano, and garlic, since they didn't taste the same. I also wanted to avoid eating so much rice; the repetition was boring, but I was paying attention to discussions about arsenic content in rice.

The restrictions led us to sample new grains that we would not have ordinarily purchased, simply because they were now safe and "for us." We could have gotten along just fine with corn, potatoes, and rice (and eventually, we would), but the hole left behind by wheat seemed so large that we felt we had to avail ourselves of every chance to fill it in. We picked up bags of millet, amaranth, and teff, and tried to work them into our meals. This might have been a good thing to do six or eight months later, but to move into such unfamiliar cooking territory in the midst of withdrawal, longing, and frustration was, I now think, a mistake.

It led me to develop an immediate hatred for millet. Bec hated it too. We *tried* to love it, but in the end could only wonder why the Chinese had called this grain "king" before rice (and wheat) cultivation moved northward. Maybe King Millet was a despotic ruler, and rice was the liberator? The history of millet is in fact longer than that of wheat, but it was not a history I could appreciate. Millet looks like birdseed (because it *is* birdseed), and it cooked up dry, gritty, and less flavorful than any other grain I had ever tasted. Over a period of several weeks I attempted to steam millet, boil it like a porridge, and use it like couscous in tagines and salads. I toasted millet in a pan, then prepared it like risotto, and loaded on the cheese. I made millet pilaf. Nothing could make me like it.

I tried to enjoy amaranth, too, but couldn't find any enthusiasm for a pile of gray mush, even though the flavor and texture appealed to me more. I had heard it was possible to pop amaranth like corn kernels, but I couldn't work up the interest to try it. I felt the same way about teff. In the next town over, an Ethiopian woman was making huge, round, flat loaves of injera, the staple bread from Ethiopia. The texture of injera is spongy, and it tastes a little like sourdough. Ethiopians use it to scoop up pieces of cooked meat and vegetables. I bought a few wheels—they aren't really loaves—from the health-food store, and although I enjoyed them, I could not commit. Injera became a food fling, an impulse buy.

There was a pattern here. Almost any grain indigenous to African and Asian cuisine (with the exception of rice) failed to appeal to me. Sorghum fit this pattern too, and so would tapioca (cassava). Intellectually, I knew that millet, amaranth, and teff had been enormously important to huge populations for eons, but I could not see them as *my* food. The millet was even regionally sourced, from the Finger Lakes, but that didn't make it taste any better. I bitterly reminded myself that being able to disparage these grains was a "first world problem." The only explanation I could come up with was that the stability of wheat supplies in the course of recent history had quite literally ruined me. I wasn't a picky eater. I was even in a mood of receptivity—I *wanted* to like these foods, and Bec did too—but it seemed that only those common to the history of Western cuisine made the cut and remained in our regular rotation.*

I had a suspicion that I might have enjoyed these grains more if other people were eating them along with me. I did not feel like a gastronomical explorer, as I did whenever I discovered a new dish and eagerly presented it to my friends. There was no way in hell I was going to prepare my guests millet or amaranth, and this made the experience of trying and disliking them feel more isolating. In the entire time I've been on a GF diet, I've talked to only one person who expressed real enthusiasm for either grain: a friend who is an adventurous traveler and true Renaissance man, an early-modern literature scholar and hobby farmer who translates Chinese by day and sees to his grove of nut and fruit trees in the evening.** There's nothing he will not eat. More power to him, I say. There will be more millet and amaranth for him if I don't buy it.

Meanwhile, we persisted with our attempts to procure, by some means, edible bread, though at this point it would have been easier to just give in and go without. But I couldn't do that, because a day without the promise of leavened bread of some kind seemed emptier to me. A breadless day did not seem as impossible as a day without salt, or without a spot of sugar, but it felt as uncomfortable as the days I've gone without coffee.

---

* Buckwheat and garbanzo bean flour would also satisfy me when I discovered them a little later on, though more occasionally than regularly.

** Actually, I *did* once prepare millet for this friend, in the form of millet cakes with Chinese herbs, GF tamari, ginger, and something like a half-dozen eggs to glue the mixture together. This was a recipe I made up on the spot because I had a lot of millet in the house and here was a man who would help me eat it. I pan-fried these millet cakes and flipped them with a surgeon's lightness of touch because, having no gluten, they wanted to come apart in the pan. He and his wife pronounced them good. I think they were being kind. After this mission, the Experimental Millet Program was forever scrubbed.

And a week without bread felt as incomplete as a week without wine. Some of this was the experience of baking loaves in the house, which had come to happen with such regularity that the smell of bread had nearly become *part* of the house—as much as the smell of wood smoke in the winter months, cut grass in the summer, and lilac in the spring. For a time, the smell of beer had also regularly wafted throughout our rooms as David and I boiled wort for stouts and ales. I have not smelled that earthy, pungent aroma since barley vanished along with wheat; when I finally do, I know it will hold me in a nostalgic swoon. But Bec and I baked far more often, and for far longer, than David and I brewed.

For all of the regularity of our baking, I never took the smell or the sight of a loaf of fresh bread for granted. I remarked it every time, not so much out of a habit of mindfulness, I'm sorry to say, as out of comfort and anticipation. I did not participate much in the preparation, the tactile experience of kneading the loaves themselves; this was Bec's job, because she both enjoyed it and excelled at it, and because touching the flour caused my hands to break out in painful blisters—one of the earliest warning signs of celiac disease, I now know.* More than anything, though, the presence of risen bread in our house had come to signify stability. Routine. Reliability. To mix the dough and allow it to rise requires time; to bake it properly requires more; to let it cool requires still more. The demands for time and focus, and for putting other things aside, may explain why so many home bakers find that bread-making is an antidote to stress.

Helpless against this personal history, and still lacking a good, reliable recipe, we stopped baking from scratch and turned to bagged mixes. The first we tried was from Bob's Red Mill, and when I opened the oven, I could hardly believe my eyes. The bread looked beauti-

---

* I had visited a dermatologist about the sores on my hands a decade before I was diagnosed with celiac disease, and instead of diagnosing me with a condition called dermatitis herpetiformis, a skin reaction to gluten, he misdiagnosed eczema and gave me some topical steroids.

ful. Finally, here was something that resembled the airbrushed cover-model loaves from the GF cookbooks. I snapped a picture of the triumph and sent it to a few friends. When the loaf cooled, though, it tasted nothing like the appearance suggested. The crumb wasn't as strange or gritty as the train wrecks we'd made or bought from the store, but the garbanzo bean flour gave it a funky taste—"beany," in the accurate words of America's Test Kitchen—and the overall flavor lacked depth. I bought a few more bags because I thought I might learn to like it, but that never happened. After the Bob's Red Mill, we switched to the bagged mix by Pamela's, another stalwart in the field of GF baking. This bread did taste fuller, a little spongier, and even like the loaves of potato bread and commercial white that Bec and I grew up on, though not at all like the *Artisan* wheat breads we had been baking. The finish was a little unpleasant, but we made our peace and started buying six-packs of bags from Amazon.

I later learned that there is a long historical precedent for these bagged mixes and the ingredients they utilize, and even for the wayward cookbook recipes we followed for a time: having a loaf of *something* on the table has long been more important than what that loaf is made from.

When wheat, barley, and even rye have been in short supply in Europe, eaters have automatically switched to making bread out of peas, beans, nuts, acorns, and even inedible material. Famine was almost always the mother of this type of innovation. During hard times, the Corsicans made cheap "tree bread" from ground chestnuts. In the 1585 famine in Naples, people were compelled to eat a bread known as *castagne e legumi*, a mixture of ground chestnuts and chickpeas. In especially ghastly times, the French foraged for acorns, which are tannic and bitter even after soaking and roasting, and mixed the acorn flour with chaff, or with straw and clay if they had no chaff. Then they baked it, and found a way to get it down. Similarly, the Scandinavians used dried, ground pine bark to stretch meager supplies of wheat flour. And when the Puritans reached the New World, they attempted to grow wheat, failed, and would have starved if the Native Americans had not shown them how to grow corn. They forsook the wheat and bread they knew, but instead of preparing the corn as the Native Americans did, they ground and attempted to leaven the cornmeal, and gave thanks for the flat, gritty result.

Above all, a loaf was an effective method of getting down chaff or sawdust, if that's all one had to fill his belly, or to make the edible ingredients go further. However, the common practice of making bread out of ingredients that were edible but poorly suited to baking—beans, peas, and tree nuts—suggests the intensity of the psychological need for something that looks like bread. An Italian with a sack of chickpeas, or an Englishwoman with a bag of chestnuts and peas, has the raw, unprocessed ingredients for a perfectly satisfying meal for her family. The breads they made could not have tasted as good as a stew or potage of those same beans, vegetables, a little bit of fat (if it was available), and herbs. To bake the peas and beans in bread form also requires more human energy for grinding and mixing. The only reason to go to the trouble to make an ersatz bread out of something you could prepare in a number of other ways is because those ingredients become "worth" more to the eater when they are converted into something that resembles a wheaten loaf.

Bec and I lived a version of this without knowing it. I never eyed the acorns on the campus where I teach (not for long, anyway), and I didn't think about grinding into flour the chestnuts we roasted on top of the woodstove, but the bread mixes we bought were made of raw ingredients we already had in the house in their whole, unprocessed forms: white rice, brown rice, and potatoes. I didn't want to eat another bowl of rice, but I eagerly ate it in bread form. We had cans of chickpeas and dried chickpeas in mason jars, and while I didn't often use them to make hummus, or simmer them in stews, I ate them in the bagged mixes. I would not have eaten tapioca, and I had *banished* millet—but these went down more smoothly when they had been blitzed into a powder and mixed into loaf form, as well. And when they came out of the oven? They looked exactly like the thing I had been hoping to eat.

My transition into GF cooking wasn't going much better when it came to other foods made of wheat, either. The worst streak began one winter's night when I foolishly decided that from now on, *there would be no difference whatsoever* between the way we had eaten before my diagnosis and the way we were eating now. I was tired of thinking against the grain. I would begin my comeback by making fresh egg pasta with a GF "all-purpose" flour blend. I took the pasta maker down from the pantry. It felt good to have it in my hands again. I opened up Jack Bishop's *Complete Italian Vegetarian Cookbook,* an old volume, spotted and worn, which had taught me how to make salads, frittatas, and granitas. I measured out my rice-and-potato-based flour and proceeded as I always had. Autopilot. Muscle memory. No problem at all.

I needed all of thirty seconds to see that I was screwed. The eggs weren't blending with the flour, which was so dry that it had sucked up all of the moisture like sand. I had anticipated moisture issues, but thought I could work around them. My solution was to crack in a few more eggs, and, when that didn't lead to a workable dough, I added a few tablespoons of water in desperation.

Now my dough was sticky, heavy, and, paradoxically, both slimy *and* gritty. There was no way it would tolerate being fed into a pasta machine and rolled into a thickness of half an inch, let alone an eighth of an inch. So I switched plans. Instead of making fettuccine, I would make ravioli. This would give me more control over the dough because I could roll it out by hand, fixing cracks and tears as they appeared.

But that didn't work either, because by this point the dough was total shit. It wound around the rolling pin and stuck there like wet cement. I gave in. I threw a fit. I tossed measuring cups and spoons into the sink, threw chunks of dough into the trash can. We ate premade rice pasta instead. It tasted fine. I would need more than a year to work up the courage to revisit the scene of this particular kitchen disaster.

About a week later, possibly even in the same week—the whole month is a blur of frustration, longing, and rage—a recipe for crêpes *also* made me its bitch.

At first glance, crêpes seemed so much easier to adapt to GF than fresh pasta. For one thing, the batter is wetter, and for another, what is simpler than a crêpe? Well, if you're counting ingredients and considering chemistry, *pasta* is simpler, but crêpes are pretty basic too: flour, milk, eggs, and either salt or sugar, depending upon whether your taste is running savory or sweet. I love them because they're like dressed-up pancakes: lighter, airier, more elegant. The possibilities expand significantly past the usual maple. We used to have them for late-night dinners with cheese and vegetables, or smoked salmon and a salad, and some wine. It had been a long time since I'd made them, and I had been pining.

I don't know whose recipe I was using—maybe from *The Joy of Cooking*, or Julia Child's, or Mark Bittman's—but it doesn't matter, because I think the results would have turned out the same with every recipe. I can't remember which GF flour blend I was using, either. Maybe Pamela's, King Arthur, or even Bob's Red Mill. I tried so many products in those days, just spraying and praying and hoping to hit the target, as a soldier I know puts it. The problem is that a *true* gluten-free equivalent of all-purpose wheat flour does not exist; "AP GF" (all-purpose gluten-free), or "cup for cup," is a marketing ploy based in good intentions or false hope, depending upon where you fit on the spectrum of GF-cookery rage.

Once again, I proceeded with poise and confidence. When the first crêpe ripped as I tried to flip it, I thought my technique was rusty. Then another one ripped, and another, because without gluten, the batter was as anemic as I was. I burned my fingers trying to flip the next ones, because it seemed that if I tried to use a spatula, I shoveled them into a mess.

Cooking was officially no longer fun.

The last crêpe was basically a pancake—I poured it thicker, thinking *why the hell not*—and when I tried it, instead of experiencing the savory, glutinous chew I anticipated, I tasted blandness and grit. That was enough for me to pull the ejection handle. The evening ended with no crêpes, burnt fingers, piles of ruined dough on the counter, hot metal flung into the sink, expletives, and my wife leaving the kitchen, unwilling to bear witness to my Gordon Ramsay-esque antics. The thing is, I wasn't *trying* to channel Gordon, or any other celebrity-chef blowhard; I was just tired of everything I touched turning to shit.

The failures kept stacking up: a cornstarch-based "panko" for pork and chicken that went from dry to charred on contact with heat, by-passing the nicely browned stage (and it *stank*, like burnt popcorn); sauces that wouldn't thicken predictably, since most GF flour blends contain potato and/or tapioca starch; the roux that would not brown but readily burned; the crisps of thawed berries that turned into fruit soup; cobblers that wouldn't cobble; cookies that wouldn't form. If I adapted a recipe that called for even a modest amount of wheat flour, the result was as if I had never cooked anything before in my life.[*]

---

[*] And I know I'm not alone here. A few Christmases ago, my mother decided that she was going to make me a GF stollen, the log-shaped, buttery, fruit-filled bread I had grown up eating every December. She sent me the recipe she was considering. I was immediately wary, because it looked like any other stollen recipe with the exceptions of GF flour and xanthan gum. Not wanting to discourage her, I told her it looked fine, and thus sent her off to her stollen doom. I never saw the stollen. I never even heard about it. And I never asked, because I already knew, before she even took the mixing bowl off the shelf, exactly how that boondoggle would go, though she would have tried it anyway.

I was not flying blind, either. I was attempting to work from my favorite cookbooks, writers, and recipes. For as often as I cooked intuitively, I also took real joy in knowing that I was following a path that had been blazed by a sage. I loved the sense that I was entering the mind of a writer like James Beard, or Claudia Roden, or any of the other authors on my shelf, and experiencing a rich tradition through their eyes, hands, and words. To be unable to follow their recipes to the letter—to have to use GF substitutions, or omit some ingredients and steps entirely—compromised and even destroyed the heart and soul of the recipes, which was their replicability. GF cookbooks were available, yes, but there weren't many good ones at the time, and I had something of a literary sensibility in the kitchen: I was loath to scrap a beloved canon just because I could no longer keep wheat flour in the house.

Unless the recipes called for no wheat or other unsafe ingredients (like oats) at all, I never knew for sure how far off the author's ideal I might have been. Quite often I was left to work purely on instinct, or, even worse than that, to guess. Sometimes I knew something that was supposed to happen had not: the meat in a stew, for example, which was supposed to develop a brown crust in the casserole after getting a light coating of flour, did nothing but get slimy; the biscuit didn't fluff or flake; the sauce didn't thicken correctly. Other times, I felt only a suspicion that I had missed the mark, and I couldn't say why. It was beyond frustrating, and I could see no easy solution, at least not in the immediate future.

One night, I had a cookbook come-to-Jesus moment. All of this hurling myself into adaptation was clearly not good for me. So I removed all of the bookmarks and unfolded all of the dog-ears identifying dishes I probably should not try again for a long time—if ever. I looked briefly at the pages, some of which were spotted, stained, or torn, and took my leave. Then I turned to the indexes. A great attribute of any literary tradition, from short stories to cookery, is durability: it holds up to different readings at different times. In *Beard on Food*, I looked under "Rice" first, of course, and read all of the recipes I had never tried before: *tian*s for the summer months, along with rice with sausage and tomato, and saffron risotto, and the list went on. There was another *tian* from Elizabeth David, and an adaptation of *mujaddarah*, a dish of lentils, fried onions, and rice, from Deborah Madison. And at the recommendation of a friend, I bought Chang and Kutscher's *Encyclopedia of Chinese Food and Cooking*, which provided enough inspiration to keep me busy for a long while. It would occur to me, much later but with a shock of understanding when it did, that *this* was what gluten-free cooking really meant: not paying attention to wheat—or trying to imitate it—at all.

9.

THE FEARFUL
GOURMAND

Sometime late in February, we were out with friends at our favorite
restaurant in town, an American bistro in an old farmhouse that
focuses on local, regional, and seasonal ingredients and dishes. I knew
this restaurant well. Bec and I had been visiting for over a decade.
When we pulled into the parking lot, I expected that my first meal out
as a person with celiac disease would be only slightly different from
the dozens of other times we had eaten there in ten years. But when
we sat down to eat, it was as though for the first time.

I froze when I looked at the menu. What was safe? Was there flour
in demi-glace? I knew there wasn't, or that there shouldn't be, but how
could I be *certain*? What about beurre blanc? It helps to know gastronomical terminology when you bring an allergy into a restaurant, but
I was encountering something different from unfamiliar vocabulary.
The idea of getting a meal I didn't have any control over filled me
with anxiety, even fear. I read the menu once, twice, three times, trying to see through the description of the finished dishes back into the
process and the ingredients. But a good menu, I knew well, never tells
you all of its secrets.

This was strange territory. I felt embarrassed. It's one of the
reasons why newly diagnosed celiacs, according to one survey, dine
out 90-percent less after diagnosis than before. The dangers of

cross-contamination, and the high probability of a buzzkill even if the meal does go well, combine to upend the very story restaurants exist to create, which is that when a diner walks in, they can be, and for a brief time are, a different person—a little wealthier, more romantic, more worldly. To walk into most restaurants with a severe allergy is to be reminded *exactly* what type of eater you are, no matter how understanding and flexible the kitchen might be.

Bec leaned over and confirmed the safest options. I noticed, for the first time, that instead of starting with a familiar feeling of expanding possibilities—for years, my approach was always to order dishes I do not have the time, knowledge, equipment, patience, or ingredients to prepare at home—this meal out began with reduction, elimination. By the time I had crossed off the definitely unsafe and the probably unsafe, I was down to two options. When the server arrived, I trotted out my new dietary needs.* At that point I was one of only a few people in town with celiac disease that I knew of. She listened carefully, and kindly offered substitutions that I found to be both a relief and problematic: in changing the dish, I wouldn't be experiencing the meal the way the chef had designed it. I had come to believe that everything on the plate at a good restaurant was there for a reason, and it bothered me to tinker with it.

The plates came. I ate hesitantly, without much enjoyment, and talked distantly with Bec and our friends. Nothing felt as it should have. Even though I experienced a victory in not getting sick, I won-

---

* In time, the entire waitstaff at this bistro would give me the great gift of relieving me from ever having to say anything about gluten-free again, because they would remember me: no bread before the meal; no croutons on the salad; no sauces, garnishes, or sides with wheat flour. They also later updated their menu to identify those dishes that could be made GF. Once, at a business dinner there, without so much as a hint, a waitress brought me an amuse-bouche on rice crackers when everyone else got theirs on crostini. Such home-field advantage, as I came to think of it, was as wonderful there as it was difficult for any other place to follow—to nobody else's fault, since other restaurants did not know me.

dered how long it would take for me to feel normal in a restaurant again.

Plenty of eaters are in the position I was, of course. Vegetarians, vegans, and those with allergies and special religious practices all approach dining out with varying degrees of caution. They've learned the ropes and figured out how to enjoy themselves. But the most sensitive have also come to know something that "normal" eaters do not often have occasion to consider: to have anyone make food for you is an implicit extension of trust. The more serious the consequences, the greater the confidence one puts in the cook. It's a happy thing for people with allergies that restaurants are offering an increasingly wide range of options and substitutions, and more information on their menus. They recognize the benefits that everyone enjoys when they take sensitivities seriously.

For me, the problem was that I hated having to extend so much trust in the first place. I had learned to love food, and travel, and dining out by doing it, of course, but also by reading books by those who had done more of it than I ever would—mostly because they had more money and time to travel, but also because, in some cases, dining out was different in the eras when they lived and wrote. I had no real gastronomical guides in my family or circle of friends, and so the writings of gourmands like M. F. K. Fisher, Julia Child, Calvin Trillin, Ruth Reichl, and many others loomed large. Reading might be the nerdiest way to become a hedonist, but it worked for me.

The most dramatic and compelling of the eating stories I read and hoped to someday replicate for myself was of a certain type. There came a point in a gourmand's travels when he arrived exhausted at a hotel or a restaurant, sat down at a table, and said to the waiter or the chef or both, *I am in your hands.*

That was it. That was how he ordered.

Sometimes he did not even have to say that much; he entered a restaurant, was shown to a table, and then food, lots of it, simply started appearing. This mythological encounter seemed to occur more in Europe, especially during the first half of the twentieth century. Miraculously (or not: they chose their venues carefully), these thoughtful eaters who had not asked for anything specific enjoyed meals from which they could not have asked anything more. I had long wanted to experience an outing like that, but not anymore; having celiac disease makes the idea of getting a meal that way terrifying. Imagine the embarrassment of having to send it all back—without even tasting it first. A prix-fixe menu is also bad news, as is a tasting menu. A short menu is challenging enough, unless the kitchen is flexible.

It wasn't until after my diagnosis that I realized where the real pleasure of these storied meals existed: it was all about the act of surrender. Give yourself over entirely to the talent and the instincts of the chef, and if the chef delivers, you will be sated in ways you could not have predicted.

This approach worked for the gourmet illuminati because there was nothing they would not eat, nothing they *could not* eat. Only the "roving gourmand" Jim Harrison, who has written eloquently of having gout, stands apart from the canon's possession of what appears to be exquisite digestive equipment. Or, maybe they *did* all have dietary restrictions, and reached for the Rolaids after their feeds, but like elite athletes who play hurt, they soldiered on. In any event, only Harrison's attitude tends toward "Damn the torpedoes and full-speed ahead. I'll have the rib-eye and a bottle of Châteauneuf." It was an act I would have followed if it were possible to do so. Gout and celiac disease are not the same thing.

Nonetheless, it was difficult for me to leave this kind of thinking behind, because I *had* experienced variations of surrender-and-satiety before visiting restaurants suddenly became threatening. There were the friends who had fed me foods I had not known I was craving but must have been, their offerings were so delightful: a perfectly roasted chicken, braised short ribs, *saag paneer,* even a plate of cheeses and olives. There were street vendors I smartly chose not to avoid, chowder houses I wandered into, and even nights in my own kitchen when a simple pasta dish, or piece of grilled fish with vegetables, tasted surprisingly good. These experiences didn't achieve the ideal of complete surrender, but I wasn't in a defensive mind-set, either.

The first such meal that I'd had in a restaurant came late one winter afternoon more than ten years ago, when Bec and I turned a corner on a side street in Ottawa's ByWard Market neighborhood and found ourselves standing at a staircase leading to an Italian restaurant below street level. We did not have to discuss whether or not to eat, even though five o'clock was typically far too early for us. We trusted the coincidence. Downstairs we found a small dining room with ten or so tables, most of them for two, all candlelit. The walls were plain stone and exposed beams, but there was nothing fake or calibrated about the atmosphere. We were alone except for two other diners, and although it strikes me now that we were young at the time—in our mid-twenties—we felt comfortable enough to shed a watchful part of ourselves, which was new for us, and is a key to the enjoyment of any meal out.

They brought us fresh bread, of course, either made in-house or at one of the nearby bakeries. The pasta was also homemade. This was the first time I ever tasted *burrata,* homemade gnocchi, brown butter sauce. We savored multiple courses followed by desserts that were not overwhelmingly sweet. Though we could not exactly afford this meal, it came with the added value of instruction in how to eat well from talented people who took pride in what they did and wished to show us a few things. All gentle persuasion, no coercion. The night concluded with that gratifying sense of feeling surprised to discover our own desires; we had not planned to eat Italian cooking, had not even talked yet about eating at all.

I wanted to feel something like that again. The disappointment of my first post-diagnosis restaurant experience made me all the more insistent on finding it. The Italian restaurant in Ottawa was out of the question, of course, so I decided a few weeks later that it was time for us to make a trip to Vermont, and one of our favorite fine restaurants. In my heart, I knew it was too soon to be making a trip like that. Finding three meals out in a one-day period is entirely different from driving just up the road from home for dinner, but I was eager to return to the way I used to eat and travel.

The place was called Butler's when we first went there—it has since changed names—and, like the restaurant in Ottawa, we had found it when we were young, and had also learned to love fine dining there. Its status as a culinary school made it approachable, and there was the bonus of an inn attached, which meant you could share a bottle of wine and then have an after-dinner drink before walking (instead of driving) to your room. One night years ago, we splurged on a bottle of Turley Vineyards zinfandel, and from the moment the cork came out I never thought about wine in the same way again. We might have encountered great food and wine at some other place, but the fact that it happened there gave Butler's a special pull on our affections. Like this whole region of Vermont, it had become synonymous to us with leisure, repose. It seemed as if nothing bad or disappointing could ever happen there.

Our trouble began when we sat down. The menu, which I hadn't checked in advance, was heavy on flour-based sauces and starches, as well as some other foods I wasn't handling well at the time. I had known I was taking a chance, but I had also expected to find *something* safe and appetizing. The server came, and when I tried to give him my spiel it came out jumbled and inarticulate. Bec finished for me, adding, as she always does, that while she's not celiac she never eats gluten, either. "In solidarity," I sometimes add with a smile. He did not seem interested.

A few minutes later, he returned with a Gruyère popover, airy and browned and gorgeous. He set it down in front of my wife.

"I know you can't have this," he said, jerking his head at me, "but I thought that you"—he nodded at Bec—"might want to try it."

Her face hardened into an expression I call The Look. Everyone who has a partner knows some version of The Look, and is happy when it's aimed at someone else. Dr. Sandwich had received The Look, albeit through the phone; others we encountered along the way would receive it. Had this server not listened to a word she'd said? What sort of arrogance was this? Or was he just stupid? Before she could latch onto him, he sped away.

When he returned, he didn't seem to have any idea which dishes might have flour in them and which might not. He didn't appear to be well versed in the menu at all, nor was he interested in helping us find substitutions. Clearly, I was a problem. This was a change from our past experiences, and it would have been annoying in other circumstances, but now it seemed threatening. Maybe we had caught him on a bad night. I don't remember what I ordered—which is saying something, because I can remember just about every other meal I had there—though I do remember not getting sick. The meal, though, was already ruined before the food arrived. We never went back. Trust was now even higher on the list of requirements than inspired dishes and ethically sourced products.

We still had to find more meals the next day. I wanted to do it the way we'd always found good restaurants—by first getting good and hungry and then trusting our luck and instincts as we read menus posted in windows. I think Bec knew how this would go, but she was willing to let me try it. We ended up standing on a Burlington sidewalk, scanning signage for phrases that would indicate there would be something—I was coming to hate this phrase—*something for me*. We were both cold, and irritable because we were hungry, and I felt stupid and frustrated because in my denial I hadn't planned ahead and written down some names. Now there were no options in sight that were safe *and* appealing. Thank God for smartphones, and also for Google Maps, OpenTable, and Urbanspoon.

The easy solution in such a case was to find a Thai restaurant. Drop a celiac in Thailand and, even though he doesn't speak a word of the language, his chances for survival are better there than anyplace else in the world (on the other hand, if you want to kill him with a country's cuisine, send him to Russia, or northern China). But I didn't *want* Thai. I could get Thai at home. Hell, I was on my way to making my own good Thai. I didn't want Vietnamese, either. I was so damned sick of rice; it seemed to be all I ever ate anymore. Well, I asked myself, what did Mr. Gourmand want, then? I didn't know. I wanted someone else to figure that out for me. Wasn't that what restaurants were for? Was that too much to ask? I wanted to look at a menu and have that moment of sudden recognition I used to have: *Yes. That sounds good.*

These first disappointing experiences suggested to me that an entire future of eating had gone up in flames. How could I feel emboldened to eat my way across a foreign city—Paris, say, or Prague, or Florence—when I knew that even a slight misstep would knock me sideways and result in the waste of thousands of dollars? It explains why one man with celiac disease I know takes a "travel kitchen," a personal Chuckwagon (minus Chucklady) complete with cookstove, whenever he travels for conferences and the like. And if I were to play the meals safe and subsist on a Paleo-styled diet for the duration of an extended trip abroad, how could I say that I had truly been to these cities without having savored the foods they were famous for? How the hell does a person go to France and not eat the bread? Go to Hong Kong or Tokyo and not eat the noodles? That was another theme in the gastronomic literature that I had hoped to weave into my own life: one visits a place by ingesting it, taking it in, making it part of him. On the other hand, this seemed a silly and reductive goal. One also visits a place for museums; one takes a place in with sightseeing and copious amounts of wine and cheese (but what about the Roquefort?). In time, I would meet people who made those trips exactly, allergies and all, and they survived to tell me the journey was not a waste. When it comes to food allergies, people in cities *get it* (European cities in particular). This was difficult for me to believe in that first period of adjustment, when venturing out of the state, let alone the country, could and did make me panic. Bec and I had, in fact, canned plans for a summer trip to Newfoundland and Labrador.

My problem, as a brutally honest friend told me not long after that weekend in Vermont, wasn't just that I was a celiac. Plenty of people with celiac disease ate safely at restaurants all over the country without crying foul. No, my problem was twofold. I was a very sensitive celiac, one whose entire body melted down when he got glutened, instead of just breaking into a skin rash like the lucky ones. When you thought about it, I had no business putting myself in a chef's hands at all. The second, bigger problem was that I was a sensitive celiac with *ideas*. I had done a little too much reading, watched a little too much food TV. I thought too hard about what I ate: how I should find it, how it should taste, be presented, and sourced. I had a philosophy of eating that was poorly matched to—how could my friend put it?—my *digestive realities*. Couldn't I just chill out, eat some oily fried rice or bad tacos, maybe bottom-feed on a chain restaurant's overcooked GF pasta or desiccated baked potato for a night, learn to forget all these ideas about gourmet serendipity, and go into the next trip with an ironclad plan? Wouldn't that be better than bitching about it?

Yes, probably.

And yes, I could do that.

Around this time, another friend of mine tried to comfort me with assurances that I would come to extensively know the pleasures of Asian food. He had in mind more than the usual pad Thai: Indonesian,

Laotian, Cambodian, and those regions of India not dependent upon wheat. Like my friend who reminded me that there was still an entire world of wine for me to drink, he was trying to be encouraging and kind, and, also like my oenophile friend, he turned out to be half right. Chinese cuisine is vast, but Chinese restaurants are dicey for celiacs—soy sauce is a ubiquitous base for many other sauces, to say nothing of the wheat-starch dumplings and noodles. I knew I would not likely return to Chinatown for dim sum anytime soon. Japanese restaurants seemed difficult too, especially if a sushi bar did not have gluten-free tamari; and what was sashimi, what were maki rolls, without the saltiness against the cool sweet fish, the pickled ginger, the wasabi? Many dishes from Korean cuisine looked likewise difficult to parse, once you stepped away from kimchi, barbecue, and rice.

Still. Not long before the start of spring, we finally figured it out when we followed a recommendation for a small, authentic Thai restaurant in Kanata, Ontario. When I looked at the menu, for the first time in months it was a challenge to order not because there was only one option and I wasn't excited about it, but because almost *everything* on this menu was valid, safe. I did not have to give my speech. I did not have to start the meal by declaring myself. One question did the trick. Which dishes had soy sauce? Very few of them, it turned out.

Our immoderate love of spicy food served us well here. We ordered deep-fried tofu because Bec had eaten it at a Chinese restaurant only once before I was diagnosed, and had been looking for a safe version of it ever since (no breading, here; just dried and dropped into the fryer). Then we ordered shellfish and vegetables with roasted chiles, Thai basil, and lemongrass over rice. The flavors were more vibrant, more exciting, than anything I'd tasted in a long while. We rarely order dessert, but we went in for a round of mango and coconut ice cream simply because we wanted the meal to last a little longer. It had been a long time since we enjoyed a restaurant so thoroughly.

In the car, on the way back home, Bec said it before I could: "That was *good.*" It was freeing to look at a menu for once and know that we could have just about anything off it we wanted. It was not the same thing as gaining the whole world back, but it was a comfort, and a start.

10

THE LESS-TRAVELED
GF ROAD

It happened one night in the early spring. It must have been April, because the winter CSA had run out but we were not into asparagus or wild leeks or fiddleheads yet. Eating and cooking locally had become a little challenging, a little lean. We were living out of the freezer and off of preserves, and supplementing it with the produce offerings at the co-op.

I was standing at the counter between the stove and the sink, prepping vegetables for a dish that now escapes me. What I remember instead, and clearly, is the music coming through the speakers as I guided the knife: the Miles Davis Quintet's rendition of "Bye-Bye Blackbird." It's a simple song, ripe for jazz embroidery, a standard about fleeing a place where the speaker can't be understood and everything is sad to a safer, kinder place. Not a love song so much as a good-bye.

This was the first time music—*any* music, whether jazz or classical or even the endless stream of feel-good pop songs churned out of recording studios like so many Chicken McNuggets—had sounded good to me in six months. And I knew, as I listened to the muted horn and brassy piano block-chords and really *heard* them, that something in my mind and in my body had cleared, recovered, been cleansed. I had punched through to the other side of the clouds. Finally.

The arrival of the warmer weather had worked some magic. It had also helped to receive my doctor's clearance to start working out again. I was still anemic, but I'd eaten so much meat, shellfish, green vegetables, and nuts that I was no longer nearly as depleted as I had been (it takes a long time—several months—for the body to convert the iron in food to iron in the blood). I had stopped taking the iron supplements, multivitamins, and probiotics.* I was putting weight back on. My fingernails were growing again, and my barber said my hair had stopped looking like straw. All good signs, and all also indicators that celiac disease was not in fact something I'd made up, which on some days I still could almost believe to be true.

Bec designed a rehabilitation plan for me, a fringe benefit of being married to a personal trainer. Instead of plunging right into my old workouts and hurting myself, she showed me how to get moving again, how to figure out which muscle groups were weakest and most prone to injury—which turned out to be just about every group. I was surprised to find out how much strength I'd lost.

I had added interval training to my runs a few years back because they made me a better recreational softball player. The motivation was that simple, that pathetic: my playground ego got a lift. Quickly, however, I came to connect training to eating—not in the sense that a workout "earned" me a meal, but because a hard run sharpened my appetite. I loved that deeper kind of hunger, loved how it increased the anticipation of sitting down at the table and the pleasures of being there. While running, gutting it up a hill, far from comfortable but not dying, either, I'd think, *Yes. Tonight I get to eat a steak.* (Vegetarians, apologies. The effect is not the same when I substitute *cauliflower.*) No form of training, however, whether running or strength, had ever

---

* Another hot topic in celiac forums. Do the probiotics work? The scholarship on microecology is compelling, and I wouldn't have continued to pay fifty bucks a bottle for billions of flora if I didn't believe—and feel—that they were doing *something* beneficial.

come easily to me. Even in college, I was always slower than I thought a lanky guy should have been. Now I wondered if celiac disease had been holding me back all those years, and whether, now that I had been diagnosed, I might see improvement.

One afternoon, I was standing in front of the coolers at the health-food store when I noticed, for the first time, bags of flour that I had never before cooked with: garbanzo bean, buckwheat, lentil, coconut. What did a cook do with these? Which cuisines did they belong to, and what was the history? I had no idea, but I suspected they contained additions to the GF diet that nobody had told me about. It occurred to me that if I truly believed that cooking and eating were among the most important things I did every day, then it wasn't reasonable for me to expect that my repertoire would remain the same. I had already made some changes, but I needed to extend my reach.

The solution to my discontentment might be to go back in time, yes, but not to raid the tables and tombs of ancient kings for ancestral wheat. What I needed to do instead was visit times and places in history *before* wheat was ubiquitous, when those who could not afford it enjoyed foods made of other things. I began to root around in the history of flatbread, which has always been the leavened loaf's poor brother. For many reasons, foremost among them convenience, economy, and versatility, mixing starches with water and salt, skipping the leaven, and rapid cooking have been at the heart of culinary traditions everywhere for thousands of years—to the degree that there's a case for calling flatbread *the* quintessential human food. Even after the Egyptians and other cultures began baking yeasted bread, the flatbreads remained a firm fixture, to the degree that "bread" was most likely synonymous with a simple barley or bean-flour flatbread, not a risen loaf.

Why did it take so long for me to discover this eating history?

For one thing, there is not much of a flatbread culture or tradition in the United States outside of pancakes and corn (or wheat) tortillas. The former is for breakfast, and usually made with wheat; the latter can be said to be important only in certain parts of the country. We eat tortillas, yes, but those of us who are not Latino tend to view them as an occasional ethnic food experience. It's unfortunate, because the thinking obscures how a well-made tortilla could, in fact, answer the same bready needs that a wheaten loaf does.

The United States is a young nation compared to European countries, and this may also have kept flatbreads distant from mainstream American eating. The Native Americans depended upon corn and squash, and the Puritans survived their first winter in New England by learning to love corn and relearning to love the beans that had sustained their ancestors in Europe when the wheat crops failed. Yet their descendants reverted back to wheat as soon as they could, and that reversion happened quickly; westward expansion in the United States roughly corresponded to rapid technological advances in wheat cultivation, processing, and shipping, all of which combined to increase crop reliability, yield, and distribution, to the effect that Americans were catapulted into a stable wheat supply. We've had our shortages, like the Dustbowl Era, but large parts of the population have mostly escaped the need to subsist on grains of poverty such as buckwheat and—God help me—millet, which for millennia have been everyday fare for many people. In fact, highly refined white flour has become so cheap that one could make a case for naming it the "food of poverty" for our time, which is an ironic twist, considering that in the nineteenth and early twentieth centuries, European immigrants came to this country for everything white risen loaves signified, including class ascendancy and economic stability.

The result of these separate but related factors is that, over time, knowledge of wheatless breads—not simply how to make them, but their existence at all—disappeared from American eaters' memories and imaginations. I never heard of them or ate them when I was growing up. I didn't know of anyone who ate them. Uncovering recipes that used bean and buckwheat flours took a little sleuthing in encyclopedias like *The Oxford Companion to Food.* I scoured the entries for mention of flours I brought home, looking for clues as to how, and where, and when they were used. Then I tracked down recipes in cookbooks and on the internet. And when I ladled the batter into a hot pan, cooked it rapidly, and sampled it, I knew immediately that I was eating something real, and satisfying, and possessed of its own storied history—which was more than I could say for many of the items in the GF section at the grocery store.

Take, for example, *socca.*

You don't see this flatbread in the United States very often. It is still made in the Provence region of France and also in northern Italy, though I suspect its tradition goes back much further, since all over the ancient world there are references not only to legumes, but also to bean breads and bean flours being used to stretch barley or wheat supplies in times of shortage. It's not hard to imagine the earliest cultivators of chickpeas experimentally pounding the dried beans down into a flour, mixing it with water, and frying it. Much later, Provençal and Italian merchants and travelers carried pouches of chickpea flour and a little salt with them, knowing they could count on someone along the road to share a fire and water so they could make a quick meal. *Socca* is traditional in Nice, where it is still cooked by street vendors.

This flatbread is blissfully simple and delicious—especially when you bump the batter up a notch with some grated Parmesan cheese, olive oil, and herbs, as America's Test Kitchen suggests in their book on gluten-free cookery. It's the perfect canvas for high-end olive oil (especially *harissa* olive oil), tapenade, caponata, or pesto. In southern France, *socca* is typically prepared on a screaming-hot cast-iron skillet pushed inside a wood oven, resulting in a crust that is crisp and slightly smoky. This experience is achievable if you remember to whip up some batter when the charcoal grill is going. Almost any flat-bread loves a charcoal fire and a cast-iron griddle; the smoke and the intensity of the heat impart flavors that an oven or range-top simply cannot. And when you stand outside in the late evening, grilling your flatbreads over the coals while the twilight slowly gives way to dusk, you feel that much closer to the long tradition of people cooking their simple flat cakes over open fires.*

Chickpeas and other beans, most importantly lentils, are vital sources of protein all over the world, and other cultures have their versions of bean-flour flatbreads. In India, especially on the Malabar Coast, chickpea (or just as often, lentil) flour is the basis of *papadum*, which is more of a crisp bread than a flatbread, because it's fried in oil like a fritter. The presence or absence of baking soda, as well as the thickness of the bread, determines whether the flatbreads belong more to the tradition of *papadums* or *papads*, the latter of which tend to be denser. But when I allowed myself to be nudged in the direction of southwestern Asia, and experimented with *papadums* one night as an accompaniment to spicy vegetarian fare, I found the linguistic distinction to be irrelevant. Although not part of my food culture, *papadum* provided an inspiring alternative to crackers.

Not long after discovering *socca*, I was eating breakfast on a patio overlooking Lake Champlain when I had my first buckwheat crêpe. In this country, we don't seem to eat buckwheat unless we have to, and I immediately wondered why, especially given its affinity with maple syrup. Technically, buckwheat is an herb (both "grass" and "wheat" are misnomers) domesticated in China around 3,000 BC, and it now comes in several varieties, from the familiar slate-gray flour, with a

---

* For a truly nerve-wracking but authentic experience, you can let the embers burn down into ashed-over coals, rake them into a single layer, and ladle the batter directly *onto* the coals. Then you must brush the ashes off the flatbread, which cooks ten thousand years ago had to do all the time. Bonus points for going old-school and using your fingers instead of tongs. I don't recommend it.

strong taste, to an Acadian white blend that is an excellent substitute for wheat.* I've used both in crêpes and pancakes and, best of all, the blini for which Brittany is famous: made with beaten egg whites, and seltzer water or beer (or GF beer) added to the batter, the cakes rise rapidly in a skillet and are so delicious they have been immortalized in literature. In "Babette's Feast," it is the first course of *Blinis Demidoff au Caviar* that makes the general Lorens Löwenhielm sit up with notice, his impressive moustache bristling; one taste and he suspects that the cook in the kitchen of the austere Berlevaag home where he is dining is the same chef whose signature dish he enjoyed once in Paris. I haven't yet had a chance to try authentic *Blinis Demidoff,* though I have made a poorer man's version with smoked salmon, quick-pickled onions, sour cream, and clippings of tiny garden-lettuce leaves.

And if I was not already convinced of the hope and satisfaction that awaited me in flatbreads, an encounter with a taco trailer in Santa Barbara sealed the deal. Prior to this tortilla breakthrough, I had been a Northeasterner who viewed tortillas as little more than an edible wrapper for the meat and vegetables inside. But when they are prepared the right way, which is to say fresh, tortillas are as good as many wheaten breads, and even have the texture and chew of a chapati or naan. Through the window where I ordered, I watched the cook flatten ovals of dough with a press, applying the full weight of his body. He cooked them on the flat-top, waiting until each side was blistered before flipping them with a metal spatula. The result was flatbreads so puffed up and covered with caramelized pockmarks that I nearly suspected someone had slipped in a little wheat flour. Hours later, I felt fine, and I was hooked. I literally ate my way from one taco place to another before we left town.

Not all of the possibilities for real GF foods offered by the eating

---

* This variety of buckwheat flour is grown in northern New England, primarily in southwestern Maine, and it can be difficult to find outside the region.

traditions from around the world are flatbreads, however. The constant thread is rendering starch of any kind into a food that is soft, chewy, and hot. *Pão de queijo,* or cheese rolls from Brazil—though there are variations scattered throughout Latin America—call for tapioca starch, which is the root of the cassava plant that is dried and ground into a fine powder. My discovery of this bread converted a kitchen enemy into a friend; I had hated using tapioca ever since I had added it to my first GF bread recipe, because it's prone to forming a slurry anywhere and everywhere (and I still hate working with it, to be honest), but the texture of the tapioca-based batter becomes intriguing when baked: sweet and chewy, even meaty, with a nicely browned crust. *Pão de queijo* does not rise so much as it balloons. The glycemic load in these rolls—unlike that of *socca* and buckwheat blini, both of which are higher in fiber and protein—does not exactly make them suitable for nightly fare, but they're great for some much-needed variation.

And where would we be without two notable Italian contributions that are not flatbreads but still indispensable: polenta and risotto? I won't be caught eating gruel, whether it's made of wheat or not, but I do love a bowl of polenta, especially on a winter evening, topped with a sauce of vegetables or meat, and accompanied by a glass of wine. Similarly, one night Bec looked up from a particularly successful bowl of risotto and declared that slow-cooked rice had become, for her, a viable replacement for mac-and-cheese. These staples, which I began cooking hopefully and then joyfully throughout the spring and into the summer, took me all over the world, and back in time. They helped to teach me how to cook again—or, how to relax into cooking again.

Some nights, I decided I would take my cues from near the coast of northern France, and I made simple buckwheat pancakes browned in bacon fat we reserve in a mason jar, and served them with some pickled vegetables and a salad of bitter greens to help cleave the fat. Or there were spring turnips, asparagus, or wild leeks. Fried eggs go nicely with these pancakes, as well. Together, these foods made for a satisfying if rather blunt eating experience: the buckwheat cakes were not as airy as blini and not as light as crêpes, but dense and filling. Afterward, I felt fortified for chores: I thought that I should go out and split some wood and haul it inside, or weed around the onions.

Other nights, I progressed up a social class or two, and adjusted the batter to be more elegant, making crêpes that I filled with some chèvre from my friend Sue's goats, and chili-tomato jam. If there was no cheese available because the goats were nursing, I used homemade applesauce, fennel-onion preserve, or a rosemary onion confit, all of which Bec had put up in the fall. Sometimes I served them with chicken breasts from my friend Kassandra's birds, which I poached or pounded flat and seared until just barely done—a chance I only take with meat from her chickens, because I know where and how they live.

The *pão* inspired me too. It cried out for meat—marinated, grilled tri-tip and *chimichurri* made of the first herbs of the year, and some new potatoes on the side. The *papadum* drew me further into Indian cuisines. *Socca*, once I'd mastered it, paired well with braised beef, or ground lamb.

And yet, I could not be too hopeful. These foods and the meals I made with them satisfied us, but they also gave me insight into why most cultures with traditions of cooking flatbreads from grains of poverty immediately converted to wheat when they could finally get it. Either they worked wheat into their diet in addition to their native grains, baking risen, wheaten loaves alongside their flatbreads, or they abandoned their flatbreads almost entirely. Even though I soon had a cupboard full of flours from which cultures around the world would have happily made the focal point of their meals, I noticed that—for as much as I enjoyed *socca*, or blini, or crisp breads made from lentil flour, and as easy as they could be to prepare, and as stimulating as it felt to once again be eating a food with a history and tradition that had some heft to it—I did not *crave* these foods. I did not find myself making them every day, or even thinking about them every week. I only craved the pancakes we made from Pamela's GF flour blend, and as far as ancient grains eaten by the lower classes were concerned, that didn't count.

SPRING AT THE MARKET

It was June in the year of the Death of Bread.

At Dan and Megan's stall at the market, I filled bags with our first CSA produce of the year, our fifth with the Kents. Dan wrote the offerings on a chalkboard that he hung from the support lines in his collapsible tent. You filled up, and off you went. He couldn't have made it any easier for his subscribers short of putting the veg in their fridge for them. We bought from other farms too, especially during the late summer and early fall months, but at least in terms of produce, we had come to think of Dan and Megan as the people who quite literally fed us, along with Kassandra Barton and her family, in nearby De Kalb, who supplied our beef, pork, chicken, and lamb.

The quantity and variety of CSAs and farmers' markets in the North Country always start small, no matter the farm; we're not the Central Valley of California. May and June typically provide humble offerings from the cool, drowsy earth: salad greens, radishes, spinach, young shallots, and sometimes turnips. This year, apparently Dan and Megan had started their summer squashes early, in the greenhouse, because here they were already, both yellow and green, the skins bright and firm. I wouldn't welcome them as warmly in August when we'd had our fill, but in mid-June there seemed to be endless possibilities.

From this slow trickle of the year's first veg, Bec and I made salads, simply dressed. We made frittatas and omelets from our friend Ellen's eggs, and went without our *Artisan* bread. Even simple stir-fries seemed to shine. I threw handfuls of spinach into some of last summer's tomato sauce, blistered ramps in smoking-hot oil, and served them all up with rice pasta and cheese.

Off and on throughout the winter CSA season, a thought had buzzed through my head, and it returned as I filled the bags at the spring market: *You're lucky.* I was lucky to be within easy reach of the growers and ranchers I had come to know so well; lucky to be able to front the money at the start of the season for a CSA subscription (we pay in advance, taking on in some senses the risks of the growing season with the farmer); and lucky as well to have the time required to prep and cook what my growers provided. Local agriculture had given Bec and me many gifts already: pleasures at the table, health, friends, and a sense of community. Ideally, everyone would be able to have these gifts, if they wanted them. Which led to a nagging question: How much harder would it have been to adjust, to "comply" with the GF diet, and simply to heal, if I didn't have access to these wonderful foods? How much slower would my recovery have been? How did people with celiac disease who lived elsewhere *do* it?

I knew something that I would never be able to prove: the reason I had recovered faster than my doctors or even my friends had predicted, going from completely trashed to mostly healed in four months, was that I had been eating almost entirely whole foods, real foods that came out of the nearby fields: cabbages, carrots, onions, winter squash, potatoes, frozen summer vegetables, frozen berries, greens. My diet was far from Paleo, but these formed the backbone of our everyday eating. I sometimes recalled the day back in February when I had watched the slow, bemused smile on my GI doc's face after I told him I was choking down raw beet juice—which tastes nasty and does not belong in anyone's diet unless their blood panel or personal trainer commands them to drink it.*

"Okay," he said, looking down and nodding into his hands, and I thought, *Race you in July.* Now we were only in the first week of June, and I knew I could own him already.

I did not believe that whole foods were a panacea; some things, many things, cannot be corrected or cured by diet alone. And yet, though I had gotten sicker than many of the people I'd been reading about in the celiac forums and blogs, I had recovered faster, my own missteps and self-glutenings notwithstanding. Even my sense of despair seemed to be less intense. My diet was the one big difference I could point to. Some of my recovery was also just plain good luck; my intolerances to fish and dairy had not lingered for long, and no new complications had appeared. For all of these reasons, it began to seem odd to me that few people in the forums and blogs I followed were talking about a whole-food (not necessarily a local-food, though that might help, too) strategy for recovering from celiac disease. As recently as 2013, a "Gluten Contamination Elimination Diet"—not quite modified-Paleo, but close, with its focus on plain white and brown rice, fruits, vegetables, meats, dairy, and basic seasonings—had been trumpeted in some gastroenterology publications for its positive effects, though it didn't seem to be catching on. The GF diet I most frequently encountered was couched in terms of substitutions for glutenous processed foods, many

---

* More guesswork on my part with the food-as-medicine approach, but this may have worked. I began juicing—pun intended—on raw beets when I read studies that indicated their high mineral content increased oxygen transport in red blood cells, and improved overall blood health in elite athletes as indicated by their VO2 max (blood-oxygen uptake) readings. It sounded like a good thing for an anemic guy to be drinking. So I juiced several pounds of raw red CSA beets a week and kept it in a mason jar in the fridge. My tasting notes? Thick and punishing from the cloying sweetness of beet, with unforgiving shockwaves of schist, quartz, and mud.

of which were high in sugar, starch, oil, and fat—known causes of gut inflammation, and not what a person recovering from celiac disease (or any other digestive disorder, for that matter) needs. A good nutritionist would have told me to avoid the mountains of crackers, sweets, energy bars, and other processed GF foods, but I had done it automatically, habitually, and because the CSA veg just kept coming whether I felt like eating it or not. It seemed a commonsense approach to recovery that everyone should be trying. I thought that all of the advocacy groups should be shouting it everywhere. My bafflement grew as I later attended conferences, panels, and expos, and at times listened to experts talk about the gluten-free diet without once mentioning those things which I had come to believe were most important: *learn to cook; make the time to do it; eat whole foods.**

At the same time, I had also noticed that celiac disease was complicating our practice of locavorism. For as hopeful and grateful as I sometimes felt about the pounds of vegetables that we carried into our house every other week, I had been dogged by an awareness that the demands of the GF diet were repeatedly shoving us out of the 150-mile circle within which we had been eating as much as possible for years. Up until January, the most important local (or, to put it more accurately, regional) staple we bought, next to meat and produce, was also the easiest staple to take for granted—wheat flour. Our AP flour came from the bulk bin at the co-op; the grain had been grown, milled, and blended nearby.

When our dietary influences swung from West to East and North to South, tilting heavily in the Pan-Asian direction, our ingredients and

---

* One reason I believe this *isn't* getting as much mention as it could is that the foundations and organizations are being sponsored, to one degree or another, by the GF prepared-products industry.

influences also moved closer to the equator, landing us squarely in rice cultures, not wheat cultures. Not much rice grows in the North Country, no matter what the variety. Neither do the iconic spices of Asian cuisines, the curries, or, obviously, the coconut milk. The ingredients for *socca, papadum,* and all of the other flatbreads we enjoyed did not come from New York. Even those GF dishes that *looked* like the foods we used to make from local flour—tagliatelle, lasagna, spaetzle, and quiche crust, all of which depended upon brown rice flour—had more in common with Vietnamese rice noodles or pad Thai. We had always eaten rice, of course, but never in such volume. And if we fled from Asia for a few days and took our dietary cues from Latin America, our locavore practice also broke down. We had plenty of local sweet corn, fresh in August and September and frozen in the winter for as long as our supplies held out. But I wasn't going to nixtamalize* my own masa and make tortillas, not when I could find excellent handmade corn tortillas from Brooklyn. At least Bec was growing the serrano and habanero chiles, tomatillos, scallions, and cilantro.

GF baking left an honest locavore with no place to hide. Tapioca root doesn't even grow in our part of the world, let alone in our zip code (at least some of the rice we bought came from the southern United States). Sorghum will grow around here, but you tend to find it in syrup form, not as flour. I *still* didn't know where the hell xanthan gum came from; judging by the name, Mars.** Almond flour, flaxseed

---

* Another case of grain poisoning (kind of) concerns the pellagra outbreaks in regions where people depended upon corn for the bulk of their calories. Unless the corn is treated with lime—a process called nixtamalization that dates in Mesoamerica to before 1,000 BC—its nutrients, in particular niacin, are not able to be absorbed by the body. The nutritional and metabolic effects of pellagra are similar to malabsorption, but more visually horrifying. Soaking corn in an alkaline solution such as lime renders the nutrients usable by the human body.

** Pretty close: xanthan gum comes from a lab. It used to be derived from a strain of black mold, but now comes from corn. The point remains that I'm not going to find this at the farmers' market any more than I'm going to find an olive.

meal, buckwheat: all foods from antiquity, but not common to my region. And not inexpensive compared to their commodity counterparts, either.

The widening distance between where our staple ingredients all grew and our kitchen counter, or table, raised a question: What would have happened to me had I lived one or two hundred years ago and celiac disease had come a-calling (provided I survived infancy and childhood)? Depending upon where I lived, it would not have been possible to convert to rice, or chickpeas, or even corn. When I told my doctor that I imagined the onset of celiac disease I'd had in November would have killed me centuries ago, he disagreed. What would have happened, he said, is I would have gotten sicker and sicker, until someone started spooning me broth. Gradually, I would have recovered. At some point, I would go back to eating wheat, causing me to get sick again. This cycle would continue, making me an invalid, which is how I would remain until something *else* finished me off, probably pneumonia in the middle of winter. Comforting.

When I started buying so much rice, tapioca, sorghum, and other products, I did it so easily that I hardly registered the "rules" I was breaking. I was simply trying to fill in the holes left behind by wheat. Once I realized that I was acquiring food from across the world and forsaking my local diet, I felt as if my hand was being forced in yet another way. The discoveries of flatbreads, which had given me hope, were also making me a hypocrite. The one available regionally sourced GF starch outside of corn was my mortal enemy in the kitchen—millet. Which I refused to buy. So it appeared that when it came to grains, at least, I believed in locavorism as long as I had access to a steady supply of wheat.

The only solution was to relax. Lighten up. Be thankful that I lived in the twenty-first century, not the nineteenth, and so had access to the staples I cooked with now: rice in the form of both whole grain and finely ground flour, the roots, the beans. As compensation, I could think that much more carefully about using my local foods with them. That way, the beliefs we had taken pride in for years—our investment in community growers and our vote with our dollars against industrial foodways—remained at least somewhat uncompromised.

Later on, I would look back on that winter and early spring and see something else: that without my knowing it and without my permission, celiac disease was making me a better cook. By necessity, I became more fearless and innovative. I curried local winter vegetables in Thai and Indian spices, learning in the process that butternut squash and—of all things—celery root from ten miles away love coconut milk from five thousand miles away. I became a scholar of stews and ragouts made from the other hearty winter veg we received. I learned to stop caring much at all about which ingredients were "traditional" to a recipe. I mastered Bolognese and then shepherd's pie, which I filled sometimes with the conventional beef but just as often with lamb, leftover chicken, and even just vegetables. I became a devotee of flatbreads with winter vegetables and meats that I roasted, braised, and grilled. Never had my range expanded so quickly.

Once spring and then summer arrived, the CSA also helped by bullying me around a little in the kitchen. Every Friday, which was pickup day, and for several days afterward, my fridge was filled with several pounds of produce. I eagerly anticipated many of the offerings: snap peas, eggplants, peppers, tomatoes, mustard greens, onions, strawberries, kale. Some of it, however, was strange to me: daikon radish, collards, kohlrabi, and pungent Asian greens. My task was clear—do something inspired with all of it, the weird and the recognizable. If some of the veg would freeze well (peppers, for example, or corn), I could do that. Bec could make a chutney or a salsa or some other preserve. But I could not waste it, not even the escarole and the dandelion greens, two foods that I had never in my life deliberately sought out, nor even seen on a plate until the day they came looking for me. I knew the growers who had sweated and worried over these plants from seeds to harvest, knew their struggles against bugs, weather, and plant diseases. If I threw away half of what they provided because I convinced myself that I did not have the time or the desire to cook it, or because I thought I didn't like to eat it, I would be doing something worse than wasting money. I wouldn't be able to look them in the eye the next time we met.

Sometimes I had to work quickly, too, because these vegetables required attention faster than conventional produce, which has often been hybridized for shelf life, sprayed, or gassed (or all of these). I had to find other foods to pair with the eggplant, the mountain of Swiss chard, or snap peas; often, I had to compose a new meal. Even in my gluten-eating days, approaching local eating with creativity day after day could be tough, and now the lack of familiar wheat-based options could sometimes make it even harder. Gone were the days of simply slicing vegetables, tossing them with some oil and seasonings, and dumping them on a pizza. A man and his wife can eat only so many salads in a week, so many stir-fries. It wasn't a good idea to be consuming dozens upon dozens of eggs in the form of frittatas and omelets, no matter how much I loved them. And it's just not as possible to hide the less-desirable vegetables on bruschetta when you lack good, crusty bread (hiding something you don't like on something else you don't like: bad idea).

Not that this is a new problem, exactly. It isn't. The plentitude and scarcity inherent to small-scale farming have presented a challenge to cooks since the first kitchen gardeners walked out to the vines early in the morning light and beheld, to their surprise, far more beans or tomatoes or cucumbers than they had bargained for. I had known for a long time that these forces could be a good thing. Surrendering some options, usually those foods that we had once chosen to eat—like salad greens in January, tomatoes in March, or chicken for a whole spring when our rancher's freezer emptied faster than she expected and no local birds were to be found anywhere else—led us to discover *more* options, in the long run, and develop a richer repertoire as we learned more ways to cook what we had on hand.

And now, focused on using my CSA veg before it became mushy or moldy, or entered a state of active fermentation, I sometimes forgot that there were other, glutenous foods that I used to eat regularly. Not always, but I tried to let the influx of summer squash, lettuce, turnips, spinach, and other produce nudge me back into an old, familiar rhythm, one that fit the GF life as well as it had fit my life before, and maybe even fit it better. Those baby turnips, I learned, lose every trace of bitterness when they are slow-cooked in a casserole with bacon; broccoli can indeed be grilled; garlic scapes make a beautiful pesto to spread on the zukes after they have been salted, drizzled with olive oil, and grilled. And if I braised the kale, roasted the carrots, quick-pickled the radishes, and could find in the fridge some yogurt or sour cream for a Mexican-styled *crema*, I was well on my way to some outstanding vegetarian tacos. A little focus, a little reorientation, and I was cooking—at the height of the growing season, when it's never too far to the next good thing—with hope and gratitude.

12

THE GOD ENZYME

The cashier at Burlington's City Market eyed me warily as I walked up to her register. I had selected the express lane because technically I had fewer than fifteen items. In my cart were two cases of Omission Pale Ale, another case or so of Glutenberg Pale Ale and Red Ale in pint-sized cans, and a few bottles of Citizen Cider. There were also a few four-packs of Alchemist's Celia Saison ale, a GF beer brewed with sorghum but cut with orange peel and coriander (in the right hands, sorghum is a good match for Belgian-style ales and yeasts), which I'd grabbed at the last minute.

"At first I thought you had too many items, but it turns out it's just a lot of alcohol," the cashier said with wonder. Her hair was dyed raven-black and she wore colorful jewelry. She couldn't have been older than twenty-five, and I wondered if she registered the irony of who was lecturing whom about alcohol consumption, here.

I looked from the cart to her, and then back into the cart. "I'm having a party."

"Right on." It was almost ten o'clock on a Friday night. The beer section was the busiest department of the co-op.

I wasn't having a party, though I felt like having one. Our first trip back to Burlington since the winter fiasco had been fruitful. Earlier in the day, we discovered a loaf of exceptionally good gluten-free bread at the farmers' market. Eliza Hale of Up the Hill Bakery had set up a table toward the end, with loaves in plastic wrap gathered around a plate of free samples: GF cinnamon-raisin, something called "mock rye," and sourdough. The traffic near the other tables was heavy. Traditional wheat breads surrounded us, burnished and rounded, glazed like beautiful pottery. If gluten contact highs were possible, I would have been stoned.

Eliza's loaves didn't appear to be in such high demand, so we talked for a while, comparing celiac-disease horror stories. She described how she had been experimenting with flour mixes for years before she hit on one she liked, and now she was producing a type of GF bread that was, at the time, difficult to find: sourdough. Eliza would turn out to be the first of several people I met who were working innovatively on GF bread-making, not settling for "good enough."

I knew after tasting a sample that this was indeed *bread.* Her sourdough had an incredibly successful texture, but it was the tang that got me, immediately reconnecting me to the spelt and multigrain loaves we used to buy. When it came time to select some bread to take home with us, the good manners and economy drilled into me throughout my upbringing worked against me. I should have bought Eliza out—should have written a check for $140 and taken home all twenty loaves at $7 each, then stacked them in the chest freezer like cordwood. At a loaf a week, Bec and I could have lived off of them until Christmas.

Instead, we bought two measly loaves. I thought I shouldn't be greedy, should leave enough for the other poor celiacs, and all that. And seven bucks for a loaf of bread sounded, at that point, a little steep, even though I was already paying that for the bagged mix. (It doesn't sound expensive anymore, though it's hard not to see such a price for bread as more evidence that the poor are priced out of good gluten-free items.) Across the country, the average cost of high-quality GF bread—which is the only GF bread worth eating—seems to fall between eight and eleven dollars *per loaf,* depending upon location and ingredients. Ironically, most are made from "grains of poverty": bean flours, nut flours, and millet. In the GF world, everything that used to be poor is now rich.

A few hours later, I thought better of my actions, and I returned to the market with the intention of buying out Eliza. But she was gone; I found only an empty space where she had set up her tent.

So I was determined not to make the same mistake with the beer. I had learned about the Omission when my neighbor, Matt, had once again returned from Rochester with treasure a few weeks prior. The Glutenbergs, Celia Saison, and cider all had emerged during a seren-dipitous beer-and-cider tasting at Burlington's Farmhouse Tap Room & Grill, which had long been one of our favorite places to eat because it served locally sourced meat and produce. Now we liked the Farm-house even more, because they had a GF-dedicated fryer. Compared to other restaurants we'd visited, the staff was fantastic; they made substitutions willingly, showing us the joys of rare-cooked burgers on beds of wilted kale with pickled jalapeños. Their variety of celiac-safe beers meant I hadn't pined—not much, anyway—for any of the other hundreds of beers they stocked. No New Planet. No Bard's. No Redbridge. Only innovative, inspired brews. I'd left the table a tad unsteady, and with the shopping list I'd brought into the City Market.

"Actually," I started over with the cashier, "I'm not having a party." I lifted the four-packs onto the belt. "I have celiac disease. Where I live we can't get good GF beer, so when we visit here, we tend to load up."

I watched as her face softened. It was the first time that I had ever played the celiac card in my defense: *That's right, don't judge me, be-cause either I buy you out or I'm drinking Bitchy Tree.*

"It will last a *long time*," Bec added from behind me, mostly for the benefit of the shoppers in line behind us.

"Well, soon Monsanto will be doing that genetically modified wheat so people with celiac's can eat it, right?" The cashier smiled at me brightly, apparently unaware that she had turned celiac disease

IN MEMORY OF BREAD

into a possessive, like Tourette's. She went on, "My wife is into GMO and Monsanto. She sees it as a good thing—the problems GMO can solve, and all that."

We had a pleasant talk about the loaded issue of GMOs and paid an absurd amount for what seemed a small quantity of beer—not 252-percent more than for all others in the cooler, but about 50 percent more than the refreshing, gluten-packed beers from Allagash and Stone, Otter Creek and Long Trail. Then Bec and I left to load up the car.

"The only bad thing about this whole damned town," I said as we drove back to our hotel, "is that we don't live here."

The contrasts in the available products were leading me to see the North Country, which I'd long thought of with pride as my home, as a GF desert. I knew that GF bakeries and even small-scale breweries were popping up all over the country, and I also knew that they would come to our region last. I didn't *want* to move, and it wasn't practical to do so. But I was tired of feeling left out, though for the time being, as long I was within striking distance of the good stuff, I could live with it.

Talk about letting a genie out of a bottle: the first time I tasted Omission Pale Ale, after a year and a half of drinking gluten-free beer, I stood stunned in the middle of my kitchen, unable to speak. The regions of my brain still sensitive to barley seemed to light up in neon. I took another sip, and then another. How could I possibly thank Matt for ending what had become, by then, a very long dry spell? He couldn't comprehend the value of the gift; nobody could, unless he had been drinking sorghum for that long.

I said to Bec, "Holy shit. This is real beer."

I knew that the other GF beers on the market, the sorghum-and-fruit brews I had been drinking and dissing, *were* real beer—in some

places, anyway, and in the academic sense. But this beer had barley flavor. There were hops—a healthy dose of them. There was no funk, no
saccharin aftertaste, no overcarbonation. Just hoppy, malty goodness.

"I have to have more of this," I told her. "I need an endless supply.
Right now."

Bec tried the beer, also loved it, and then read the label. She gave
me a look that said, *Hold on there.* Omission is in fact brewed with barley, and through a special process the gluten is removed, or stripped,
down to 20 PPM or less. This fact was all over the packaging, like a
disclaimer. "There's some poison in here," she said.

I considered that while I drank some more beer. "Well, yes. I suppose there is. But it's minimal and it's probably safe and that's what
makes this *beer.*"

"The poison makes it beer?"

"Well? *Doesn't* it?"

It was a hard argument to counter. She, too, had given up beer. She,
too, had come to believe that, the brewing traditions of the world notwithstanding, in our part of the world, barley inhabits beer like wood
does trees, to paraphrase a poet-friend of mine.

"We'll impose a strict one-beer limit," I said. "And I'll adhere to
it. I promise."

"First we'll see how you feel in a few hours."

She looked worried, and I suppose she had reason to be. This was
new territory. Prior to Omission's introduction to the market in 2012,
the debate over the safety of beers from which the gluten has been
reduced ("GR" beers) was relatively quiet, perhaps because the available brews were imported from Spain and Belgium in small amounts.
When I sampled Daura Damm and Brunehaut that first winter, immediately after I was diagnosed, I definitely liked them, but I also
quickly forgot about them. Even in cities that are well stocked with
GF options, Brunehaut and Daura Damm can be difficult to find. But
Omission thrust questions about GR beer safety for those with celiac

disease into the spotlight. Some groups, like the Celiac Support Association, have approved Omission. The CSA views the instruments designed to test for gluten—in particular, what's known as the R-5 ELISA (enzyme-linked immunosorbent assay) test, which checks for the presence of antigens like gluten epitopes—as accurate and reliable. Other organizations, however, have been outwardly critical or quietly skeptical of beers like Omission. Many gastroenterologists will say that any gluten at all is too much for someone like me, even though recent scientific studies have concluded that 20 PPM a day is "quite safe" for most people with celiac disease. The real worry, the skeptics of GR beers note, is that the R-5 ELISA test was not designed to measure gluten content in hydrolyzed and fermented beverages. Thus the readings in the tests could be inaccurate, which is why the packaging of a beer like Omission Pale Ale or Lager does not say "Gluten-Free." The FDA will not allow it. Instead, the packaging says "Crafted to Remove Gluten" and "Tested to 20 PPM."

I felt fine after drinking my first Omission. I still felt fine the next morning. Would I have told my wife if I felt like shit? I would have tried damn hard to hide it, though it's difficult for me to cover up the effects of getting glutened. I'm a bit like Dr. Jekyll turning into Mr. Hyde when something gets me—mood swings, greenish tinge to my face, and all—often prompting Bec to ask, *Did you eat something?* I would have turned in an Oscar-worthy performance to keep this beer in my fridge. Then I would have pounded one hundred ounces of water, waited a few hours, and gone for a hard 5K run to sweat out the toxins.

My discovery of Omission came around the time when researchers in particle acceleration were closing in on isolating the Higgs-Boson "God" particle. In that spirit I took to calling the ingredient that put *beer* back into "GF beer" the God Enzyme. (I also wondered if it would be possible, someday, to do the same thing for bread.)

David and I immediately started wondering how to get our hands on some of this God Enzyme, known commercially as Brewers Clarex. Derived from a mold, *Aspergillus niger,* Clarex has for a long time been used to prevent chill-haze in cold-fermented beers like lagers and pilsners, so that the beer pours clear and golden. When introduced to the wort in the proper proportions, at the right point in the brewing process, *A. niger* renders a beer clear *and* reduced of a significant amount of its gluten. Simply stated, Clarex inhibits the formation of the chemical bonds in beer that lead to an autoimmune reaction in a person with celiac disease. It disrupts the formation of antigens.

It turns out that Clarex, and other products like it, are widely available from home-brewing supply companies. Perhaps, David and I thought, we could order an IPA kit, brew it up like we used to, and then dose it with some of this stuff? How great would that be?

I did a little research—and, unfortunately, the GR brewmasters I talked with said that Clarex needs to be used in a specific way in order to remove gluten. It's pretty easy if you know what you're doing, but for a home brewer with celiac disease, the stakes are high. I decided not to go dabbling in this myself, though I did start to wonder why, if it's a straightforward process, more breweries both in the United States and abroad are not producing GR beers instead of relying on sorghum.

As Amy Jeuck at Omission Beer told me, Omission Pale Ale came out of a "deeply felt internal need" to make a good barley-based beer safe for people who are intolerant to gluten, not from the trend in gluten-free eating. Their timing was simply fortuitous. Omission would have launched their beers whether the GF diet was popular or not. Development of their GR pale ale began around 2006, when Terry Michaelson, former CEO of the Craft Brew Alliance— Omission's brewer—was diagnosed with celiac disease, introducing an even crueler irony than the one that befell me: whereas I was a home brewer, here was a guy who *owned* a whole damned beer company, and he couldn't even drink his own beer (the Craft Brew Alliance also includes Widmer Brothers, Redhook, and Kona, none of which are gluten-free or gluten-reduced).

The research and the early batches of beer, according to Jeuck, were highly secretive. The people at Omission knew they did not want to replicate the industry practices of using sorghum. "We wanted to make *real* beer gluten-free," Jeuck told me, emphasizing what she thought made beer real: barley. She noted that sorghum is perfectly fine brewing material in other food cultures and traditions, and plenty of celiacs claim that they do not mind the taste of sorghum,[*] but she believed that many American drinkers resist the flavor because it's not part of our food culture. We weren't brought up with it.

After a few years of experimentation, Omission launched their Pale Ale and Lager, and, later on, their IPA. According to Omission's brewmaster, Joe Casey, it's possible to reduce the gluten content in all kinds of beers, from lagers to stouts, pale ales to porters.[**] The question, as with all specialty gluten-free items, is about how much product a producer, in this case a brewery, can sell. Casey told me he believes that people tend to drink darker beers in lower numbers than lighter beers, regardless of the time of year. Darker beers are just too rich and heavy to drink in quantity, and when you combine the low consumption with the lower demand for GF beer, a GR stout or porter doesn't look profitable. (I disagree on the effect of a beer's darkness, or strength, on its drinkability, but I might not be representative of the beer-drinking culture in America.)

Another prohibitive factor in GR beer brewing is the special demands on processing. Even in a dedicated facility, tanks and lines must

---

[*] I suspect they're lying.

[**] Yes, please.

be carefully cleaned, inspected, and tested. Jeuck described something like a lockdown occurring at the facility on bottling day, with no one allowed in or out except at specific times, to eliminate any risk of cross-contamination. The beer is tested internally for gluten, and it's also tested by external third parties who post the results online, so that drinkers of Omission can verify the gluten-content scores of the bottles they hold in their hands. Jeuck said that Omission has "blasted everywhere that we are made from barley. We're committed to transparency." All of these steps are necessary to win the trust of a customer base who will bolt and never come back if a product makes them sick.

But wait. Before we go stripping the gluten from beer, just how much gluten is *in* beer?

I never stopped to ask this question after my diagnosis. I just followed the conventional wisdom: "Beer is made from barley, and barley contains gluten. Sucks to be you."

Ancestral beers in Babylon, Egypt, or Sumeria might have been more gluten-rich than most of today's brews, because they were unfiltered and unclarified. Fortifying the barley mash with emmer, einkorn, or spelt would have resulted in brews with even higher gluten potency. But if the Neolithic grains were indeed different from today's plants, packing lower concentrations of the harmful 33-mer gliadin peptides, then, like ancestral bread, these brews might also have been less detrimental no matter how much gluten they contained. Gluten content in modern beer is more variable for several reasons, but mostly due to the different approaches to brewing (mashing), fermenting, and filtering that have led to the wide variety in beer styles. The differences between modern and Neolithic brewing practices aside, high-gluten beers are commonly on the shelf today. For example, according to one Swedish study, a single UK pint of Guinness clocks in at 5,000 to 6,000 PPM of gluten. The study's authors even broke the

stylistic conventions of scientific writing and appended an exclamation point to the results—"5-6000!"—as if to say, while leaning back
in their lab coats, *Whoa, baby!* I find these data astonishing, especially
given how frequently I enjoyed all stouts, including Guinness. Did I
ever drink the entire four-pack of widget cans? Sure, once or twice,
on a cold winter's night with a dinner of lamb-and-bacon stew ladled
over roasted fingerling potatoes, and some crusty bread on the side for
the gravy—thus ingesting 24,000 PPM gluten from beer alone in one
sitting. And I enjoyed every drop.

Measurement of gluten content in beer has advanced since 2005,
when the Swedish study was published, but even if the study's findings for Guinness were revised down 1,000 PPM, I think I can now
explain why my gastrointestinal decline was so rapid. I was drinking
stouts in the fall of my diagnosis (to wash down all the bread), and just
one Guinness exceeds my 20 PPM limit by 250 times. If gluten had
something like a radioactive half-life—which in a sense it does in the
form of gliadin antibodies that live on in the blood for a while after
exposure, along with razed intestinal microvilli and mucosa—my intestines might still be glowing.

The winner of the Swedish study was Kronenbourg 1664, a pale
lager measured at 10,000 PPM gluten (curiously, no exclamation
mark here). In the celiac world, this is nuclear weapons–grade gluten.
The fact that it's a lager and not a stout also reveals the difficulty of
predicting gluten content based on style. While it's generally accurate
to say that darker beers have higher gluten contents, Kronenbourg
1664 does not look like Guinness in the glass. If you were to point
to the pint of stout and say to a celiac, "That will kill you, friend,"
many would think the light, golden Kronenbourg safer. They would
be wrong. And yet, Carlsberg beer, which the Swedish study found to
be "safe" at under 20 PPM—though it's not sold as "gluten-reduced"
and is not widely known for having low gluten—is also pale gold and

translucent. Budweiser, which looks much the same as Carlsberg, is not safe, but Coors Light, Modelo, Pilsner Urquell, Pabst, and even Duvel—at 8.5% ABV, fruity, hoppy, and strong—potentially *are* all as safe as any GR beer, because the breweries use Clarex in the same way as Omission. They just don't advertise that fact. The gluten reduction is coincidental, their facilities are not dedicated, and they aren't paying for third-party testing.

So I never tried any of these beers, not even when I was out of Omission or Glutenberg and hating on the sorghum brews that always seemed to find their way into my fridge out of hope and desperation. I wasn't willing to take the chance on a Carlsberg, and certainly not a Duvel; it would be like playing Russian roulette with my gut. Losing an entire week to GI issues, chills, and foggy thinking has a way of making a guy walk the line. I also had come to believe that every time I got glutened, there was a good chance I was setting back the recovery of my intestines a little more. I might have been exaggerating, but even if I wasn't, it is an awful feeling to have absolutely no control over the way your body is reacting to a toxin.

This was why I came to love a beer like Glutenberg, which appeared on the market at about the same time as Omission, but is entirely gluten-free, since it is made from malted corn, millet, quinoa, buckwheat, sometimes chestnuts (in the case of their Red Ale, which is excellent), demerara candy syrup, and hops. Though it doesn't taste quite the same as Omission, this beer is without risk, and, of all the completely GF beers on the market, comes closest to imitating the body and hop flavors of the pale ales and IPAs that I loved. Ground Breaker Brewing's Harvester IPA, Pale Ale, and Dark Ale—which include in the mash tapioca maltodextrin and *lentils*, of all things—are also especially good beers with carefully chosen mixes of hops. They're less easy to obtain, especially on the East Coast. (I once spent as much on shipping as on the beer itself, just to check out their latest offerings, and to confirm that, yes, lentils *work*—and so the makers of Mumm might not have been totally crazy for including beans.)

In the midst of the GF beer renaissance, a question arose: If I had alternatives, and if I wouldn't drink those beers that are GR by coincidence, then why did I keep drinking the Omission? For one thing, at the time, I didn't know about the debate over the validity of R-5 ELISA test results for beers. By the time I read the salvos being launched at GR beers, it was too late; I wasn't going to give it up. I also trust my body. It's basically a Geiger counter for gluten, and it comes through a bottle of Omission fine. If I'm going to be completely honest, I do sometimes wonder about "silent" side effects—even though my symptoms over the last couple of years have never been close to silent when I get glutened.

If I was knowingly putting gluten into my system, albeit in microscopic amounts, I had to justify, or at least explain, the risks I was taking—to myself, but also to others who sometimes raised their eyebrows as if wondering whether my drinking a GR beer meant that I was making celiac disease up, or wasn't as disciplined as I claimed to be. It seemed odd to some people, even stupid, that the only gluten I ever deliberately came in contact with anymore was in the form of beer. After all, I wasn't attempting to estimate 20 PPM's worth of crumbs of bread or cracker or cake, and eating them just to experience the momentary neurological fireworks.

That tiny amount of barley in the bottle of Omission (or any other GR beer I later encountered) was a thin, tenuous tie back to the eater and drinker—and so, in some ways, to the person—I used to be. My feelings would be exactly the same, I imagined, if I were eating bread that had been rendered safe with the God Enzyme. When I brought this beer to parties, or had one with friends, I felt as if I had been returned to an equal footing. Unless you're eating and drinking alone, the rituals around food and drink are about inclusion, and sometimes you feel the pangs to be included.

So I made a deal with myself. I only drank one bottle of Omission at a time, and usually only one bottle in a week. It was a good strategy for preserving something we could not get easily, anyway. Slow beer to match the slow food: I poured and I savored. And when the glass was empty, I looked forward to the next time.

13

SUMMER RITUALS

Late afternoon, midsummer. Someone was throwing one of the season's many parties: a backyard barbecue on the river with friends, an evening in the lengthening shadows with colleagues from work, or the annual "Food, Games, and Shit for the Kids" event given by a teammate on my summer softball team (who doesn't have kids, and thus his curious umbrella term). The fare was always much the same: meat for the grill, salads, chips, and cakes and brownies for dessert. In the coolers were assorted beers, gin, and bottles of tonic water. The forecast called for full sun, humidity, and a 70-percent chance of eating foods—and an amount of food—that you wouldn't eat at home. Kids would be everywhere, and if any group of humans can bring disorder to a table of food faster than drunk people, it's kids. For someone with allergies, the whole scene could get dicey in a hurry.

When I came out of hiding, as I thought of it, and started attending these parties, I noticed that two things were beginning to happen. The first was that the hosts, and sometimes the other guests, made sure to bring things for me, foods that I could enjoy—rice salads, GF quiches, GF buns for burgers and sausages—which they kept in a sad, dark corner of their own freezer they had voluntarily made so on our account. Oddly, or perhaps not, such kindness had a way of making the fake breads taste a little better; generosity of spirit is an excellent seasoning. We threw them on the grill, toasted them, and ate them. We were together outside in the summer, and that was all that mattered.

The second thing that happened was that, by midsummer, I had stopped feeling much interest in many of the foods that everyone else at these events could eat but I could not. Mostly. It depended upon the genre of the food. At a certain point I noticed that I barely registered the presence of the tabbouleh, the cold salads of couscous and bulgur, the pasta dishes. I learned to ignore the hotdogs I could not source, or those sausages not made by the Bartons, because many others contained gluten or chemicals that could hurt me as badly as gluten. The Doritos ceased to trouble me. I did not for one minute miss the veggie burgers. For breads and certain cheeses and noodles I felt a momentary pang—*nope, though it looks good*—and then my eyes just ticked right by. It was almost as if, in my mind, these foods had ceased to exist as food.

Some of the forgetfulness I had cultivated came from discipline, a determination not to get sick. I knew that not everyone with celiac disease found it as easy to be disciplined, that plenty of people were willing to risk losing a few days in return for enjoying a piece of cake or something else that they loved—a fair trade for the eating experience, or at least that was how they said they saw it. I could never quite get there. Like many people with allergies, I found fear and suffering to be powerful behavioral modifiers.

I knew that discipline came from more than simple fear, though. Plenty of well-meaning, conscientious people I had spoken with had learned their personal threshold for a reaction to gluten—and then bumped up against it as hard as they could.

Much later, I attended a conference panel on the recurrence of symptoms in people with celiac disease who should have technically been in remission because they had been self-reporting as gluten-free for months, even years. They were not intentionally cheating on the diet. I was shocked to hear that many in the survey were still symptomatic, experiencing a range of maladies, from GI distress to neurological issues, as frequently as two or three times a *week*. Furthermore, their intestinal biopsies revealed that they were not in remission. In some cases they weren't even close. Yet these people didn't quite fit the profile for refractory celiac disease, either. The study made me wonder: How often were these people who were suffering several times a week eating out at restaurants? What was their attitude toward sacrifice and risk? How clean were their kitchens? How much or how little time had they been able to take to educate themselves, given the demands of work, family, and chores? And, especially, how much support were they getting at home? Many of the people I had spoken to in the audience at that conference—and many people with celiac disease whom I have met since then—lived in houses divided. Gluten for him, not for her.

Among the greatest gifts Bec gave me was her own decision to eliminate gluten. She didn't even ask me, *Do you want me to do this?* I would have said no, and she knew that. So she just did it—although some people assumed that I must have asked, even demanded it of her, or else she would have stuck to her old diet. Our friends quickly came to understand and admire her sacrifice, but whenever we met someone new, they were surprised. Some referred to her decision to give up wheat as martyrdom, which pissed me off—I knew that she had done it out of love, and that she wasn't enjoying the GF life any more than I was. It seemed we were the exception and not the rule in how we were going about managing this.

The truth is that for many people with celiac disease, as well as those with other gluten-related disorders, cross-contamination is a real threat, and long-term medical complications can come from continued exposure to minuscule amounts. Supporting a partner is not an empty gesture. I would have done the same for her. If we believe that food can and does convey love, then turning away from food in certain circumstances must be a gesture of unconditional love as well. Anyone who wakes up one day with a condition that raises his risk for early mortality and diminished quality of life, if he does not heed the puzzling new demands of his body, should be so lucky as to have a partner who will sacrifice that much for him.

I understood, of course, why people who do not have intolerances are loath to make the sacrifice. Our eating choices are intimately personal, and they are far from rational. It can be tough enough to self-impose restrictions, let alone take up someone else's.

Especially early on in our days as GF eaters, I asked Bec several times what she missed. I did this partly out of an ongoing curiosity, a measurement against my own experience, and partly to keep myself mindful of her. Although our eating habits are the same, our relationships to food are different; whereas I've come to acknowledge gluten as poison, she knows that it is theoretically still an option for her. Bread always made her list. Blue cheese. Dark beer. Like me, she pined for French toast or brioche when she saw them on menus. For a long while she walked around with a mysterious craving for a layer cake. She reconciled to losing pasta, but not the breaded, fried buffalo shrimp from our favorite restaurant, or sandwiches. She didn't miss the stuff that no one ever longs after: soy sauce, teriyaki, raisin bran. Like me, she most longed for the freedom to walk into a restaurant and order whatever sounded good that day, instead of searching for the two or three options that would not violate the sacrifice. She said she couldn't eat any of those other foods in front of me, not with any enjoyment. And, now that she herself had been GF for so long, she would feel sickened as well, and that wasn't worthwhile.

Never encountering wheaten foods at home smoothed the road for me, though the sight of homemade bread in someone else's kitchen continued to fill me with longing. Many homemade desserts that showed up at those summer parties cued the wistfulness, as well. Nobody in their right mind uses GF flour to make a carrot cake or a strawberry pie if they don't have to, and I don't blame them. The seasonal pies especially drove a dagger into me. On the "pie or cake?" personality test, I was always "pie," though if given the chance to hedge I would say both. When I looked at the buffet table and saw these pastries, my eyes did not gloss right over them. There's a reason desserts possess the power to make people immoderately happy. For this part of the backyard party, the potluck in someone's spacious kitchen, Bec and I had no answer. If there was nothing safe, no ice cream or sorbet, and we hadn't brought something ourselves, we grabbed some grapes, or another glass of wine, and wandered away.

I make it sound as if our life at the table was all discipline and sacrifice, but that is not true. Beyond the health reasons, beyond fairness and solidarity, beyond the inescapable truth that it's easier to be "compliant" with medical mandates if you have support, and beyond the promises implicit in vows of unconditional love, we had found, by midsummer, some good gastronomical reasons for both partners in a household to relinquish wheaten foods if one of them must do so—or to make any sacrifice together for that matter, from dairy to peanuts to cholesterol. We discovered, together, the pleasures of Korean-style barbecue: beef and lamb sliders wrapped in red leaf or butter lettuce, or served, as one restaurant taught us, on a bed of sautéed kale or arugula. We explored the sea of gluten-free pastas until we encountered our ultimate favorite, a fresh egg pasta made with rice flour. We smiled the first time we cooked it, knowing we'd made a significant discovery and were closer to a total victory over longing. Bean noodles, glass vermicelli, seed-based crackers, and legume chips: we compared notes on all of them, determining which would make regular appearances in our cupboards, which we'd use occasionally, and those we'd never buy again. It was a comfort to decide together to keep tweaking certain recipes and to banish others. We scrutinized the results of flour mixes, and innovated solutions for oat substitutes in apple crisps, the best of which involved pecan meal. At times our opinions divided, but these happy disagreements were part of the exploration, too. I had not thought this new feature of my life could make eating better, and more companionable, but sometimes that was exactly what seemed to be happening.

The most difficult social situation I encountered that summer came on Friday nights. It wasn't a backyard party or cookout, or wing-and-trivia night at a bar, or trip to watch a game. For the last several years, Friday night had been Softball Night, when, along with ten other men who had become my friends, I played modified fast-pitch at diamonds across our part of St. Lawrence County.

We played ball at a beautiful field with horse pastures beyond the fences and a river not far behind home plate; we played at a miserable dump known as "The Pit," where the fences were so short that I saw balls go up but never saw or even heard them come back down; we played on freshly mown high-school fields, and in the shadows of water towers. Grown men, all of us, running hard and pulling—and, in a few cases, breaking—parts of our bodies, all because some flame of boyhood still burned within us. Most of us grew up on baseball fields, buying baseball cards from corner markets, and playing Wiffle ball with ghost runners. Now, every Friday night, some man over forty dove or slid or gathered up a difficult ground ball without even having to think about it, all because his muscles still remembered what to do. It was a beautiful thing to see, and even more gratifying to feel.

And after every game, there were always beer and snacks.

We climbed into our cars and headed a few miles from our home field to Eben's Hearth, the restaurant that sponsored us because the owner was generous, and also because we drank their sponsorship costs back and then some. Or, if we were playing away, we stopped at a place called the Skunk's Nest, or Zorro's. And if there was no watering hole nearby, we drank beer out of a cooler at the field.

The Hearth had more than a dozen beers on tap. Omission and

Glutenberg were not included in the rotation. They famously sold the Big Beer, a frozen glass mug that held a liter. That's 33.8 ounces, only 2.2 ounces shy of three bottles of beer in one glass. A draft Big Beer of something good, a craft IPA or hoppy amber ale, cost only seven dollars, a bargain. A Big Beer hid your face when you drank it, sometimes demanded two hands, took about an hour to drain, and tasted best after two hours in the field. A sign behind the bar proclaimed the rules: LIMIT OF THREE (3) BIG BEERS PER CUSTOMER PER VISIT. I never put back three, though I did once struggle through the last sips of a second.

For years, after every home game, I ordered a Big Beer of a West Coast–style IPA or Lake Placid Ubu. On especially hot nights I went for something lighter, like a Sam Adams Summer Ale, a Switchback, or a Long Trail. Then I sat with my buddies, smelling the effervescence of the hops and savoring the first bittersweet mouthfuls as our talk drifted from the game to work to vacation plans. Everyone bought rounds for everyone else. No one kept track. We knew it all worked out by the end of the season; and if it didn't, well, that didn't matter much.

When the season began, I thought I would be happy just to be able to play, which I was. Then I discovered that my only draft option at the Hearth was Bitchy Tree (there was a bottle of Redbridge or two, way in the forgotten caverns of the beer cooler; once when I asked for one I watched the bartender disappear shoulder-deep trying to retrieve it). I had always thought this cider was hard on a beer lover, but the food historian David Buchanan killed any remaining enjoyment when I read his observation that most commercial hard ciders, none of which he names, are wine coolers compared to the dry ciders drunk in the early American Republic. I knew immediately that he was right. Ciders made according to early practices are indeed making a comeback, including a local hard cider I've found, and I'm also always on the lookout for those that have been dry-hopped into a beer-cider lovechild. But I was never going to find ciders like those in the kegs at the Hearth, through no fault of the owners. The few times I gave into longing and drank a Big Beer of Bitchy Tree, I was sorry. I woke up feeling a little as though I *had* drunk a real beer. Too much sugar, too much malic acid.

Most other times when I went out with friends, I wasn't troubled as much by the lack of a beer option. But on Softball Night, I regressed to a younger age—in many ways *during* the game, my teammates would say, and also at the postgame ritual. I was no different from celiac kids across the country who want to have what everyone else on their Little League team has after the game, whether pizza or burgers or ice cream sandwiches. I also frequently craved the salt and grease of fries, which I never ordered because the fryer wasn't "clean." Rarely, but intensely, wings or a burger sounded good. But mostly I wanted to join in the clinking of glasses filled with beer.

As I'd done with so many other foods and experiences I had given up, I tried to think my way out of the trap. I wondered if I wanted the beer after the game because I *truly* wanted it, because it could satisfy me at that moment more than anything else could, or if I wanted the beer only because the story I had been told all my life about men and games and camaraderie and celebration had convinced me that softball night was incomplete, a letdown, without a beer. I loved playing the game, but I loved the postgame more: the brief stops at double-wide bars and old hotels where we shared an hour with people we would not have met otherwise, or the evenings we gathered around a cooler on the tailgate of someone's pickup truck beside a lazily flowing river as the heat and the light softened, drinking sweaty cans and quietly talking as the fish stirred the water's surface in ripples. Back when I could still drink any beer at all, every one of them, even the lower-quality brews, tasted decent as I stood in my cleats, adrenaline still pumping. There's a spot only certain foods and drinks will hit at certain times.

And that was why the beer I was drinking—or not drinking—ultimately did matter.

After my discovery of Omission and Glutenberg, I started tucking a bottle into the cooler I took to the game, along with water and a banana (since I still couldn't handle the dyes in sports drinks). I never brought them into the Hearth with me, but I considered it. (Once, I did in fact sneak a beer into another local place, as punishment for many wrongs committed by the owner, the least of which was stocking nothing better than Woodchuck raspberry cider; I ordered a glass of water, drained it in three gulps, and then stealthily refilled it with an Omission, using a ball cap as a screen.) Packing my own chute, so to speak, didn't mean I was unappreciative of my teammates when they thought about me, as they increasingly tended to do, by dropping a can of Smith & Forge or Stella Cidre into the cooler they filled with Labatt or Yuengling. I drank the cider, because it was their gift to me. But first I opened my beer, and I stood with my pals in the dying light on a baseball diamond, drinking rich malt and hops and feeling, for a short while, so wonderfully complete.

14.

GF by Choice

For reasons I could not understand, the distance and time I spent running had both been getting longer. Back in the winter, I would have been happy to run any distance at all without collapsing on the shoulder of the road. But after a few weeks I wanted to be in 5K shape, and then 10K. In the middle of the summer I passed the 10K marker, pushed my way to 15K, and then close to a half marathon.

Since classes were over for the summer I could run in the daytime, and I did, pounding pavement in the teeth of the afternoon heat and glare. I ran without a dog at my hip, without music, without a watch. I didn't even care about exact mileage; I was content to estimate the distances. I had no goals, no race on the horizon, no plan. I followed a vector away from the house and back amid the whir of cicadas and the dizzying smell of hot tar. My route took me out of the village and along the roads that led, eventually, to some of the farms that grew the produce we cooked and ate. I primarily ran to find that zone of perfection in which I forgot I was running. I hardly knew who I was; I was unaware of anything except for the road and the approaching cars.

Lots of runners and other athletes, I knew, reported they felt better after adopting a GF diet. I was diagnosed around the time Peter Bronski's book *The Gluten-Free Edge* was published. Bec had a professional interest in the concept. According to Bronski's accounts, it was as if the athletes he'd met had been putting low-grade fuel into their bodies before cutting gluten. Once they were free of wheat pasta and bread, and of all the gluten in processed foods, their performance data improved—but, more important, they also claimed that they *felt* noticeably better. They no longer feared they might crap themselves on their runs; they experienced less gas. They did not suffer as much afterward from that sensation I've always thought of as runner's bends—that hot, greasy, cramped feeling low in the gut.[*]

All of this was true for me, though not all of the time. I did feel like I was running cleaner. I wasn't sure I believed the GF diet always led to a performance edge, though. It's a difficult claim to back up with hard science. Plenty of athletes eat diets high in gluten—think of all of those Subway endorsements!—and perform at peak levels. Plenty of athletes *abuse* their bodies and compete well, too. So much of running, of any athletic routine, whether indoor cycling, weight training, or playing baseball, is psychological, even superstitious. I've run well simply because I expected to, and I've also had my ass handed to me under nearly the same conditions. I could not always point to an objectively verifiable difference.

It's possible that many athletes and active people in studies like Bronski's, who feel they train and turn out better efforts off gluten, might have silent celiac disease. Or they might have responded to a GF diet because they had one of the other gluten-related disorders that are more challenging to diagnose but can also sap a person's strength. I took two full minutes off my per-mile time after my body stopped destroying itself, but cutting gluten hadn't turned me into an elite Kenyan marathoner. Even when I was fully recovered, I had some ter-

---

[*] Some studies suggest that GI distress after long or hard runs has nothing to do with diet, but instead results from a "shunting mechanism" in the body that restricts blood flow from the GI tract and redirects it to the legs and lungs, where it's most needed. Other research notes that the differences in discomfort experienced by cyclists (which tends to be less severe) might mean that the jostling of the organs that happens on hard runs, whether long or short, explains the aftereffects. There is even a name: "Runner's Colitis."

rible outings, stretches of three or four miles where I felt as if I were leaving a trail of body parts behind me. The improved times led me to enjoy running, and it was starting to look like I was pretty good at it, but I would have given all of the great runs back in exchange for my old diet, to be able to move and eat my way through the world as I once did. I'd surrender the lighter, faster feeling on the road; the ring of heat pleasantly buzzing around my face; the sensation, afterward, like a breaker somewhere in my chest had been thrown. I'd have taken a minute slower, or five miles shorter.

Like all runners, I turned over ideas as I ran, musings and sources of contentment and old bitter bones I for some reason couldn't stop gnawing on. One of the thoughts I kept coming back to, out on the road, was my continued discomfort with, and exasperation for, the question "Oh, you're gluten-free?"

I had come to despise the phrase "gluten-free" almost as much as I hated millet. I hated it even in the midst of the peace and resignation I was beginning to feel, *because* of the resignation, the sense of being checkmated. I admit that I think about the precision of language a little too much—it's an occupational hazard—but from the first time I entered the GF world, the "free" part seemed a misnomer, unless by "free" one meant freedom from sickness, which is so obviously desirable a condition that it hardly merits comment. I disliked the "gluten" part, too, for being reductive, obscuring the panoply of foods that disappeared. It reminded me of my doctor's careful word choice when he'd diagnosed me.

What, then, would I suggest in its place? I liked *wheat-free* better, if for no reason other than that it named a recognizable foodstuff, but there was the issue of "free" again. *Without wheat? Wheat-poor? Breadless?* All equally bad; they missed the other foods that weren't bread, the lost places and experiences.

For my part, I had come to prefer "celiac." I found it a fittingly ugly word for an unfortunate stroke of alimentary luck. It was the medical description for my case, and though I knew it didn't apply to everyone, I found "celiac" perfect right down to the etymology—it is derived from the Latin *coeliacus*, which comes from the Greek *koiliá* for "belly." The Greeks first chose the word to describe the intestinal anatomy because *koiliá* referred also to geographical features such as caves and cavities. The abdominal cavity and the intestines are both hollows—hollows within a hollow. But more to the point, celiac disease *creates* such holes. Any severe allergy or sensitivity does this: it clears spaces on the table, in the pantry, and on the travel and social itinerary. It clears spaces in one's mind, hollows out corners of the memory, and empties certain traditions of a little of their pleasure.

The more I identified as a celiac, the more I felt caught between the abrupt emergence of my own new dietary needs, which were absolute and irrevocable, and the whims, as I often encountered them, of people I met who had decided to cut gluten simply because they had heard doing so would make them feel "amazing." They would lose weight, their workouts would be better, they would have more energy, and their lives, overall, would improve. I read about such people in their blogs and elsewhere on the Web, and I met them at parties or gatherings, where they sometimes sidled up to me and asked me if I had noticed, since going gluten-free, improved mental clarity, focus, and energy levels, or if I believed that the stomach was indeed a second brain. I had no response to these questions except to say that I was not the best yardstick by which to measure. Yes, I supposed I felt pretty "amazing" of late, but all things were relative: I had also required two bags of someone else's blood just to make it from feeling wretched to feeling awful. And I had really, *really* liked foods made with gluten.

I began to assume that every eater who went voluntarily GF was a fad dieter. I knew they were fad dieters if gluten was off-again/on-again like a bad relationship. Unless they suffered from any of the gluten-related disorders—the detection of which could be difficult, as any doctor knows—I didn't see a good reason for them to cut wheat and other glutenous grains. Not that their eating habits were my business. They weren't. But I was still so uncomfortable with my own gluten-free diet, and with everything that came with it, that I could not see the virtue or the sense in voluntarily taking those restrictions on. It especially offended me if the person seeking "amazement" and "clarity" seemed to think that my life as a GF eater was as easy and as fun as they so often made their GF life sound, usually by citing all the delicious new products (oh?), the way chain restaurants had responded by putting GF items on the menu (happy day!), and the weight they'd lost. In the early days, I told them I still had ten pounds to gain back. Ironically, I might have gained the weight back faster on a commercial, prepared GF diet, since many GF foods are more calorically dense to compensate for lost flavor and texture. As I once heard a registered dietician put it, "A brownie is still a brownie," which is both true and not true, as you need more sugar and fat in a GF brownie to get you to a real brownie experience. Many of the professional GF bakers I met were both grateful for the eating trend and realistic about its ephemerality: "Sooner or later," one baker told me, "some of my customers are going to realize these baked goods aren't making them skinny, and the bubble is going to burst."

I've since evolved in my view of those who voluntarily take on GF diets. If special eating practices help a person—physiologically or psychologically or both—to be a genuinely better human being, to contribute more to the world, then sure, go ahead and eat whatever you need to eat. It took me a while to get there, though. My response to the GFers-by-choice I met that summer and throughout the year was to step back and use my newly reclaimed mental clarity to judge middle-class American eating practices. With the exception of pregnancy, allergies, or certain moral or religious beliefs, like those of vegetarians or people who kept kosher, why limit oneself? There was so much *good food* out there. This was America post–Slow Food

Revolution, not suburbia circa 1950. The urge to exclude, to slash, astounded me. Moderation and mindfulness seemed better routes to well-being, which, after all, was the goal of every diet without a moral or a medical grounding.

More than that, though, I began to think it privileged to alter one's diet so severely on a whim, whether by choosing Paleo, GF, or even organic. I investigated the degree of privilege firsthand when I visited a local food pantry to check out the GF offerings (substitutions, not inherently GF foods, like canned beans or vegetables). As I had predicted, I found the options to be thin—virtually nonexistent. What do you do if you can't afford the substitutions, the grains that used to be the thriftiest but are now the most expensive? The answer was obvious: you kept eating wheat and feeling like crap, and, as a result, everything else suffered. Most eaters in the world, including plenty in this country, have no recourse when the staples of their diet, whether wheat, rice, or beans, suddenly become unobtainable. They don't have the flexibility to just pick up other options. Americans are among the wealthiest eaters in the world, and yet we have the tensest, most dysfunctional relationships with food. It's a testament to how confused I was that even as I leveled such criticisms at the voluntarily gluten-free, I had completely lost sight of the privilege that formed the foundation of my *own* eating habits: local, organic, seasonal, homemade, and now GF. I had not undertaken these practices on a whim—I was deeply committed to them—but still, the option to do so is undoubtedly symbolic of life going your way.

Eventually I saw that although those who were voluntarily GF might have offended me by squandering their choice, unless they were spreading factual misinformation about what the GF diet truly *meant*, they weren't causing any problems. Some of them did in fact loosen their restrictions in front of their friends by drinking beers, cooking with real soy sauce, or telling the server to leave the ponzu sauce or blue cheese on the entrée because these things were fine for people who ate gluten-free, or at least they were fine for *them*. This behavior does no celiac any favors. I didn't encounter many such eaters, though. Mostly I met people who hadn't been feeling as well as they hoped, and were trying to eat their way to feeling better. And in the best cases, these voluntarily GF eaters were helping to fund more research into good GF products, and also filling the coffers of GF food companies who donated to foundations at work on finding real, permanent cures for gluten-related disorders. This made them more useful to the team effort than an eater like me, who had turned his back on most commercial GF offerings—albeit for good gastronomical reasons—and stepped into a culinary time machine aimed at the poorer rural neighborhoods of seventeenth-century Western Europe.

The biggest reason for my tension with those who went GF by choice was this: so much did I love gluten, and so badly did I still miss it, that I thought everyone, but especially all of my friends, should be consuming my share of gluten as well as theirs. My only option was to eat and drink vicariously through them. Therefore it would excite me and gratify me if they ate *more* gluten, not less. They could even eat it in front of me, if they cared to. Just, please, eat the real stuff.

So I was delighted when, sometime in the summer, the era of the beer texts started. Usually my father, but also David (who by then had moved with Mere to California), and other beer lovers who lived just across town, would text me a picture of the exciting new beer they had found. At first, Bec thought this was about as cruel as hating on a celiac got, but I saw right away what was going on. I did not reply, *Hey man, I hope the tap lines at that place are crawling with bacteria and you have the runs in the morning.* Instead I told them to drink two, or four: always one for me and one for them. I knew the beer texts (which continue to this day) were a greeting card, a way of saying, *I'm still taking you to the bar with me, man, and I'm thinking right now of how much you'd like this pint of porter.* But being men, we didn't feel like we could actually *say* that, so my friends and father just snapped a picture of a Weapons Grade IPA or the latest recipe from Lagunitas and wrote, "Mmmmmm. Beer." How was I certain of their meaning? I was not snapping pictures of gluten-free beers and replying in kind, that's how. I never drank a GF beer, not even the good ones, with my friends in mind, because I knew they wouldn't like the beer I was drinking as much as I did, since their taste was as yet uncorrupted. They were doing just fine in the beer department.

I did, however, begin to take photos of the occasional sausage—blistered lamb kielbasa, its snappy skin about to burst on the grill—and text them to my father, because my mother is a vegetarian and no meat, let alone offal, makes its way into that house. I usually sent just the picture. No message. The subtext: *I'm thinking of you, Dad. I know how much you'd like this sausage you can't eat in your own house. Now we're even, kind of.*

PS: I have rib-eyes where this came from.

15.

Two Anniversaries

A man I once worked with told me about a time shortly after he and his wife were married, when they ate three excellent dinners over the course of the same evening. Each meal was small and different enough from the previous meal that instead of gluttonous repetition, the sequence acquired an indulgent luminosity that you could see in this man's eyes as he described it. Certain tastes and meals can stay with you like that; they have a way of lingering more intensely than other kinds of experiences. Every person has his own mental recipe book, or food scrapbook, filled with dishes and snacks that continue to feed him for long after the encounter. The hope of repeating them provides motivation to keep exploring—or, if left unsated, it becomes a form of haunting.

I, for my part, was haunted by Eliza's sourdough bread months after we discovered it at the Burlington Farmers' Market. We had brought the loaves home and rationed them out, stunned by how much fuller and more *bread-like* they were than the bagged mixes from Pamela's or Bob's, and certainly any of the disasters we had baked from cookbooks. The next time I saw her table, I wasn't going to blow it. I would buy every crumb she had, no matter what she thought of me.

We returned to Burlington again in the fall. No Eliza. No table of breads in three flavors, all of which were safe. Nothing for me. *What the hell*, I muttered to myself as I retraced my steps past the same tables again and again, just to make sure I hadn't missed her.

I feared the worst. Had she been unable to build enough of a customer base, pay the bills, stay solvent? After all, she was not baking in Los Angeles, Philadelphia, or Chicago. She was in Vermont, the land of cows and kale and maple syrup, and while it was true that I'd met more people there than in my own town who were sympathetic to the challenges of celiac disease, that didn't mean there were enough people like me to keep a small business like hers afloat, no matter how good the bread.

It was, I would come to know well, one of the cruelties of the market for small-scale GF producers, those who made the artisanal versions of the shadowy Udi's and Schär breads. Apparently I had to be cautious about loving these discoveries too much. We had gone back to the bagged mixes from Pamela's as soon as we ran out of Eliza's sourdough. And it looked like that was where we would have to stay.

There were also some bright spots in the late summer and early fall. I had experienced the "food is love" metaphor before, but never as frequently as I did now. The summer parties gave way to more formal invitations to dinner, when friends invited us to meals and abandoned, for a night, their typical repertoire. I never once sat down to a dinner where the food consisted of theirs and ours, safe and not safe. We gathered around the table as equals, everyone GF for a night. They cleaned cutting boards and counters, read ingredient labels, and took the potential of hurting me so seriously that they were not afraid to check on the obvious: Does mustard oil contain gluten? Could I have quinoa?

Our friends did not have to learn to cook new dishes just to have something to share with us—it doesn't get any safer and simpler than rice—but many of them acquired, for our benefit, new kitchen skills, new ways of cooking. They threw themselves into polentas and white beans, inventive salads, ethnic dishes. They visited the GF corner of the grocery store where they stared at strange brands of crackers and snacks, wondering which were the lesser evils to put on their buffets. They brought back fine ciders from the Finger Lakes, my favorite GF beers from sojourns in cities, and honey mead from Maine. (Even at the office, our department secretary stocked a file cabinet with my own stash of snacks for long meetings.) Coincidentally, at this time, the cookbooks and websites were getting better, and the trend seemed to be helping everyone along. This did not change the fact that converting to cooking GF with any ambition did take time, and it took effort. Remembering my own attitude toward people with allergies before I developed celiac disease—I had found them inconvenient, more often than not—now made me blush, especially in the face of my friends' generosity.

Their skills with GF baking in particular had improved. I have to assume that along the way, they'd experienced their own kitchen disasters just as we had, and thus learned the hard way. They too had looked into the bowl of the KitchenAid, thinking, *What the hell is happening in there?* For all I knew, every dessert they presented us had at least one failure in its wake. They had likely also wasted ingredients, money, and time. I didn't have the heart to ask how much. I just enjoyed their experiments with cheesecake, pies, and fruit crisps. One friend arrived to dinner one night with an amaranth pudding (not too bad). Another stocked her kitchen with baking chocolate and butter, and made impromptu desserts of rehydrated figs and honey. Others dropped ice cream into booze. Most impressively, nobody resorted to GF boxed cookies. They seemed to know what awaited down that road.

At the end of the meal, after the dessert, the friend who had made the cake, or the pie, would often declare in equal measures of disbelief and pleasure, "That wasn't too bad for gluten-free, was it?"

Then they sent us home with the leftovers.

· · ·

There were some things we hadn't figured out how to do yet, and were still a long way from doing.

In October, I began to anticipate my birthday with anxiety, even a little dread, simply because of the cake. Bec and I usually made cakes only around our birthdays, preferring desserts with fruit throughout the year because we had so much of it. Consequently, it had taken us a long time to master cakes, and in recent years we had perfected our go-to, which came out of the 1997 edition of *The Joy of Cooking*—a simple but rich chocolate layer cake with vanilla icing that we nailed every time and took to calling the Oreo on 'Roids. We could have branched out and discovered other recipes, but we never seemed to feel the need to.

After spending the better part of a year trying to bake without wheat, we knew better than to just wander into the *Joy* recipe with GF cup-for-cup flour and good intentions. The hard lessons about the limits of baking chemistry had stuck. We had become pessimistic, cautious about destroying recipes and memories that we loved—or maybe we had just become GF realists.

It didn't help matters that long before the days of our own home-made cakes, I had formed pleasant associations with birthday cakes. I could still clearly remember the Italian bakery favored by my mother in Newton, New Jersey, when I was growing up. D'Angelo's sat beside a dry cleaner's in an unassuming strip mall. The moment you stepped through the glass door, you were immediately greeted by the heady, velvety scent of creamed butter and vanilla. Every year, my mother, brother, and I would enter the cool, bright shop in the middle of August to pick up my brother's birthday cake (for some reason I cannot remember picking up my own cake, probably because my birthday fell during the school year, and so I arrived home from the bus to find the cake magically there on the counter, waiting for me). My brother, David, always chose chocolate with white butter-cream icing, and often strawberries or candied cherries between the two layers. I think these cakes were the first gourmet foods we ever ate, though I don't think my mother necessarily saw them that way. In going to a bakery run by a large, pale-faced Italian woman with hair piled on top of her head, who offered us pignoli cookies on the house, my mother was simply doing the sensible thing: patronizing a fellow Italian. The experience of walking into a bakery and selecting from so many options the one thing you desired was, in the days before supermarket bakeries, a powerful annual rite. I never forgot it. Most people never do.

A familiar feeling came over me and intensified the nearer my birthday drew: something about not being able to have a real birthday cake, whether our cake or one from a bakery, made me want a cake even more.

It did not help that, at about the same time, I had a bad visit with my GI, who had wanted to talk about some concerns he had over my routine blood work. His receptionist called me because he'd been concerned to discover that my hemoglobin and total iron-binding capacity scores had dipped. At my appointment, I told him not to be concerned; the explanation was that I had briefly tried to reintroduce steel-cut oats to my diet. I blamed that bad decision entirely on the arrival of autumn: walking the dog in the early mornings, past the frosted lawns and orange-capped trees, through air filled with the scent of dried leaves and wood smoke, made me come back to the house wanting a hot bowl of oatmeal (and it wasn't even below zero yet). I wondered if my tolerance for it might have returned along with my tolerance for fish and dairy. I needed only one serving—prepared the right way, I'll add, with thawed blueberries, maple syrup, a little nutmeg and cinnamon, and some toasted, slivered almonds—and about two hours before I started to feel off. All day long I was agitated and light-headed. I threw the bag of oats away, downed some water, and went for a run. The symptoms cleared up fast, but apparently the effects of my experiment had lingered in my blood, and ratted me out.

When I told my doctor all of this, he looked at me as if I were stupid. "Everything you get from oats," he told me, "you can get from some other food"—as if mere nutrition, acquiring fuel, comprised the only goal of eating. Even my dog knew there was more to food than getting the calories you needed.

If I couldn't have one of the most humble breakfasts a man could cook (and part of my heritage, too: think about Dr. Johnson slighting the Scottish by noting how in England oats are fed to horses, but in Scotland "they sustain the people"), then I wasn't willing to compromise on cake. In time, I would grow to be fine with a flourless chocolate cake at the end of a special meal, or even a plate of my favorite cheeses. I would come to realize that cake is tradition, but if I can't go back to the Italian lady and get the cake that lives on in my mind, or make the Oreo on 'Roids, then a generous tumbler of single malt is as deep a pleasure. But that October, not for the first time and certainly not for the last, I regressed to being a kid. I asked my wife what she thought she could do. She did her best, and hit the Pamela's website for a spice cake recipe that used their all-purpose baking and pancake mix. Best not to take chances, she thought; no crazy internet recipes, nothing that hadn't been tested. The Pamela's recipe might have seemed uninspired, but it had the virtue of being a pretty sure bet.

While Bec baked I hit the road. I remember pounding out that run, breaking seven-minute miles for the first time. The air was cool and bright and clean and I ran like an animal that had been let out of a cage. I knew that *this* was my gift to myself; that, strange though it sounded, the run, the sweat burning my eyes, was my cake. I had not become a crazed, ascetic runner—time would prove that I could balance running hard and playing hard well enough—but I realized, as my focus sharpened with my footfalls, that at this time a year ago, I'd been a month away from going down the drain.

Afterward, the hunger and fatigue felt so intense that, even though the cake for my first birthday tasted like glorified pancakes, I felt satisfied nonetheless.

Six weeks later, in the first week of December, there was another anniversary of sorts: it was a year from the time I'd gone into the hospital, a season that I will associate for a long while with dizzying sickness. I was running again, in the streets of Canton in the dark, in the snow.

Three inches had fallen already. Snow accumulated on my shoulders, on the top of my head, in the folds of my jacket. We are connoisseurs of snow in the North Country, and this one was light and powdery, completely manageable, though I still felt strange running in it. The drivers who passed me looked annoyed, as if they thought I was purposely on the shoulder of the road to make their evening commute more difficult. The real reason behind the snowy run was that I had seen the gunmetal clouds moving in as I walked home from work and I thought, *Now.*

I was out for only thirty minutes, working time instead of distance. At home the oven was preheating for dinner, which I intended to determine on the run, though as usual, I quickly forgot what I was supposed to be thinking about. Not being able to hear my footfalls allowed me to pretend I was floating. I liked watching the vapor from my breath shoot out in sharp gray plumes. It was easy to stay cool.

Somewhere near the one-mile mark I removed my hat. By two miles my face was crusted with a mixture of melted snow and sweat. Near the street corner, on the bottom limb of a bare birch tree, a wind chime stirred gently. The sound of it as I passed by, light and summery, made the sudden onset of the winter snows seem like a mistake. I descended into the trees and shadows at Bend in the River Park and, as I expected, found myself completely alone. A hush enfolded me. The Grasse River flowed thickly past, dark and slow. I kept my head up, hoping to be rewarded with a glimpse of an owl.

For nearly six months now, I had been training hard. I made my intervals as grueling as I could stand, and I didn't avoid the difficult runs, the long hills, the hot days. I had adhered to my GF diet. Yet as recently as October, I had been returning from long runs overheated and banged up. The breakdown point seemed to be right around ten miles. Why, then, had I kept running past it, to eleven miles, and twelve? The fatigue I felt for hours afterward made it difficult for me to cook with attention or patience. The dehydration made it hard for me to hold my wine, and that annoyed me. Still, I didn't quit. What the hell was I doing this for?

Right around Halloween I had realized the answer. I was far into a twelve-miler when I rounded a corner and the reason seemed to be waiting for me on the trailside, so simple and obvious I couldn't believe I hadn't figured it out sooner.

I was still so goddamned mad.

I still was angry about the diet, the challenges, feeling different, Bec having to change, and the lack of a good explanation for why these things had occurred. I had tried to content myself by tapping into forgotten traditions, by eating those non-wheaten foods that people had been eating with gratitude for thousands of years; I had tried to see the connections between my local eating and history. In some ways this had made things easier, but the approach of the one-year mark allowed me to see that, paradoxically, I had made progress and had not made much at all. I especially felt pained whenever we traveled, or went out to eat. Lately I had been thinking that Bec and I had become like animals that always returned to the same feeding grounds: Thai and Vietnamese restaurants in Ottawa, our favorite bistro and Thai restaurant in nearby Potsdam, and our stops in Burlington and Lake Placid. I had not yet ditched my grand—or maybe they were just inflexible—ideas about eating. That explained my tendency to spoil a perfectly good meal by thinking, *It's always the same place.*

You're not exploring, not doing anything new. And then: *Be grateful. Shut up and eat.*

So I had decided to see if I could burn a hole right through all of the frustration in another way. I chose December 11—the date I went into the hospital and spent three days looking out the windows—for a 13.5-mile run. I wanted a private half marathon, but I was continuing to estimate my distances—I refused to run with a GPS, or expensive gear—and I didn't always want to wonder if I'd run 12.99, so I tacked on the extra half mile.

I wanted a personal-best pace. I was willing to completely trash my body to get it. When winter arrived for real, I could hang up my shoes and repair for as long as I needed.

Then, suddenly, winter did arrive for real, and earlier than I had anticipated. The snow that I was running through now was the vanguard of a system that intended to hang around for a week, through my celiac anniversary and past it. More snows were coming. After that, subzero temperatures. It all came on before I had the chance to taper my miles, ease back my pace. While I could have gutted out 13.5 in the dark right now, it would not have been the run—the event, the tribute, the vengeance—I wanted and needed.

You take what the land, the climate, gives you.

What else could I do? It seemed, as I climbed the hill leading out of the park and turned away from the river, that what I had learned about food, and agriculture, and even about celiac disease, also applied to the land I was running across. Yield to where you are instead of fighting it. Figure out how to work within that frame. It's not necessarily easier that way, but it's better, saner.

The same climate that had helped me recover, given me respite from the GF diet with Adirondack blue and Siberian red potatoes, kabocha and butternut squash, sweet corn, globe eggplants, red and poblano peppers, blueberries, cranberries, molasses, maple syrup, lamb and chicken and turkey—that same sky and soil seemed to want me to quit the running season a little earlier than I had planned. I appeared to have no choice. In a way, I was relieved.

I turned up my street and hit the bright lights of our house at the half-hour mark. By the time I had my shoes off, I knew what we would be eating for dinner: a pan of Dan's root vegetables, celery root and carrots and beets and shallots, tossed with dried herbs from the garden and olive oil and roasted, along with some of Kassandra's pork loin, seared and topped with the spiced apple chutney Bec had put up back in September when we were buried in apples and onions.

Even as I cooked, though, I thought that somewhere out there, someone knew how to turn rice into wheat. People like Eliza Hale: there had to be more of them. There had to be. If we could put a man on the moon, as the saying went.

I resolved to find them, as many as I could.

16.

Avoiding the Doctor

One day early in the spring of 2014, my gastroenterologist fired me. Or did he dump me? Either fails to capture the end of a relationship where one person sent a camera down another person's throat, determined the cause of their suffering, and told them the "cure" was eliminating the cornerstone of Western cuisine. Who, I wondered, was working for whom, here? Apparently, it didn't matter anymore.

His receptionist informed me that I'd broken too many appointments for upper endoscopies. By my awkward silence, I confessed that this was true. I had canceled three appointments, to be exact. In the span of two months. At more or less the last minute. In medicine, this constitutes giving a physician the runaround. It's normal for doctors to want to follow up with severe cases a year later and make sure everything looks good, and the clock had now expired. We were way past a year. The receptionist conveyed that my GI wanted his patients to take their health seriously. That's a paraphrase on the verge of quotation. His real interest, I knew, was in being a good doctor, being careful. I had gotten what I deserved.

It was the first time I'd been fired or dumped since college.

I tend to be a bad patient for two reasons: I research and think critically about what I'm being told by my physicians, even though medicine is about as far from my skill set as I can get; and I don't sit still and convalesce for long. Only the first character flaw applied in this case. The need for endoscopies in patients who are asymptomatic remained an open question in some celiac forums, and I knew that (funny, how I subscribed only to those forums that corroborated my own thoughts). So any assumptions that I was not serious burned in my gut like a chunk of Triscuit.

I decided to take control of the situation. I fired him back. I didn't call the next day. I didn't say, "Oh, please read my blood panels." I didn't say, "I'll change!" I knew that's what I was supposed to do, though I didn't think he was worrying, particularly, over anything specific having to do with my recovery. Rather, I was on the receiving end of standard practice: the old warning shot across the bow to make the other boat change course.

My decision felt validating. I told myself that he needed a certain number of ailing asses and stomachs coming through the door to keep the lights burning, the jar of thermometer condoms stocked, that sort of thing. But I'm sure my silence was also an empty gesture. Someone had no doubt already taken my place. It is a sad fact of the medical field, and no small discouragement, I would imagine, that whenever one person heals, two new sick ones walk in to take his place.

None of my doctors had any proof that my wife and I were cooking our own food and rigorously maintaining the gluten-free lifestyle. They had no proof that I had not deliberately cheated on the diet since the month after my diagnosis, more than a year ago. There had been no furtive rendezvous with Reubens in desultory hotel parking lots, wrappers hurriedly shed in the car. I hadn't tooted a sip of someone's porter or pale ale when they weren't looking since New Year's Eve of 2012. The worst I had done was to lower my nose to the rim of many a friend's pint glass and sniff deeply, inhaling the malt and the hops while the glass's owner looked on with awkwardness and concern.

So if I had nothing to hide, then why not have the endoscopy and be done with it? That was Bec's question to me. Other people with celiac disease asked me the same thing. Why not wow the guy with my splendid intestinal mucosa, my complete recovery?

It wasn't about the procedure, which isn't too bad when you consider the nature of the intrusion. They start an IV, knock you out, spelunk their way down your esophagus, nose around the neighborhood of your small bowel, collect their data, depart, and wake you up. The first time I bailed, I had some New York strips thawed and I refused to fast beforehand. The next time, I realized that softball season started the same day as the procedure and I was scheduled to pitch. Both of these were, admittedly, minor events and major dodges. The last time I canceled, I just didn't want to be bothered.

No, I had avoided the endoscopy because I was afraid. Not of the experience, not that I'd fail to resurface on the other end of the anesthesia. If I hadn't croaked when my body was fragile two years ago, I didn't expect a surgical team to kill me when I was healthy.

I was afraid that, the good signals from my body to the contrary, my GI would still find something amiss in my gut, and then we'd have to *act* on it. I would have to make further changes—to my diet, to my life, to more of the things I lived for. I had no reason to believe this in fact would happen to me, but I had heard enough stories from people who continued, for apparently no good reason, their free-fall into the dietary wasteland of fruits, nuts, and occasional scraps of meat. I read about such unfortunate souls all the time, and I had met and talked to some as well. A man I spoke with from the Celiac Support Association described how he had been fine for a long while—decades—and then, boom: new intolerances left and right. No one could explain it. All anyone in a situation like that could do was keep eliminating foods. Sometimes you didn't even feel awful; your body just wasn't healing as well as it should, and the tests showed it.

And so it seemed that I was entering, far earlier in my life than I'd expected to, the long history of suspicion and antipathy between lovers of food—good food, real food, not processed garbage that kills you, which is the root of a specific evil and should never get a pass—and their physicians. I could not help but be reminded of the immortal gourmand A. J. Liebling's writings about his friend, Yves Mirande, "a small, merry author of farces and musical comedy books" who would "dazzle his juniors," including Liebling himself, by

> dispatching a lunch of raw Bayonne ham and fresh figs, a hot sausage in crust, spindles of filleted pike in a rich rose sauce Nantua, a leg of lamb larded with anchovies, artichokes on a pedestal of foie gras, and four or five kinds of cheese, with a good bottle of Bordeaux and one of champagne, after which he would call for the Armagnac and remind Madame to have ready for dinner the larks and ortolans she had promised him, with a few langoustes and a turbot...

Well, now. That is *a meal*. It occurs to me that while almost everything on Mirande's table is gluten-free (well, except for that sauce, which, according to *Larousse*, has a base of béchamel, so no spindles of filleted pike for me), the spread is not, as those who have been doubly cursed with gluten intolerance and editorial deficiencies sometimes write, *glutton-free*. I leave it up to the reader to decide whether the report of Mirande's appetite, which verges on gargantuan in the classical sense, is an accurate portrayal, or merely Liebling's attempt to marry two beloved pastimes, food and sports, by painting his friend as a table-gladiator.

The point is that Yves Mirande apparently made it to *eighty* eating like this, and Liebling seems to think he might have become a centenarian, had his physician not severely restricted his diet after he fell ill one day in Liebling's company as the two sat in a favorite restaurant, dispatching a couple dozen *escargots en pots* (served with crusty bread to sop the butter) as a first course. Thereafter, Mirande's family strictly enforced the physician's prescribed dietary changes. Liebling does not disclose the exact physiological source of his comrade's end, but he makes it clear that Mirande's real downward slide began when the doctor, whom Liebling calls a fool, killed the man's spirit by putting him on such dismal fare as kidney-and-mushroom mince served in a giant popover, paired with third-rate wines.

Put simply, the guy died of a broken heart.

Perhaps Mirande was a miracle of genetics from top to toe. Certainly his gut was. I have never aspired to equal his voracity at the table, but I was learning a thing or two about his aversion to physicians, and Liebling's, too.

I would happily remain glutton-free, but I did not want to suffer my own version of this gastronomical exile. Why go looking for trouble? There was a small chance that the endoscopy could reveal that my intestinal microvilli were not healing as quickly as they should be, and what would happen then? I would have to start eliminating other "inflammatory" foods from my diet. Wine. Cheese. Maybe even rice. And to be sure, the first thing I would have to toss onto the fire would be Omission, my beer brewed with the God Enzyme.

I knew that technically I was not 100-percent gluten-free, and I worried about being found out. Or I *was* GF, inasmuch as under 20 PPM once a week or so still qualified me, and the scholarship said that it did. What was I, then? Gluten-minuscule? Gluten-safe?

Good enough, is what I said.

I had come to feel toward my beer and every other food, from fish to yogurt, rice to almonds, like some of my North Country neighbors apparently feel about their assault rifles, if the stickers on their trucks and the signs in front of their houses were any indication: *Just try and take it away from me. I dare you.*

If cheese or eggs or quinoa or beans or coffee or anything at all was hurting me, I didn't want to know. I could imagine my gastroenterologist's response: Was this thinking mature? Was it rational? Of course it wasn't. Many of those who develop allergies and intolerances to foods they love say the same thing, though. I feared more intolerances coming over me like a pestilence coming down out of the sky or up out of the ground, like insects or fungi ravaging the garden before we had the chance to savor what grew in it.

At the same time, I knew that I was all bravado.

Knowing that something else was hurting me would mean that, logically speaking, for my own good and also for my wife's—who would have to deal with the consequences and complications both short- and long-term—I'd have to compromise once again. And so I would.

For the time being, though, wheat was enough. It wasn't possible for me to be a protégé of Yves Mirande, or A. J. Liebling, but nobody eats like that anymore, anyway (nor should they). Celiac disease had cleared many things from my table, but one thing it had given me was the ability to listen to my body closer than ever before. I would involve the professionals when it seemed like something was up. Until then, I would continue to pound the pavement, and keep listening.

17.

GETTING GF
WITH AMERICA'S
TEST KITCHEN

I didn't know it at the time, but even as I had been searching for real bread and crying foul almost everywhere I looked, about three hundred miles away in Boston, the staff at America's Test Kitchen were throwing themselves into a similar project to restore joy to gluten-free eating. And because they're the Test Kitchen, they were doing it with a hell of a lot more scientific and culinary firepower than I was able to bring to bear in my own kitchen. More than many people, it would seem.

In the last half decade or so, lots of cooks, from both amateur and professional kitchens, in print and online, have been exploring gluten-free cooking and sharing recipes. In the same way that social media has helped build businesses like gluten-free bakeries, those interested in GF cookery have been able to trade ideas and processes via blogs and comment threads. It's a good thing. There's a real community out there, and the result is that a careful and discerning cook can pick up a few good recipes and some new techniques in an afternoon. By the end of my first year on the GF diet, I'd had plenty of occasions to think that if I had to get celiac disease, the diagnosis came at a pretty good time. My experience had never been as isolating as it once was for people I had met, and GF eating and cooking were getting better, and easier, all the time.

Nonetheless, they had a long way to go. Few of the cookbooks I read seemed to approach the challenges of GF cookery with any true scientific backing. The same could be said of many of the GF options I had encountered on menus at restaurants. Generally speaking, they tended toward safe, rice-based recipes, plenty of xanthan gum, and raiding the cooking traditions of non-wheat-based food cultures for inspiration. And the most innovative recipes could get a little strange, like a popular online recipe for a gluten-free bread that called for no starch of any kind—it was a brick of nuts and seeds. My friend Sarah forwarded me the recipe with the subject line, *This is not bread.* I never made it.

America's Test Kitchen (ATK), however, has always attracted a nerdy type of cook, one with an appreciation of history and science to accompany his keen palate. The ATK keeps a chemist on staff to clear up any debates about what's happening on the molecular level of, say, a pan of scrambled eggs or boiling corn kernels. I can't remember the first Test Kitchen television show I ever saw, or when I began watching *Cook's Country,* or when I first subscribed to *Cook's Illustrated,* but like many home cooks, I instantly became a fan. Our public TV station featured their program, complete with bucolic New England location, on an evening lineup of cooking shows. Because I had read Hervé This's *Molecular Gastronomy* and Harold McGee's *On Food and Cooking* without the looming threat of a final exam—and so did not *read* them—*Cook's Country* always seemed to be more instructive than other food TV. I even enjoyed the philosophical conflicts I sometimes felt with the Test Kitchen, who seemed unworried about locality or even seasonality. Their emphasis fell on one question: What works best?

In 2014, they brought their scientific methodology to *The How Can It Be Gluten Free Cookbook* (*HCIBGF*). It was an approach to gluten-free cooking—and, more important, gluten-free baking—like none other I had encountered, though other groundbreaking GF projects were in progress elsewhere at the same time, and would appear shortly after.* Some of the recipes in *HCIBGF* were grounded in the flatbreads and flours historically eaten by the poorer classes, and thus represented the trip back in time that I had already taken. Some borrowed from Asian cuisines. Their substitutions for wheat, and changes in approach when baking pastas and breads, however, struck me as innovative, even cutting-edge.

I had met *HCIBGF*'s lead editor, Jack Bishop, before—sort of. In my early twenties, I received as a gift his *Complete Italian Vegetarian Cookbook*. It was one of the first real cookbooks I ever owned. For some reason, in those days I approached cookbooks like I did every other book I picked up, working my way from beginning to end, and so over one summer he taught me how to make risotto and a real pizza, and how to mix up a granita. I learned, from his sidebars, how to contrast and pair flavors in different courses. It was a good follow-up to the very first cookbook I ever bought for myself, a stained copy of *The Frugal Gourmet*, from the Books in General used bookstore in Ann Arbor; the title seemed to promise just the experience a broke graduate student needed, and the simplicity allowed me to experience both instructive successes (broiled salmon in a half-sauce/half-marinade of orange juice, soy sauce, and cloves) and dismal failures (shirred eggs) quickly and for cheap. Bishop's book amounted to higher costs, but the payoff was also greater.

So, that spring, I did what writers do. I wrote to him. I thanked him for his hard work. I asked him to talk with me about this "quantum

---

* Among them, Nancy Cain's *Against the Grain* GF cookbook, which adapts some recipes from Against the Grain Gourmet, a GF bakery in Brattleboro, Vermont, and provides plenty more that the bakery does not feature. This book was released a year later than and provides a nice contrast to *HCIBGF*, in that it eschews many of the ingredients and processes the ATK uses, and with good results.

leap forward." Then I set to cooking my way through *HCIBGF* while I waited to hear back.

I found myself in conflict almost immediately.

I knew before I even opened the cookbook that this was going to happen. The ATK and I are like two badly paired zodiac signs, like cat people and dog people. I love learning about the science of cooking, but I'm not a scientist in the kitchen. Most of the time, to be completely honest, I don't *do* precision. I will carefully follow recipes the first few times I cook something new, but I'm always after a template or a set of techniques more than an exact recipe. Unless I'm making sauces or baking, I work off of recipes like a jazz musician embroiders and leaps around a standard. This necessitated labor-division in the kitchen. Bec usually handled the baking, because baking requires weights, measurements, exactitude. For the same reason, I would hesitate to eat in January anything I had canned by myself in July, so she put up the preserves. It's nice to have orderly rows in the garden instead of a wild, gnarled patch of onions or greens, so she planted the seeds. Most of the time my approach worked quite well (for me, anyway), and it was well suited to the flexibility required when a person cooks mostly local food that the farmer picks out for him, because you don't always have exactly what a given recipe calls for. But every time I delude myself with the thought that I could have gone to cooking school, I remember this character trait of mine and know beyond a doubt that I would have been expelled.

Why, then, was I baking at all?

Losing wheat had changed things for me. I was baking because I wanted to know my enemies: tapioca starch, millet, sorghum flour. I was on a quest. I wanted to beat the game.

The trouble with *HCIBGF* started with the ATK's signature flour blend: a mix of white rice, brown rice, tapioca starch, potato starch, and nonfat milk powder. It turned out to be the best GF blend I had encountered, and the milk powder in particular was a stroke of genius for giving body to those flatter, grittier flours. It was expensive to assemble, though: buying all of those bags amounted to a startup cost of nearly twenty-five dollars at my store, a little less than ten times the price of a five-pound sack of King Arthur all-purpose flour. I was uncomfortable with paying that much; it felt like a privilege just to be able to rail at the cost. Mixing my own flour blend also reminded me that I still resented being a different type of eater, one who had traded a recipe of four ingredients for a recipe of ten or more. The ATK recommended King Arthur Flour's GF all-purpose blend if I didn't want to make my own, but the King Arthur GF was expensive as well (more than six bucks for a twenty-four-ounce box, which works out to $21.63 for a five-pound bag), and the milk powder clearly made a difference when I tested the Test Kitchen by making loaves with each. Those nerdy cooks had me. I didn't like it.

Blending starches was fussy and not my idea of fun. I had to weigh out each of the flours, combine them, and then mix (sift, preferably) them for uniformity. I also needed to purchase and incorporate *additional* flours and meals to make many of the bread recipes in the cookbook: oat flour,* almond meal, flaxseed meal, and hot cereal mix. So now we were up to about forty dollars, and our fridge looked like the GF section at the health-food store, because some of these flours—the nut and seed meals especially—are prone to going rancid and have to be kept cool.

We didn't have enough of those brilliant OXO vacuum-seal con-

---

* And here we had another problem. I couldn't eat oat flour, not even GF oat flour, because I had discovered, or rather confirmed, that my shoot-first/ask-questions-later immune system mistook the avenin protein in oats as a foreign invader too, responding to it as if it were gluten. Oat flour is important in GF baking because of its protein content and the way it absorbs moisture. It appeared that now I was baking with not one but two hands tied behind my back.

tainers for all of them. The flours made a mess. I got pissed off about the slurries of spilled tapioca starch all over the counter, all over me. My own damn fault, obviously, but it was not my fault that none of the ingredients came in the right proportions, so that as time passed I always found myself out of *something*: usually the white rice flour, though also the brown, and less frequently but no less annoyingly the tapioca or potato starches. And then, on the day when I praised myself for finally being prepared in the flour department, I would reach for the box of nonfat milk powder, which comes in a package the size of a cereal box (and costs ten bucks), only to discover that now I didn't have enough of *that*. Or I was out of the psyllium. Why did I keep forgetting to restock my supplies of these things? Because none of them normally goes into bread, that's why, and my internal ledger apparently had not taken the quantum evolutionary leap forward along with the Test Kitchen.

And what the hell is psyllium?

At first it sounded unpromising to me—not an ingredient but a bacterial infection that commonly afflicts careless travelers to equatorial regions. Someone goes to Costa Rica, say, tries to find a waterfall in the jungle, and comes home with a rash: *You have psyllium.* Technically an herb, psyllium grows knee-high in India and Pakistan,* and produces small white flowers. The husks of these flowers get harvested, dried, and ground into a high-fiber powder that you can stir into a glass of water where it easily dilutes, which is how it came to be the basis of supplements like Metamucil. Like sorghum, psyllium appears to have been of marginal value to Western bakers until our guts started exploding and we needed to cut back on the wheat.

It's not the first ingredient one would think of adding to gluten-free dough, but it turns out that psyllium is a gift to GF bakers. (Not

---

* Where it is known as *Isabgol*, which sounds like it could be the Epic Glutenator's nemesis.

quite as awesome a gift as the God Enzyme in beer, but still revolutionary.) According to the ATK, psyllium readily bonds to the proteins in GF flour blends, allowing the dough to create sturdier protein chains. Thus the dough can trap the carbon dioxide produced by yeast, providing lift, structure, and a chew reminiscent of the experience of eating real bread. Outside of tapioca starch, which also gets naturally chewy when it gelatinizes, psyllium is, for those eaters who can handle it—your colon will thank you later!—possibly as close to gluten-free gluten as we're going to find. Xanthan gum, for years the standby in GF bread-making, lags far behind.

The first loaf of bread I made from *HCIBGF* was the basic white sandwich bread. Even with the benefits of psyllium, the process was vastly different from making the real thing. I never experienced the relaxing, rhythmical kneading that led M. F. K. Fisher to liken baking bread to practicing yoga. Not once. I often ended up cursing. Sometimes I threw things—usually fingerfuls of tapioca starch. I wanted to dump the ATK during every one of the six minutes when the lump of batter thunked around in the KitchenAid bowl like a shoe in a dryer, launching crumbs onto the floor for the dog (could she eat psyllium? did I want to know?). When I was done bashing the hell out of the bread batter—it would be a stretch to call it dough—I was doubtful about the results. It didn't even go into a baking pan evenly. It stuck to everything, but it especially stuck to my hands.

From that point on, the dough behaved like bread dough was supposed to. An hour later, I peered flinchingly at the pan and saw that it had risen. Substantially. More than any loaf we'd ever made.

After it had been in the oven for about forty-five minutes, the house filled with that incomparable smell of baking bread. It smelled better than any of the bagged mixes or other recipes we'd tried. Could I even remember what the real stuff smelled like? Not really, to be honest, and this realization troubled me. But this smell was similar, warm and yeasty and comforting. The loaf, after it had cooled, yielded easily to the slicing knife, and there were—I could hardly believe it—*air pockets,* and some spring. When we tasted a slice, unadorned so as to be objective, there was no funky aftertaste at all.

Suddenly the whole process seemed worth it. After nearly eighteen months, we were baking loaves in our house once again.

Okay, Test Kitchen, that wasn't even close to fun. Or convenient. Or economical. But you win.

We rationed the bread over the week. When we ran out, I made more.

An artisan flaxseed loaf drew my attention next, but I took one look at the recipe, which spanned two pages and featured photographs to help the novice along, and cried foul. What kind of madness was this? Bread didn't require ten ingredients, parchment paper, and a skillet. Now the scientists at the Test Kitchen were going too far.

As usual, Bec figured out that my fury meant I *wanted* the loaf, but I didn't want to suffer the disappointment and wasted time if it totally tanked.

"Fine," she said. "I'll make it."

I walked the dog and returned to find that the process was not as hard as it looked. What had appeared to be a call for weird equipment turned out to be the ATK's clever substitution for the baking stone used for free-form, bakery-style loaves: you put the dough in an oven-proof skillet lined with parchment paper and slid that into the oven on top of the baking stone, because the loaf would collapse and get deformed with too much handling (it doesn't tolerate any handling at all).

When Bec pulled this bread out of the oven ninety—*ninety!*—minutes later, I immediately liked the looks of it: round, domed, the crust browned and ridged where she had slashed it with a knife before leaving it to rise. It resembled the *Artisan* breads she used to make;

and it inspired the same feelings. The heft, the shape, and the smell made me want to tear pieces off right away, the way I used to.

We took a walk together so I couldn't attack it. The evening was beautiful, the sky moody and gray in some places, and gilt in others where the sunlight broke through after the recent rainstorms. A loamy, fertile smell floated up from the soaked ground. The garden was growing well in our raised beds, and soon the real fun would begin. Could it be that everything was coming together, finally?

Later that night we cut ourselves each a slice. The texture was chewy from the flaxseed and slightly sweet from the almond flour Bec had substituted for the oat flour. It was a hearty loaf with the spirit of whole wheat.

"What do you think?" I asked her.

"I think it's great."

"So do I."

And just like that, by going *ahead* in time, not back, by using baking science and a weird assembly of ingredients that nobody would have considered dropping into a bread dough recipe twenty years ago, we had bread—not one type, but two. We felt wealthy, and our kitchen seemed to be full.

When I finally spoke to Jack Bishop about *HCIBGF* and how the book came to be written, he told me the ATK's goal was not to frustrate the home cook (and to be fair, many people might not find the bread recipes fussy at all, and most of the others are quite easy). Rather, the ATK wanted recipes for GF breads and other foods that would appeal to everyone, not just those with intolerances. If that's your aim, then you have to focus on the foods that people come together to share— pizzas, pastas, cakes, breads, and cookies. Basically, anything with gluten. The better privately owned GF bakeries had already figured that out, but among cookbooks this thinking in itself seemed to me a revolutionary starting point. Few available GF cookbooks were taking as their premise that the cook desired to create a GF meal or bake something that would bring *everyone* at the table pleasure. A goal like that sets the bar very high. You're asking the available starches to do things they're not designed to do, which was why bakers were slow to figure out how to do it. According to Bishop, people knew what the ATK was capable of, and they had been asking them to do a book like this for a long time.

"I think there's something about baked goods that people just have a need for in a deep and emotional way," Bishop told me. "Tofu, that is not a food that's likely to have deep emotional connections for you." And so, for your average American, losing tofu would not amount to any great sacrifice. Indeed, it's a trade I would readily make. "But chocolate chip cookies, and bread, they do have deep emotional connections."

When I asked him which foods provide those feelings for him, and so would be the most difficult to surrender, he did not hesitate. "That's easy. Bread!" At the start of the process of writing *HCIBGF*, he told me he might have said pasta, but in assembling the book the ATK discovered that there are some good GF pastas available now (and I would agree). "All bread," he clarified, "but especially baguettes."

In order to achieve the broad appeal they sought, when the ATK editors taste-tested the results, at least half the tasters had to like the dish. The test group was comprised of both people with gluten and wheat sensitivities and people who could eat anything safely. In Bishop's memory, it was the most difficult cookbook project the ATK had ever done. They completed it in nine months, an astonishing pace. Doing so required six people testing recipes in the kitchen every day (two of them on gluten-free diets for medical reasons), plus two editors to synthesize the results. The endpoint, compared to where they started, surprised even Bishop, who told me that while he tries never to spit food out in the Test Kitchen because he feels it's rude, in the early stages of writing this cookbook, the results of the recipes were beyond bad. "They were inedible," he said. The thought of spectacular failures at the ATK amused me, especially when I recalled how the tone of the Test Kitchen's cooking shows and magazines is so confident and calm as to make a perfect dish seem like an inevitability, even an anticlimax. Putting a camera in the kitchen for this book might have made for some entertaining food TV.

The most profound insight the ATK uncovered in their nine months of recipe-testing, in my view, is that cooking and baking successfully without wheat and gluten requires counterintuition—or maybe it's countertraining. In order to make not just edible but truly successful cakes, or biscuits, or muffins, for instance, the cooks had to go against cardinal rules and processes they had been taught and even humbled by their instructors and superiors for not following. These adjustments in approach seemed to be just as important as the discovery of psyllium or nonfat milk powder, or the addition of vinegar to the GF grains in their piecrust. In some cases, the adjustments to process were more important.

For example, GF bread gets more bread-like when you beat the batter on high speed for six minutes, which is something that you would never, ever do with wheat. Even existing GF recipes, like that on the bag of Pamela's bread mix, only call for three minutes of high-speed mixing. The extra mixing time allows the psyllium to work into the rice and other proteins. Similarly, you don't walk away from muffin batters made of wheat flour and let them sit for an hour before baking. The result, Bishop pointed out, would be a tough muffin. But allowing low-moisture rice-based flours time to hydrate was an important breakthrough in many of the recipes.

Bishop's description of the way gluten-free cooking forces a cook to reroute his approach revealed the sources of my own early catastrophes: the fresh raviolis that tore and then turned into gritty balls; the breads that crumbled to dust as soon as they cooled, or went stale in only six hours; the roux that would not brown; the breading that came off; the crêpes that tore like tissue paper. I lacked some key substitutions and additions, yes, but more important than that, my *ways* of cooking, the practices that had made me a good cook, were on autopilot and foiling me. The old rules didn't apply anymore.

When I thought back on my rare successes, I saw that they often came at times when I ditched the "right way," mumbled some expletives, and watched what was happening in the pan or the bowl closely, adjusting as I went. Some things, however, I never would have figured out on my own.

Among the adaptations the Test Kitchen found most difficult were, surprisingly, cookies. "Cookies are really hard [to convert to gluten-free]," Bishop told me. "People think, oh, cookies must be easy because they're the first things kids learn to make." The GF food industry's offerings back this up; bad GF cookies are everywhere. But a good cookie in the sense that we think of as "good"—as the ATK went on to observe, through multiple object lessons—is the result of specific chemical reactions. Cookies have to spread properly, because there's no mold or form for them, and they rely on gluten to do this. They're also complicated because they contain little added moisture—a few eggs, some oil or butter, and that's about it. In a gluten-free environment, the recipe adaptations that start out wet tend to be more forgiving than drier recipes.

Cookies are also more forgiving than bread because of the presence of sugar and butter. The absence of sugar and fat in bread meant that the many loaves in the book were not at all easy for the Test Kitchen to perfect. Psyllium and flax, and even almond flour, can approximate some of the properties of wheat, but they can never imitate it exactly, and an eater tends to notice un-wheatlike qualities more in breads that do not have a high sugar content, like brioche, or eggy mixtures like challah. The ATK found the basic breads turned out more successfully with the addition of eggs, sometimes butter, oil, or all three.

These ingredients do work, but I've always been bothered by a sense that each addition takes the loaf further away from the simplicity and purity that bread has known for thousands of years. I couldn't help but wonder, Was this bread I was pulling out of my oven, or something else? Was it closer to a quick bread, or a cake? Did it even matter, as long as I was trembling with anticipation?

Jack Bishop and I didn't talk about this, but I think I know what his answer would be. The ATK's modus operandi, for as long as I've been following them, has always been the quality of the food on the plate, not a recipe's ties to its historical roots. Taste, texture, and a pleasurable eating experience trump everything else. They can be frugal when it makes sense (and like all true Yankee institutions seem to enjoy being so), but they'll break the bank if the test results indicate that expensive ingredients make a difference. They love an easy night in the kitchen, but they'll set you up for a climb if necessary. They can be unsentimental, even iconoclastic, about the sanctity of a traditional recipe, as, for example, when they deconstructed Julia Child's boeuf Bourguignon to make it easier to prepare. Though effective, many of their shortcuts and innovations would give members of the culinary old guard—chefs and writers like Escoffier, maybe—fits. Thinking about the results of their philosophy encouraged me to let go of some of my long-held beliefs about purity.

As the old saying goes, discretion is the better part of valor, and the ATK also know when to back down. When I asked Bishop what they *couldn't* do without gluten that they wished they could, he noted that respondents have asked for three things: bagels, baguettes, and croissants. Each is a form of bread with its own ties to cultural tradition and eating practices. Each also has a low bullshit tolerance; it demands adherence to traditional processes and ingredients.

Bishop believed that the ATK would tackle bagels in a future book. About baguettes, he was skeptical, like many GF bakers I've talked to. And on the subject of croissants, he laughed out loud. There are some things you just can't do. It's better to acknowledge that fact from the start and put your energy into the battles you can win.

After the bread, our reclamations kept piling up: muffins, cake, fresh pasta.

I adjusted to the rigors of the ATK process, which turned out to be good training for the rigors of just about every GF recipe worth cooking that I would encounter over the next few years. Most of the time, I felt as if Christopher Kimball stood in the corner of my kitchen, over by the water cooler, where he watched in that red monogrammed apron (no apron for me; I hadn't earned it yet), stroking his chin as I looked for shortcuts. Which, by the way, I never found. Ever. I did have to make some substitutions for oat flour on more than one occasion, which annoyed me, but the bread recipes turned out to be surprisingly forgiving on that score. Or, I might have been eating bad bread for so long that everything excited me.

One night, I decided to revisit the scene of an earlier crime. I made crêpes.

It had taken me a long time to forget that disaster, and I returned to it only after things started going my way again. Anyone who cooks seriously at home knows that you have winning streaks and losing streaks, a stretch of days when for some reason scrambling an egg kicks your ass, and then a long period where you're ambitious, playful, and cannot seem to screw anything up even though you might get a little lax. The ATK's book had given me back my confidence, and I'd recently been riding a winning streak that began with the most beautiful seared scallops I'd ever made, followed by a perfectly grilled strip steak with a strong *chimichurri* atop a crispy shredded potato–leek cake. For dessert I decided to bump up a flourless chocolate cake by lacing the batter with cayenne. In deference to cholesterol content, I dialed the evening meal down the next night, making tofu—nope, still no deep emotional triggers there—and by the next, when we had Sarah coming for dinner, I was ready to cook with a little swagger again.

Since switching to the GF diet, I had been wondering something: Would it ever be possible to fool a dinner guest who would readily eat as much gluten as she could hold when she was in the mood for it—the one who had started the yearlong *Artisan Bread* feed among us—by serving her gluten-free baked goods? Was now the time to try, with GF crêpes? She wouldn't *really* be fooled—she knew which house she was coming to—but was it time to test the Test Kitchen's guiding premise?

I made the decision to try about fifteen minutes before Sarah arrived. There's a school of kitchen wisdom that says this is never a good idea. Plan your menu three days in advance, and don't deviate unless you're unafraid to admit defeat and order a pizza—which was like an escape pod that would now forever have an OUT OF ORDER sign taped to the door in our kitchen. But I liked a challenge, and would continue to like it well into the future: Just how much rice dressed up as wheat could I serve my guests and have them *like* it? I was moving from hating the game to trying to beat the game.

Crêpes, as I had well learned, don't leave a cook much room to hide. Either the recipe works or it chokes. They are delicate, unforgiving of lapses in attention and temperature variations, and they would appear to rely absolutely on gluten to hold together. Nevertheless, I was even up to my old tricks again: I decided to convert the *HCIBGF* recipe into a savory version. I followed my instincts, turning the sugar way down and guessing about the salt.

The crêpes worked. Or, we worked together, the Test Kitchen and I. Splendidly. Thin but not so delicate that they broke, chewy but not too rubbery. Sarah, Bec, and I ate them on our deck with smoked salmon and cheese and salad, a bottle of rosé—one of our first meals outdoors after a long, hard winter.

.   .   .

This left the final frontier: pizza.

I had learned well that the road to eating hell is cobbled with awful GF pizza as much as it's cobbled with GF bread. My experience had told me that most GF pizzas, whether homemade, frozen at the store, or from a restaurant, couldn't be called a pizza any more than you can call a toaster-oven pizza bagel or a microwaved Pizza Pocket a pizza. Once I ordered a GF pie from the local pizza place when a friend was in town; he wanted the specialty of the house, which is basically a cheese-filled doughnut, a pizza that has been folded over and deep-fried. I tried to avoid bitterness as he ate his and I ate mine, but all I could think was, *This is some grim shit right here.*

It took me weeks to work my way up to the Test Kitchen's pizza dough recipe. I had read the recipe before and it scared me off. Here was not a process that one just wandered into at four o'clock of a Saturday afternoon, when friends were coming over and you wanted a pizza to go with some beers and the ballgame on the TV. *Oh, I think we'll have us a pizza.* The price of admission was high: five hours start to finish, from the mixing, proofing, and shaping to the par-baking, finishing, and cooling. You have to want a pizza badly, though as a bonus you get to freeze one par-baked crust for later use (if you don't share it with your friends, who won't want it anyway, having been scarred, as I was, by gluten-free pizzas in the past; we've never made pizza for any of our guests, ever, and we probably never will). Once again, an apparition of Christopher Kimball seemed to be hovering in the corner of my kitchen, scrutinizing me, asking me just how badly I wanted a legit adaptation of a food I loved.

Pretty badly, I guess.

One of the magic ingredients in this pizza recipe, elevating it from Neolithic flatbread topped with cheese, is almond flour in high volume, which provides the depth and body and a good deal of expense, at eight dollars for a twelve-ounce bag (you don't use the *whole* bag, at least). And you haven't even topped this pie, yet. Like so many other conventional foods that go GF, this pizza severs ties with peasant traditions, with working-class Italian-American neighborhoods, in order to taste like something that my Italian grandfather, who enjoyed his pizza and knew a good one when he ate it—and a bad one, too— might truly enjoy.

After beating the hell out of the dough for the required six minutes with the stand mixer, I immediately noticed something different. This mixture was a little messy, a little wet and heavy, yes, but it seemed to have some elasticity. I covered it with a damp, warm towel. I walked away for an hour.

And when I came back, it had risen substantially. I poked it, and the dough sprang back. It almost looked *alive*.

I worked the ball into a circle as directed. The feeling of the dough giving beneath my hands was so wonderfully familiar, and yet so long gone, that I kept on with it. After all, it wasn't like there was gluten for me to overwork. The recipe called for me to keep a sheet of greased plastic wrap between my fingers and the dough. I started out this way, but soon I couldn't help myself: I said the hell with the plastic wrap and used the tips of my bare fingers to press and stretch. I did so gently at first, afraid that I would kill it.

I didn't kill it. *This was happening.* I was kneading dough. With a smile on my face. *Now* I might have been experiencing M. F. K. Fisher's yoga analogy, except that I was far from tranquil. I was elated, because the ATK had restored one of the biggest casualties of gluten-free bread-making and pizza-making: you never touch that stuff. You don't want to; it's wet, and slimy, and completely unpleasant. And as a result, you don't develop a relationship with the dough, don't feel that sensation that so many bakers and cooks have known and loved for so long, the methodical pressing and turning and folding, the knowledge that something is taking shape beneath your hands.

I did not turn and fold this dough. But I did press my luck (literally). When I had finished shaping the second crust, I went back and perfected the first. Then I returned to the second and pinched the edges. I shoved them into the oven to par-bake.

Who the hell figured this out? A laxative puts pizza back in pizza. Such a far cry. It sounded like a joke. The things we human beings will do. Will try. Will eat, even when the chances of gratification seem minimal at best, and, while chewing the bland grit of disappointment, proceed to plot the next innovation, the next attempt, until, finally, we triumph. All that for a pizza. Our love of food indeed has us by the short hairs.

The rest of the pizza story? Nearly anticlimactic. It baked up just like it was supposed to; the crust browned; it looked beautiful. I topped it with cheese made with milk from our friend Susan's goat, Luna; green shallots; kalamata olives; and broccoli florets. Then I added a sprinkling of fresh thyme. Our kitchen smelled like pizza for the first time in two years, and as the pie baked, I remembered how regularly we used to eat pizza, our own pizza, and only rarely from the local place that catered to the college students. We topped our pies with things like dried Black Mission figs and red onions, prosciutto and scallions. But, back then, every time I ate a few slices—always washing it down with a Saranac Pale Ale or an IPA—I felt slightly off all night and into the next day.

Bec and I sat down and poured a can of Glutenberg each. Since it was the first time trying the pizza, we ate a little more cautiously than we might normally, knowing, as we did, that this pie had been brought to us in part by Metamucil. But the pizza tasted like pizza. It tasted like Friday night, like days as a child when I rode home in the car with the hot box level on my legs, like late-night feeds at college— and not like flatbread or a cardboard box or anything other than what it was supposed to taste like. As far as I could tell, anyway. It had, after all, been a long time. We kept saying to each other, with amazement, "We're eating pizza. *Pizza!* I'd honestly left it for dead."

18

RISING HOPES

It was a testament to how far I'd come in one year as a celiac and a traveler that I should find myself, that June, in a Pasadena civic center ballroom looking for the nearest exit as the Celiac Disease Foundation Conference kicked off with an invocation of sorts: a song, "Don't Cry for Me, Gluten-Eaters," sung to the tune of—you guessed it—"Don't Cry for Me, Argentina."

I glanced at Bec. I've never felt comfortable when people burst into song in front of me. I spent the entire three minutes of musical shout-outs to the GF corporate sponsors of the conference and star physicians—many of whom had dedicated their life's work to celiac-disease research, and, in so doing, had prepared a softer place for me to crash-land when my time came to go down in flames—with my face in my hands. Gluten-eaters *should* cry for us, I thought. Every last one of them. They should try to cook with birdseed; they should make French toast with the Styrofoam GF loaves available in stores; they should throw a Fourth of July party featuring GF pretzels and Toleration beer and watch their guests' faces. I knew the song was all in good fun. I had come to do serious work, and once the conference started, I wasn't disappointed. Prominent physicians spoke on the past, present, and future of the disease; pharmaceutical reps talked about pathways to treatment and cures; and researchers presented the stark data on the results of "noncompliance."

Following the conference, we circled the GF product expo. In less than an hour, Bec and I had both filled mesh bags with free samples of crackers, cookies, cereals, energy bars, and other products. The battle for market share seemed to be palpable in the room. Later, back at the hotel, I was unable to resist carrying out an obnoxious experiment: I added up the caloric value of our GF take, and was shocked to find that we had amassed more than ten thousand calories each in pre-pared GF snack samples. I encountered few examples of whole food in the entire room—a researcher from California was selling mesquite bean flour, which tastes a little like smoky cacao and long ago was a staple of southwestern Native Americans. And nearby, a prominent physician performed a cooking demo of GF eggplant Parmesan. It was good to see some actual cooking going on amid all the snacks. Curiously, not one privately owned, independent GF bakery was rep-resented at the expo (there were, however, three beers: Bard's, Green's, and New Planet).

The next day, we visited a bakery that had run a table at the expo in previous years. It had become a feature of our travel, no matter how short the distance, to seek out new GF bakeries wherever we went. Yes, we were finally making good bread at home, but we had become like the Europeans from the Middle Ages forward, who were always in search of a better loaf: one that was less gritty, crustier, tastier. In this way, we came to know about Pete's Gluten Free in Ottawa; Against the Grain Gourmet, out of Brattleboro, Vermont; and, in Pasadena, Whisk Gluten-Free Bakery, run by Lynn McKay and her sister, Stephanie Angle.

When we met them, Lynn and Stephanie had just moved into a commercial kitchen in an industrial park. They had been riding a long winning streak fueled by increasing demand for gourmet GF products in the greater Los Angeles area, and also by the fact that they were extremely good at GF baking. In keeping with the GF trend, the increase in celiac diagnoses, or both, they could barely meet the orders for breads, cakes, and cupcakes.

For all their recent triumph, Whisk had experienced the humble start typical of GF bakeries. Following a sense that GF baked goods did not have to be as sad and disappointing as they so often were, Lynn and Stephanie baked out of their homes at first and ran samples around town in their cars. Like me, both were in their thirties, and neither had experienced the truly dark days of GF eating several decades ago. Those baked goods they had tasted did not impress them, though. Now they were part of a GF-cookery renaissance that seemed to be taking place all over the country.

Their baked goods were extremely successful GF versions of the real thing—to this day, some of the best I've tasted. One particular factor seemed to explain Whisk's overall success, including their ability to appeal to eaters without allergies in addition to those who were intolerant to gluten: while Lynn has celiac disease, Stephanie does not. In the kitchen, this pairing is an enormous advantage. It reminded me that Jack Bishop had said some of the ATK cooks on the *HCIBGF* project also did not have allergies. Having someone who could move safely between GF and conventional bread and cakes allowed for a better evaluation of an adaptation's success. I knew that one of the most disturbing aspects of my own experience with celiac disease was my decreasing ability to remember what gluten-based foods really taste like. I was dismayed (yet also a little relieved) the first time I realized that I no longer knew the eating experience I was trying to replicate. Stephanie's ability to refresh her memory explained her uncanny instincts for creating a flour blend, which featured only three starches: brown rice, potato, and tapioca flour (many commercially blended GF flours use twice that many). Could my flying blind explain why I had so many early failures? If I'd been willing to humble myself to share my GF attempts with wheat eaters, would I have improved faster? It was too late to ask, though it seemed that my pride—or my low tolerance for bad news—had indeed held me back.

Lynn and Stephanie's original forte was baked goods, in particular cakes for "allergy parties" for kids and celiacs who had become convinced they would never again taste a real celebratory cake—for birthday, wedding, baby shower, going-away, or any other event. But it seems that no matter how many people with allergies a GF bakery reconnects with birthdays, no matter how many weddings they save from disappointment with beautiful GF confections, in time their customers always begin asking for bread. Sugar is good and treats are nice, but if a person cannot live on bread alone, neither is it possible to survive on butter, sugar, chocolate, and vanilla.

"You grow up with bread," Lynn told me when she described how they just seemed to find themselves baking more and more loaves, and adding different varieties. "If you were lucky, you grew up with your mom baking bread. That smell—it's so strongly nostalgic."

We loaded up on Lynn and Stephanie's bread—as much as we could, given that we had to fly it home. White, Italian herb, cinnamon-raisin. It was better than the bread that we were making with the ATK book, and I struggled to understand why. The industrial mixer? The simpler recipe, with fewer ingredients? The oven? Or was it simply the fact that someone else had made it?

As anyone in the GF industry might have predicted, the rise and success of Omission Beer—which was the best-selling craft beer in America in *any* category, GF or not, in 2014—made the production of GR beers tempting for other breweries. My contact at Omission had told me that California-based Stone Brewing had been working on one, and in January 2015 they launched their Delicious IPA, a gluten-reduced beer that uses almost the same process as Omission, with the difference (some would say a problematic difference) that their GR brew is not made in a dedicated facility. While the brewing process is ostensibly safe, Stone's GR beer is nonetheless right next door to some high-octane gluten. The GR IPA is only brewed seasonally, after the equipment is scrupulously cleaned. It is tested by a third party, White Labs, and, as with Omission, the test results are available for consumers to access online. On their website, Stone Brewing notes that the gluten-stripping process is so thorough that the actual level of gluten in their IPA is too low to be picked up by the current testing technology. Even though they leave no doubt that they take cross-contamination seriously, a lot of celiacs might say there is no good reason to pop a cap on a Stone Delicious.

Well, almost.

I wanted to try this beer from Stone. True, I was doing pretty well in the beer department of late, but I expected this new brew would be like so many of the IPAs I had loved and left behind. Like the Omission, Glutenberg, New Grist, Celia Saison, and Plasma, I couldn't find the Stone GR anywhere in my area. (It did eventually show up in town, as part of a twelve-pack sampler, prompting me to mull entering into the economically unsound strategy of buying the box of beer for eighteen dollars, keeping three I could drink, and giving the other nine to my friend Jon. While he eagerly endorsed this, I never bought the Stones, not even when the fridge was empty of Omission and Glutenberg.)

I texted David, who now lived in Petaluma. I asked him to keep a lookout since he now lived within striking distance of the Stone mother ship. He found a six-pack, drank half of it as a shipping and handling fee, and sent the remaining three bottles to me. Later on, I realized I had not even paused to consider the absurdity of shipping three beers across the country. What the hell was happening to my mind? And yet, I knew I was in good company. History is full of people going to incredible lengths to secure foodstuffs from basic to fancy. Charlemagne, for example, had as much Roquefort as a monk could fit onto a horse cart brought from the wilds of France back to his imperial capital of Aachen, which, if you think about the condition of roads (and carts) in the year 800 is even crazier than priority-mailing beer. Ernest Shackleton famously brought Bass Ale on his expedition to the South Pole. He and his team would have had to pound the beers early in the journey, before they could freeze, leaving him to pine the rest of the way.

Still, as my own gestures went, this one stood out. I did not regularly have food shipped to me. Once—I still pretend not to know why—I ordered fresh duck breasts from Pekin Paradise, a farm in Pennsylvania. They were wonderful seared rare and served with an Earl Grey tea-infused sauce at a dinner party, but I felt my grandmother scowling at my decadence from the Other Side, and never ordered duck again, even though Pekin Paradise sent me a Christmas card every year. For a while Jim Harrison's essays had me wondering about flying in some grouper or snapper when Larry the Fish Guy[*] retired, though I opted not to in the end. Like many people, we had ordered cheese online to fill the gaps in our area's offerings in our pre-locavore days, and we still order wine. I perceived, when the three IPAs arrived from California, a tempting if expensive solution to the dearth of options. I promised myself that I was involving the postal service only in the spirit of exploration and that I wouldn't develop an internet-order

---

[*] Here, once again, I feel the need to explain the weird idiosyncrasies of the place I call home. There are no fish markets within a few hundred miles outside of the grocery store, and an entrepreneur made himself a good living by picking up fish from Boston in an F350 box truck (complete with an image of a smiling lobster) that he filled with coolers. He parked outside the post office on Fridays, making sure to keep feeding the meter, from 9:00 a.m. to noon. Eventually he retired. For a while there was no fresh fish. Then a gas station picked up where Larry left off, filling its deli cooler with dry scallops, wild salmon, halibut, flounder, haddock, and the best smoked salmon I've ever eaten, also trucked in from Boston once a week. You can't make this up. Did I find it curious, and more than a little annoying, that we could contrive an arrangement to get sushi-grade tuna to my area, but we could not get good GF bread and beer? You bet I did.

bread or beer habit. I tore through the tape and held the bottles up to the light, a little giddy.

Then the bottles of IPA sat in the refrigerator. For weeks.

It wasn't that I didn't *want* to sample these malty, hophead IPAs. I did, and pretty desperately. But I kept looking at the label and packaging, which David had included, and which stressed even more strongly than the Omission packaging that the beer contained gluten. The repeated references to "barley" and "gluten" spoke louder than the assurances on the website. I attributed the caution to the fact that the facility was not dedicated. And it freaked me out. I was receiving a lesson in the powers of aversion, the way all animals, including humans, know certain foods and liquids are poisonous because they are repellent. However, usually it was the smells of volatile compounds that indicated poison, not an *idea*.

On the other hand, what if this beer was actually safe? No different from Omission? Then I was missing a chance to enjoy it.

I finally took a deep breath and poured one into a pint glass one night. I looked at the beautiful copper color, breathed in the citrusy hops. When I took the first sip, I closed my eyes and felt, as I had felt the first time I tasted a beer made with the God Enzyme, as if I were back in a different time of my life, when the beer tasted this good all the time and I had more options than I could drink in a month. I stretched the Stone-tasting over an hour, sipping and listening for the telltale whirring of my blood in my ears, the rumbling and popping in my gut that told me I was screwed. The symptoms of poisoning never came; I suffered nary a scratch.

No doubt about it: Bec and I felt rich, compared to where we had been a year ago. I had even found the courage to offer slices of the ATK bread to Sarah, who pronounced the flaxseed loaf good, just like real bread ("Yeah, I'd eat this for sure") and to our friends Jon and Jess, whose perspective may have been swayed by the generous dollop of chicken-liver mousse that came on top. Still, these were the first times that we shared "our" bread with any of our friends, and it gave me hope to see it so well received. We had pizza back, if we were willing to go to the work to make it; with a lot of help, we had reclaimed crêpes and pasta, and would eventually reclaim cake. There was no more Stone in the house, but there was plenty of Omission—I saw to that whenever I had the chance—and plenty of Glutenberg, as well.

The fact remained, though, that the ATK bread was unpleasant to make. We baked it regularly, but late in the summer I had come to look at the task of making bread as drudgery. Bec saw it in much the same way. And then, a sudden turn of bad luck: the psyllium that I bought at the health-food store stopped working. I couldn't say how or why. The dough refused to rise even though the yeast was alive. I made several flaxseed loaves that looked as flat as the breads entombed in the ashes of Pompeii. They smelled a little loamy—*fibrous*, I thought, remembering the Metamucil connection—and they tasted fibrous, too. I kept on with the defective psyllium, because it was all we had, but as I measured flours, opened cans, and created a pile of dishes, it was far too easy to think that I would be going through *none* of this if I could still walk into a bakery and buy a loaf of good bread like a normal person.

Normal-person days were over, though. I had two choices, and I acted on both of them. The first was to have my mother ship me psyllium from a health-food store in Maryland. This did, eventually, do the trick, though now there was *another* step to go through, since the psyllium she sent was not powdered: I had to get out the food processor and blitz it into a powder myself.

The second option was to track down Eliza Hale—which I did. I found her e-mail address, contacted her, and drove down to Chelsea, Vermont, in the middle of the state, on a Monday morning in the late summer. I climbed twisting roads until I punched through the fog surrounding the base of the Green Mountains, then drove several miles on a dirt road and found myself in smooth green swells, under a sky that was incredibly blue, and among white clapboard structures like something out of a New England pastoral dream. I was in a town so small it made Canton look like Chicago. And yet, the celiacs who lived here—all two or three of them, according to the statistics—had access to a great loaf of GF bread.

Her bakery, compared to the others I'd visited, was no-frills: clean but spare, no steamy windows, no hidden kitchen area where the magic happened, and no display cases of loaves, rolls, bâtards, and baguettes. Eliza's kitchen was the smallest part of the building, which had formerly been a tavern and, after that, a neighborhood grocery store. There was a stainless baker's rack on which work bowls sat inverted, large containers of spices and oils, a standard KitchenAid, a commercial mixer that looked big enough to me but apparently already was too small, and a powerful Garland stove vented through the old woodstove thimble. The place looked more like a rebel outpost than an idyllic bakery.

As if to prove the point, when she had finished putting dough into tins, Eliza cued up Notorious B.I.G.'s "Hypnotize" on her Spotify mix. I asked her about her flour blend, and was surprised to find that unlike other bakers I'd met, she leaned heavily on sorghum and flaxseed meal. Nobody, it seemed, solved the bread problem in the same way. She wouldn't tell me the other ingredients or the proportions.

"No rice flour," I said, fishing a little. "That's unique."

She was quiet for a long moment as she reached down into her tub to get a scoop of sourdough starter for the next batch of bread. Biggie rapped a verse and then, in the pause, she said, "Yeah, I don't fuck around with rice."

She started Up the Hill Bakery in 2012, naming it after the cabin in the Vermont woods where she first began experimenting with flour blends, loaf types, and, eventually, her sourdough recipe. Now she was baking several days a week, producing upward of seventy-five loaves. A few of them stayed in Chelsea or went to nearby towns. The rest she hustled down the hill and across the interstate to Montpelier. She had recently begun to mull internet sales.

I hadn't met anyone else who made GF sourdough—Stephanie at Whisk had it on her wish list—and I asked Eliza if she had any idea why. One reason, she said, is that sourdough is high-maintenance. Eliza thought of her tub of starter, which lived in the corner of the kitchen a safe distance from the oven, as a little farm animal. You need to feed the sourdough and watch over it. You need to keep the temperature constantly agreeable. This requires time and focus (especially in the mountains of Vermont). The starter will let you know if you've gone lax by dying on you. Thus travel is nearly as difficult when you're feeding and looking after sourdough as it is when you have a rabbit or a dog. People who have sourdoughs tend, for this reason, to be fanatically devoted to them.

While the first batch of loaves baked, Eliza and I debated a pet question of hers: whether or not her finished products could even be called bread. From the moment I first tasted her mock rye, I never doubted that I was eating bread, but she didn't think she was making bread.

"Bread," she explained, "especially leavened bread, *is* wheat. You can't separate the two. If you don't have wheat, you don't have gluten. No gluten, no bread."

I'd been chasing after these questions myself for more than a year, and I had come to find them wearying. I should have asked, *Why is it so important to* call *it bread, then, even if it's* not? People had been calling ersatz bread by the same name as the real thing for thousands of years, for what seemed to me a simple reason: we cannot bear *not* to have bread. We would probably always continue to do so. Nobody wants to be excluded from the fellowship, the history.

"Maybe 'bread' is an ideal," I offered. "The gold standard."

Eliza looked at me doubtfully, as if to say plenty of people who knew far less about baking than she did baked every day, and *they* achieved the ideal. Why? Because they had gluten.

"So what about just calling them 'loaves'?" I suggested. The etymology was proximate, at least.

Eliza tried it out, saying the word repeatedly under her breath.

"I don't know," she said. "It doesn't seem right. You can't have a loaf of anything but bread."

Later in the day, we finally ate some bread. Eliza liked her breads best when toasted, with generous pats of butter. First we had the mock rye, the bread that had hooked itself into my brain, refused to leave, and brought me here. The sourdough brought a pleasing depth and intensity to the sorghum (which makes a far better bread than a beer), yet the crumb was light and airy, filled with the little air pockets that I've come to know foretell good GF bread. The sourdough was a magical component, a flavor so full, so commanding, so incontestably itself, that combined with the caraway it deflected my attention away from all that wasn't there to its vibrant, heady center. I felt like—no, I *knew*—I was eating the real thing, no matter what Eliza thought. *A man could make a killer Reuben out of this.* I kept thinking of pairings: eggs, of course, but also smoked salmon. Turkey. Bacon.

So how many loaves of bread did I leave Vermont with this time?

Three: a mock rye, a cinnamon-raisin, and a sourdough. Which was plenty of bread, I told myself on the drive home in a car redolent of freshly baked grains. I did indeed want every loaf she had made that day, and I remembered my mission, but I didn't know how many orders Eliza had committed to filling. Now I knew where to find her. I could come back anytime, though driving four hours to stock the freezer with bread seemed a little, well, desperate. Perhaps she would do mail-order. She was thinking about going in that direction anyway, and she could use me to work out the issues with packaging.

Once again, I was wrong.

A few months after my visit, I learned that Eliza had decided to close her bakery for a while, possibly permanently. The reasons were health-related—a resumption of allergy symptoms connected to Leaky Gut Syndrome, a complication of celiac disease in which the intestines refuse to heal and malabsorption continues. It's not refractory celiac disease, because the antibody counts have usually dropped, but more of a slowness or resistance to healing. Such a diagnosis strikes fear into the heart of every food-loving celiac. I hear others talk about it and I flinch, knowing my lot could get worse at any time, and for no apparent reason. When this trouble arrives, it is usually a final blow to bread-eating. Yeast gets stripped from the diet, along with dairy, legumes, grains, and any proteins that are difficult to digest.

When she made the decision to close, Eliza's business, like Whisk—like many great GF bakeries across the country—had been booming. She had more orders than she could fill. But health was more important, and sad though it made me to know that once again, the object of my quest was receding further away just as I was closing in on it—one of these days, I swore, I was going to fill the trunk of the car with great bread and just be done with it—I was glad to hear that she was feeling better. She sounded optimistic. Healthy. That was all that mattered.

19.

Harvest Time

The harvest season comes to the North Country sooner than it comes to most other places in the United States. Killing frosts can arrive as early as the end of September—six months, more or less, from the week that the first thunderstorm comes in the early spring, according to some of the farmers I've spoken with. And by early October, the heat that fueled the fruiting and plentitude of the iconic summer vegetables—the tomatoes, eggplants, peppers, chiles, and corn—dies off quickly. It is almost as if someone flips a damper in the sky. We've seen snow in October.

Over on our CSA farm, Dan, Megan, and their team of workers were furiously harvesting vegetables. They froze some of the perishable ones for the winter shares, and stashed the storage veg away in the giant cooler. Some went to wholesale. The rest they toted to the market for CSA shares and retail sales. It was a mad dash until the air and ground turned too cold for anything to grow. That could still take a while; in November, I was often still pulling kale, leeks, and hardy onions from our raised beds.

When this harvest season came around, I had been gluten-free for almost two years. I was still running, but not nearly as much as I had been the year prior; maybe I wasn't as angry, not as afraid. I'd learned to trust my body and didn't feel as if I had as much to run *from*. I'd transitioned back into a life that for the most part felt measured and balanced, both in my mind and at the table.

In the village park, the farmers' market was filled with a polarity of seasonal foods, and when I visited on Friday mornings in the early autumn I reflected that, for this brief time, I did indeed have it all. There were both tomatoes and apples; pumpkins and the last of the sweet corn (less, that year, because a black bear had been ravaging the fields of our largest local grower); shiitake and oyster mushrooms; raspberries, watermelons, fennel, carrots, onions, turnips, and beets. Only cucumbers and strawberries and peas were long gone, already memories except in pickled or frozen form.

The list kept expanding as I walked past the tables: new potatoes in red, blue, yellow, purple, and white; leeks; greens; freshly dried black, kidney, and navy beans; herbs; acorn and butternut and many of other squashes; pears; and the last of the cantaloupes. There were people selling pastured chicken, Cornish hens, eggs, and turkey. Heritage breeds of pork, lamb, beef. Honey. Molasses. Maple syrup that had been boiled down and bottled in the late winter. Preserves, apple cider, and offbeat items like Cape gooseberries (ground cherries), spicy black radishes, and North Country wines. Ours was not a big market, either—about a dozen growers in all, from within twenty-five miles of town.

The market always had bread for sale, as well as pies and cookies. Doughnuts, too. But I didn't begrudge these loaves or the people who made and brought them. At other times of the year I might have. I knew that I had given up trying to give up bread. Something deep in my brain, in my heart, refused to surrender. I still wished weekly if not daily for a bakery like Whisk or Up the Hill, or any of those that were popping up across the country, to come to our town. Recently I had heard rumors that someone was thinking of opening such a bakery nearby, but I was trying not to pay too much attention. The path sounded long. I didn't want to jinx it.

And for right now, anyway, with so much produce and meat all around, celiac disease felt more manageable than ever. It was the easiest time of year to cook; there seemed to be endless variety, and all you had to do with food so fresh was stay out of its way. Almost everything I saw on the tables at market was, for me, freeing.

One day closer to the winter, my friend Karen, an anthropologist at a local college, took me to an Amish household where a two-year-old girl had been recently diagnosed with celiac disease. We have several Amish communities in the North Country, and I had assumed, based on the statistical data, that there were likely to be celiacs, either silent or presenting symptoms, in their population. I also knew that if this was true, the diagnosis rates would rapidly increase and even create an upheaval. Amish families are tightly knit, endogamous. They will only marry someone within their own church, or someone from a place where they fellowship. This means that not much new blood, genetically speaking, enters into the area. And their culture is absolutely based in bread, as well as in sweets. They mix bread with their traditional bean soup for their symbolic Sunday meal. They eat more pasta and noodles and baked goods than any people I know or have heard of. Ever the masters of economy, the Amish *can* the bread they do not eat, in addition to making the usual bread pudding and bread crumbs. It is common for outsiders to know they live several hundred years in the past technologically; but in many respects, this is also true gastronomically.

I sat in a chair by the woodstove while the mother, Rachel,[*] talked about her struggles to get her two-year-old daughter to eat gluten-free foods. Her siblings continued on with their conventional, wheat-based diet, and it sounded as if the girl had been recently awakening to an

---

[*] Her name has been changed out of respect for the Amish culture.

awareness of being different, and to the social role food plays. She wouldn't eat her rice pasta if her father wouldn't eat it too; she wanted the pretzels her siblings enjoyed. The malabsorption had clearly taken a toll on her both physically and cognitively. She was tiny for her age, and she still lacked the language to even begin to describe to her mother how bad she felt, or why. When they ran out of rice flour, Rachel said, her daughter ate wheat and spelt flour until they got more.

Later on, Karen would tell me that the odds of this family being able to make a 100-percent commitment to a gluten-free diet were slim. Lifestyle and social factors combined to make full compliance difficult, even impossible. The girl's mother was doing what she could, though. And the father, importantly, was supportive and flexible about the family's diet. In a community so patriarchal, a father's consent was a huge asset, and Karen could think of families that would never change their diet, because the men in the family did not want to. There was a chance that, over time, broader acceptance of the GF diet might be aided by the increasing number of diagnoses in the Amish community, but that would take a while.

Some Amish communities were already well versed in GF eating, though. Rachel had a GF baking cookbook written by an Amish woman in southern New York, complete with a medically accurate description of celiac disease and religious poems for inspiration. For a moment the existence of an Amish GF baking book surprised me. But as in so many Western cultures throughout history—as in my own household—the goal of the Amish would of course be to find a way to keep the symbolism of bread alive while making it safe. They weren't heading in the direction of reclaiming flatbreads, though. This cookbook author was using rice flour, gelatin, seltzer water, and xanthan gum. The recipes were clever, but without even tasting them, I knew they lagged seriously behind even the more disappointing cookbooks Bec and I had sampled.

Halfway through the visit, I realized that Rachel might have been thinking of me as an expert. I wondered if she viewed me in the same way that I had viewed Lynn McKay and Stephanie Angle, Eliza Hale, Jack Bishop, and the Test Kitchen—as a person who had been navigating the world of gluten-free foods for a little while and had outwitted longing. I didn't have any quick fixes or easy answers to offer her, though. All I could think was: *Here is a situation that makes my own look comparatively good.* At least I could drive around, search out, and order the best GF products. I had access to technology and, therefore, knowledge. I was not subsistence farming.

I had brought with me a loaf of bread I'd made from a bagged mix (Pamela's) as a gift for the family, but really for the little girl. This too was a moment of weird symmetry, reminiscent of my neighbor Matt dropping by my house with assorted beers of solace from a distance place. I left the bread with Rachel, and then Karen and I went next door so she could catch up with the parents in the "doughty house," as it was known, where the grandparents lived.

We had been sitting at the kitchen table, sampling, of all things, mashed potato candies,[*] when the girl's siblings appeared with a butternut squash for me; then they brought me a jar of pickles. These were gifts; the girl had loved the bread I'd brought. It was the closest thing to real bread she had tasted that was safe for her. And I remembered the relief Bec and I felt when we found the Pamela's mix after months of making bad recipes, our sense that here—at last—was a food that we could at least live with until we discovered the next good thing.

In Dutch, the children told Karen that their mother wanted the recipe.

---

[*] Talk about an experience that shot me into the World War II rationing era from which came M. F. K. Fisher's *How to Cook a Wolf.* What, you ask, are mashed potato candies? Three ingredients—a boiled, peeled, and mashed russet potato, a *whole bag* of powdered sugar, and half a bag, more or less, of sweetened shredded coconut—mixed together until the dough is formable, and shaped into little discs. They're not bad. They're gluten-free. And they have a screaming glycemic load. My fillings hurt, eating these things.

I saw my miscalculation too late. Rachel thought I had made the loaf from scratch. How could I explain to her that she had little hope of getting this bread, because it wasn't available locally and required an internet connection to order it? And even if they *could* get it through the company this Amish community ordered their staples from, they would need a stand mixer to make it taste the same. It simply wasn't possible to achieve the texture the girl was responding to if you mixed it by hand. Process, I had learned, mattered.

I didn't know what to do. It might be possible to approximate the recipe from the side of the bag. Do a little experimenting, see if I could break it down into ingredients the Amish could order and mix themselves. In the meantime, they might even forget about it.

Rachel and her daughter didn't forget, of course, just as I had never forgotten about each better loaf I found along the way. The bread may have even haunted them, as all of my discoveries haunted me after we had eaten the last slice, with no immediate hope of getting more. My solution was to write up as many recipes as I could find—from the Test Kitchen, from sites on the internet, from other cookbooks in my kitchen. I brought them out and told Rachel she had to experiment. She needed to work the dough for as long as possible by hand. Nothing she did with real bread applied when she was working with rice, sorghum, or potato flours. In fact, if a baker did everything she could think of to ruin a conventional loaf of bread, she just might get a good gluten-free loaf. That won me a grin.

20

A Bakery of
Our Own

I stood on a street corner in Vancouver in the January fog. Jet-lagged, hungry, and more than a little wary, I was casing the Gastown district for something to eat. No apps, no GPS: just my instincts and the conviction that something that was safe for me awaited nearby— something I wanted to eat.

Not that there weren't plenty of places right in front of me to get a safe and adequate meal. Finding GF in cities, as compared to rural places, has become quite easy. My hotel had a restaurant with GF menu items, for starters. There were sushi houses if I wanted to take the risk of getting glutened by some errant soy sauce in the midst of business travel. I passed several bistros where I could have found a few items on the menu, cafés that almost certainly offered sandwiches on gluten-free bread. Earlier that morning I had stumbled onto the best GF doughnuts I'd ever eaten (first, pineapple upside-down cake; then vanilla crème; and then, because it wasn't like I was coming back anytime soon, plain cinnamon-and-sugar). I didn't want any of the options I had already passed by. I didn't know what I wanted, exactly. My intention was to roam around until I found something that sounded unmistakably *good*.

I stopped in front of a Lebanese restaurant to read the menu for kicks. Lebanon! The Levant! The birthplace of wheat and barley! I laughed out loud.

This was not a fun way to snag a meal. This was work. The night before, I had walked eight blocks only to find that a highly reviewed Vietnamese restaurant, listed on the Web as open, was in fact closed. So much for advance research. I wanted to cry in the doorway. I settled for a self-important gastropub and the one item that my waitress said was sure not to kill me: braised beef cheeks. They were good, but they were not what I wanted. As I ate and sipped a glass of British Columbia red (no GF beer in the house), I wondered when and how getting what we wanted to eat had become such an imprisoning expectation.

Evidently, I still had not unlearned what little gourmandism I'd come to command. I still had *ideas* about what dining out in a city should be like: serendipitous, exotic, totally satisfying. I had once aspired to eat like the literary gastronomes, like M. F. K. Fisher and Elizabeth David, but I realized that I never would have gotten there, celiac disease or no. Few of us ever do, and that is why we love them. They possessed more freedom, more money, more time, and the world was different then. What they provided, and what some of them still do provide, is a glimpse of the ideal. We live—and eat—vicariously through them, as we do through all hopeful, luminous stories, and in the process we learn some things that better our own experiences at the table. It was not possible for me to eat my way across Vancouver now, but it never would have been possible anyway.

Nonetheless, I was willing to walk a long way in an unfamiliar city to sniff out the one dish I did not yet know I wanted to eat. That counted for something. I was still something of the eater I used to be. I still cared about good food, meals that have been prepared with attention and mindfulness.

I had walked an expanding grid of about ten blocks when I saw the place across the street: a tiny taquería with a spray-painted Virgin Mary over the door.

Oh, yes.

That was the place. I knew it immediately. Along the way I had passed three or four Tex-Mex-looking restaurants and a Chipotle chain franchise, without a single one tempting me. But clearly, my search needed to end here, at the line that snaked out the door along with the beat of Mexican hip-hop, beneath the Blessed Mother's brightly colored robes. She seemed to be saying, *Come, eat real tacos, and be relieved of the burden of your intolerances.*

I waited in line and ordered in Spanish when my turn came. In a tiny dining room where the walls were decorated, floor to ceiling, with Catholic-themed platters, I sat down to a dinner of four tacos—fresh fish, chicken, beans, and beef tongue—and quick-pickled vegetables on the side. I had to tell myself to slow down. I had to tell myself to enjoy this, because these tacos were a victory as much as they were a meal. And what a meal it was: spicy and sweet, tart from the pickled carrots, the tortillas caramelized on the flat-top before they were filled enough to be generous but not so much as to be difficult to eat. No cheese, no fake sauces. Just awesome, honest food.

A hell of a lot of trouble, this meal. I still had to hoof it back to my hotel. But it was well worth every tired footfall down the last block. Nothing else could have satisfied me so much. And the best part was that I had not even known I'd wanted tacos.

Shortly after I returned home, the North Country's first gluten-free bakery opened its doors. It was in Potsdam, only ten minutes away. The owners named it Three Bears Gluten-Free Bakery and More. From the earliest days, their goal seemed to be to fill as many holes in the diets of people who were sensitive to wheat as possible. Eventually they would install a salad bar and offer soups, sandwiches, and gluten-free pizza. A bona fide GF utopia.

On the day I visited for the first time, the temperature was five degrees above zero. Thirty inches of snow was piled on the sidewalks. Not the best time of year to stir excitement for a new business, not by a long shot. I knew there had been anticipation in the community, though. Friends had been mentioning it to me for months, happy to give me the news and happy for themselves, too. How many events can bring excitement to a small town like the opening of any new eatery— especially a new bakery? I kept checking in throughout the early winter as the owners of Three Bears posted about attending workshops and classes offered by King Arthur Flour in Vermont, where they also consulted with the staff at America's Test Kitchen. There were challenges with the space, the equipment, the materials. The opening date was pushed back, pushed back again. From my vantage point, they were taking their time and appeared to be doing everything right.

When I opened the door, I stepped into that familiar, pillowy warmth. The smell of baking bread, sugar, and butter mingled together. The café was inviting, the focal point a glass case filled with more pastries, cakes, and cookies than most kids with wheat allergies had seen in one place, ever (and more than most adults had seen in one place in a long time). I knew from a prior phone conversation with one of the owners, Chris Durand, that children had been a big motivator in opening the bakery. He had been diagnosed with celiac disease years ago (his wife and principal baker, Faye Ori, could eat wheat), but at least his childhood, like mine, had been filled with all of the iconic baked goods. He used to work as an entertainer at children's parties, and it had broken his heart to see certain kids left out because of their allergies.

I tried a sample of white bread and pronounced it good. Ten minutes later I carried a bag of fresh bread out of a bakery ten miles from home. Only a block away sat the bakery in the old carriage house where for years Bec and I used to buy loaves, before we started baking so much ourselves. I still passed the breads on their wooden racks every week when we went to the co-op for groceries: multigrain, spelt, whole wheat, apple bâtard, ficelle. I had trained myself not to notice the bread shelf anymore; it barely existed. And now, life had come full circle.

We went back when the bread ran out, and then, as Bec's birthday drew near, I began to consider getting her a cake from a bakery for the first time in as long as I could remember, possibly the first time ever.

Cakes had continued to be a sore spot for us. We still hadn't found a replacement for the Oreo on 'Roids, and the ATK recipe had proven a little too fussy and elusive for us to perfect. In search of a viable replacement, I had come up with "Brûlée-Your-Own Night," when I made custard with cardamom or vanilla bean and then passed the sugar around the kitchen table, followed by my mini-torch, the trigger locked into the full-automatic position and a cone of blue flame roaring out the end. It was a real showstopper. No one seemed to miss a cake with such pyrotechnics going on.

Nonetheless, I returned to Three Bears and sat down with Faye, who jotted my order down on a pad: a gluten-free version of the Oreo on 'Roids. It wasn't a complex order. I didn't want anything too fancy, for my part, and the bakery, for theirs, was still learning. Faye wasn't even sure what to charge me because she had never made a six-inch cake before. I left feeling a connection with all of those afternoons my mother had walked into D'Angelo's and ordered a birthday cake. Two days later, when I returned for the cake, the experience was just as I remembered: the white box brought out from the back, cold and sweet-smelling in my hands. I lifted the flap, glimpsed the icing, and resisted an urge to swipe a taste off the bottom like I used to when I was a kid.

We invited friends over. I seared scallops (from the gas station), roasted potatoes and onions with herbs, and made Deborah Madison's warm cabbage salad because the red cabbage population in the crisper was getting out of control. As a hedge against disappointment when it came time to have dessert, I filled everyone's glasses early and often with plenty of Finger Lakes Grüner Veltliner. I presented the cake along with a bottle of single malt. Then we toasted my wife and the new bakery and pronounced the cake as good as any other we'd ever had.

The comfort, the splendor, of locally made GF bread seemed to come unraveled—just a little—sometime later that week. We sat down to a breakfast of eggs and toast after I had walked the dog and stoked the fire. It was minus-twenty outside. I was hungry.

I was absently pulling away the crust from a piece of toast, which I'd buttered and topped with strawberry jam that Bec had put up last June—solace in a jar, on a morning like that—when I noticed fine, spiderweb-like strings spanning between the two pieces. This was new. Or, if the bread had been doing this from the start, I had been too blinded with joy to notice. Now I raised my eyebrows, and held the toast up to the light.

"I know," Bec said. "I saw it too."

What did these strings look like? Well, they resembled melted nylon, but they also reminded me of a food I couldn't quite place. The whole time we'd been toasting this bread, a cakey smell filled the kitchen, teasing me to name its source. Was this effect somehow connected with that aroma? Something in the flour blend? A new, ingenious additive for structure, mouth-feel, or flavor?

After a minute, Bec had it. "You know, Rice Krispies Treats do that."

I struggled to recall the recipe. When had I last eaten one, let alone made a batch? When I was twelve? At summer camp? For a while Rice Krispies were on the no-go list—the original recipe contained malt coloring derived from barley. Now there were gluten-free versions, as there were of so many foods that had been unavailable when I first eliminated gluten. Every day, in fact, more GF counterparts of traditional and popular foods seemed to appear. I rarely ate them, though, because I seemed to have forgotten that the original versions even existed, at least until something forced me to remember.

"So you're saying," I asked her as I concentrated on the taste, searching for intimations of childhood, "that there are marshmallows in this bread?"

I wasn't alarmed, exactly. Marshmallows contained no wheat, just chemicals.

"I'll bet it's corn syrup," Bec said. "Corn syrup is in Rice Krispies Treats, right?"

"No idea. But it goes into marshmallows for sure."

That was all it took. I was out. I wanted sourdough, and flaxseed, and rye. I wanted the hearty loaves eaten by my ancestors, near and ancient. I wanted bread that could stand up to stews and chowders and could do justice to chicken-liver pâté, confits, artisan cheese, and spicy jams. Most of all, I wanted bread that was so good it required none of those accoutrements. Was this snobbery? I remembered the day we bailed in the middle of a GF lunch at a conference we'd paid for in advance because we both sensed, at the same instant, that the mashed potatoes had come from a powder, the dressing on the salad contained thirty ingredients, and the chicken had been injected with salt solution. All GF, but—*We're such snobs*, Bec said as we hustled to a restaurant that made excellent Pan-Asian dishes featuring fresh vegetables. I had no good comeback for her, except to admit that if she was right, at least I believed wholly in what we were doing and was willing to work hard for it.

"Bread is tough to do," I said. "It's just so damned hard." I remembered her birthday cake. "That cake was pretty great, though. At least we have that problem solved."

A little while after, I went back to the bakery and asked Chris about the bread. I described the gossamer threads and offered our guesses as to the source—which amused him. He said no, he was not putting marshmallows in his bread. Or corn syrup. Or anything weird. The recipe was more or less the same one I followed in *How Can It Be Gluten Free,* with a key difference: when you're baking GF for high volume, the yeast needs a better supply of sugar to produce enough carbon dioxide to get the fake gluten—the psyllium, rice flour, tapioca starch, and potato flour—to expand. The best solution he had found was to feed the yeast honey. That was the smell wafting out of our toaster, and it was honey I had seen stretching between the torn pieces.

If there's a moral to this story, it's that good GF bread is *so* hard to make, it can seem possible for anything to end up in the dough. Even marshmallows.

Chris told me that Three Bears planned to bring out an oat bread next, which would have a different recipe and might not behave so strangely. I told him I wouldn't be able to try it, though it sounded good. I would keep rooting for them anyway, rooting hard.

My quest for bread, then, ended where it began: not in a bakery, but in our own kitchen, where we once again baked as we used to. Thanks to a few good recipes, some modern and some ancient, some leavened, some partially leavened, and some flat as pot holders, some alarmingly expensive and some poor as rutabagas (which show up in our share and make delicious fries, but apparently are fodder in France), Bec and I restored our weekly ritual. I didn't eat through a loaf nearly as fast as I'd eaten the bygone Swedish limpa, or soda bread, or homemade whole wheat. A person shouldn't eat that much psyllium, for one thing, and for another, the chore of making GF bread finally taught me restraint. If I ate less, there was more time before one of us suffered through the process again. And whenever we did, the house filled with the smell of baking grains, and I felt, as I used to feel, the familiar sense of anticipation, not unlike when a good friend is coming to dinner. I felt a sense of equilibrium, as well. And wealth, and joy.

Most of the time, the loaves we baked satisfied us. When they lost their appeal, we had our bakery up the road, and we had pushpins in a mental map representing places where we could find those breads we could not get at home, as well as the beers we may never be able to brew for ourselves. This is more or less what it's always meant to be a person who loves food and who lives in a rural place he'd be slow to trade for all the culinary wealth of the suburbs, or the city. I know of no person who has everything he wants, just so.

Despite its shortcomings, our wheatless bread did eventually look and taste "real" to us. This happened because of the spirit in which we baked it: the perseverance through the trials and errors, the inspirations from history and the teachings of science, whether we found them in books or bakeries, and the ancient traditions we made our own.

What made it realer still was that we came, in time, to share these loaves with trusted friends. Our guests enjoyed them as if the bread that awaited them at home in their own kitchens were no different. It *was* different, of course. Deep down, I still know this. I will always long for the loaves on their counters. But when we gathered around our table and passed the steaming dishes, or reached for the board spread with cheeses and salted meats, we never questioned whether the tastes were good. We never doubted whether the companionship was real.

EPILOGUE

I had wondered how I'd know when I was cured. Not cured of celiac disease, but of the longing for wheat, and gluten, and the old ways at the table. Of the confusion, the despair. I wanted the kind of proof no doctor could provide.

It came without my noticing: when I remembered, and rediscovered, that extended evenings spent at the table—either the one in our own kitchen or at a favorite restaurant, or at the homes of good friends—are among my favorite parts of my marriage. I long for such evenings more than I get them and relish them when they come, as they often do in the winter, when the sky darkens at four o'clock and the air outside turns brittle, and there is nothing more desirable to do than cook, drink wine, listen to good music, and eat. Or in the summer, when the college campus and the town are quiet and our CSA explodes with produce both strange and familiar—fennel and fava beans, Romanesco cauliflower and snow peas—a challenge that renews weekly with a demand for attention, innovation, and, often, simplicity.

On those nights, weekends, invariably, I ditch the afternoon chores and start cooking hours before we eat, simmering a stock, crisping bacon, browning meat, chopping vegetables. Often I make dessert first, something with berries or other fruits, unless the dessert is a soufflé or a dish that will not wait. Mousse is good and gluten-free, as is sorbet, or a granita. Then I go back to the beginning of the meal, working off one of the ingredients, whether cabbage or lentils or lamb, and following its suggestions associatively to other dishes, as I figured out how to do years ago, and then relearned how to do. I do not think about cholesterol, or fat, or sugar. I make pan sauces, aiolis, gastriques. I prepare small bites out of something left over in the fridge—duxelles, risotto cakes, roulades of smoked salmon. I quick-pickle some of the more numerous vegetables. Shortly before we eat, we pull out one of our better wines. I attempt to plate each course—mine first, so I can learn from the mistakes, and then hers.

Then we sit, and we eat. We drink. Something about the pace of the meal combined with the wine unspools new strands in our conversation, and we find ourselves talking more deeply than at other meals. The food is not always as good as we could get if we went out to eat, but the talk is more intimate, more hopeful, more deliberate.

And the truth about these meals is that all the good in them, alimentary and otherwise, would not exist if my wife and I were eating different foods. If Bec were eating bread and I were eating rice crackers, if she were eating semolina pasta and I were eating GF, if her sauce were thickened with wheat flour and mine with arrowroot, if her breading came from an artisanal loaf and mine from a bag of rice-and-cornstarch dust imported from Italy, then the experience would be tilted, askew. Never mind the mountain of dishes from two meals cooked simultaneously. The act of sharing the meal, and its symbolism, would not be the same. It would not be sharing at all. We might hurry through instead of lingering. One of us might be embarrassed, the other longing. We would not be able to revel in our success—not only what's on the plate, but what we've canned, what's come out of the garden, the local soil, the nearby pastures. And we would not wonder out loud at how far we've come, together, from those early days when the pasta wasn't pasta and the sauce wasn't thick and the food tasted safe but never tasted familiar, or inspired.

To share three hours at a table with the one person you chose from many—there is no loaf, no noodle, no ale so good as that.

ACKNOWLEDGMENTS

The list of people who have had a part in this book begins in the stacks of the Owen D. Young Library at St. Lawrence University: the authors in the bibliography, and others, are in some way behind every page I've written, and I appreciate the effort they have put into their books more than I can express. My thanks to Theresa Simoni for the translations, Dr. Karin Heckman for the assistance with immunology and nanoparticles, Dan Marenda for his cogent breakdown of genetics, and Joe Casey and Amy Jeuck for information on the ins and outs of Clarex and Omission beer. Dr. Gregory Healey and Dr. Xiaosong Song took time from their busy practices to speak with me in the early stages of researching this book, and the Rev. Joel Miller generously told me his story, providing context and corroboration at an important time. Karen M. Johnson-Weiner brought me into the Amish community to learn about their experience with celiac disease, and a certain Amish household in particular gave me their time and their trust. In the early stages of writing this book, I received huge support from a number of people, and even if their gestures looked small to them at the time, I saw nothing small about them: Stephanie Elizondo Griest, Kirsten Kaschock, Margaret Kent Bass, Mary Hussmann, Brian Walker, Sarah Gates, John Dermott-Woods, Bob Thacker, and Mark Sturges. I'm especially grateful for the grant-funding from the Office of the Associate Dean for Faculty Affairs at St. Lawrence University; many chapters simply would not exist without it. Every person who sent me a link to a story on celiac-disease research, or brought me a new GF product to try, has had a part in the making of this book: Howard Eissenstat, Matt Carotenuto, Jon Rosales, Daina Carvel, June Peoples, Amy Feiereisel, Tom and Naomi Wilder, and Erik Johnson.

I'm indebted to those who took extended time to talk with me about their own projects, businesses, and research: Jack Bishop, Lynn McKay and Stephanie Angle, Nancy Cain, Mary Schluckebier, Eliza Chace Hale Kelman, Chris Durand, and Faye Ori. I've grounded this book in stories of good eating as much as in research about celiac disease. Many friends have adjusted their own cooking for a night or longer, providing gifts in taste and spirit, especially David and Meredith Kratzmann, Sarah Barber and Cory Vineyard, Sid Sondergard and Ramona Ralston, Jon Sklaroff and Jessica Prody, my parents, and Jennifer Cockerill. Dan and Megan Kent, Kassandra Barton, Sue Wilson, and Ellen Rocco and the Feathered Lovelies have a special place in my kitchen and in my heart: together, you almost—*almost*—render wheat irrelevant. This project began at *Graze* magazine, where Brian Solem and Cyndi Fecher first published an essay that was the seed of it all. Thanks also to Paulette Lucitra, Peter Selgin, and Holly Hughes for the support in the earliest stages of my career as a writer who focuses on food. I'm grateful for the hard work and fabulous results of the entire team at Potter: Ian Dingman, Mark Birkey, Phil Leung, Annie Nelson, Anna Mintz, and Carly Gorga. Doris Cooper offered keen insights at the end of the process and supported me from the very beginning. My agent, Richard Florest, has been an unfaltering advisor; from the start, he believed in this book more than I did, and his sure hand and encouraging refrain—*Onward!*—have been among the greatest gifts a writer can receive. My editor at Potter, Rica Allannic, coaxed out my best and saved me from myself on just about every page. And, most of all, to my wife, Becky, companion at the table and everywhere else, I give my deepest admiration and gratitude: you gave me so much more than I can express, though I have tried.

Notes and Sources

1. Last Meals

5 some anthropologists believe: Thomas and Carol Sinclair, *Bread, Beer, and the Seeds of Change: Agriculture's Imprint on World History* (Oxford and Cambridge, UK: CABI, 2010), 11.

5 a share of 900 fine wheat breads: H. E. Jacob, *Six Thousand Years of Bread: Its Holy and Unholy History,* trans. Richard and Clara Winston (New York: Lyons Press, 1944), 32.

8 has for a long time been 20 PPM: The Prolamin Working Group (Working Group on Prolamin Analysis and Toxicity) established the toxicity threshold at 20 PPM because this was the lowest number gluten could be reliably tested down to, and it remains the limit as of the FDA's 2014 ruling on the definition of "gluten-free foods." More recently it has been determined that the LS3600 gluten test can measure the presence of reactive peptides down to 10 PPM. My thanks to Mary Schluckebier, of the Celiac Support Association, for the conversation on the history. A recent study explored levels of gluten toxicity: Gilbert Kruizinga et al., "Threshold for Gluten-Induced Mucosal Damage," *American Journal of Clinical Nutrition,* November 28, 2012.

2. The Perfect Immunological Trojan Horse

14 Few foods can measure up: Rachel Laudan, *Cuisine and Empire: Cooking in World History* (Berkeley: University of California Press, 2015), 30.

14 Ceres . . . the Latinate root: H. E. Jacob, *Six Thousand Years of Bread: Its Holy and Unholy History* (New York: Lyons Press, 1944), 81.

14 argued about which kinds: Anthony Bobrow-Strain, *White Bread: A Social History of the Store-Bought Loaf* (Boston: Beacon Press), 2012, 7.

14 unscrupulous millers and bakers: John Marchant et al., *Bread: A Slice of History* (Stroud, Gloucester, UK: The History Press, 2007), 74–76.

14 Widespread "panophobia" does not appear: Darline Gay Levi, *The Ideas*

and Careers of Simon-Nicolas-Henri Linguet (Carbondale: University of Illinois Press, 1980), 100–103, 130–31.

15   can be found in the history of ergotism: Mary Kilbourne Matossian, *Poisons of the Past: Molds, Epidemics, and History* (New Haven: Yale University Press, 1989), 12–14.

15   In Limoges in 857: Jacob, *Six Thousand Years of Bread,* 121–23.

15   Suspicion of demonic possession: Matossian, *Poisons of the Past,* 12–14, 56–57, 60–61.

15   The first known description: Aretaeus, *The Extant Works of Aretaeus the Cappadocian,* ed. and trans. Francis Adams (London, 1856).

16   after the Greek word for "belly": Alberto Tommasini et al., "Ages of Celiac Disease: From Changing Environment to Improved Diagnostics," *World Journal of Gastroenterology* 17 (32), 2011: 3665–71.

16   consistent with malabsorption: Tommasini et al., "Ages of Celiac Disease."

16   Aretaeus also appears to have noted: Aretaeus, *Extant Works.*

16   blaming, instead of wheat or barley: Ibid.

16   diet was the most important factor: See, for example, Tommasini et al., "Ages of Celiac Disease," and Hugh J. Freeman, "Celiac Disease: A Disorder Emerging from Antiquity, Its Evolving Classification and Risk, and New Potential Treatment Paradigms," *Gut and Liver* 9 (1), January 2015: 28–37. In the research, there is disagreement over whether Samuel Gee accurately identified wheat as the cause of celiac disease; some scholars point to Dicke, and others note that Gee indeed, in his 1888 monograph, "states that the allowance of farinaceous foods must be small," which they point to as proof of wheat being known to cause celiac symptoms since at least 1888. ("Letter: Samuel Gee, Aretaeus, and the Coeliac Affection," *British Medical Journal* 2 (5916), May 25, 1974: 442.) Notably, a "small" amount of wheaten foods is not the same thing as *eliminating* wheaten foods.

17   He paid close attention to a child: Tommasini et al., "Ages of Celiac Disease."

17   "could not be prevailed upon": A. Fasano et al., eds., *Frontiers in Celiac Disease* (Basel: Karger, 2008), 5.

17   effects of a banana diet: G. P. van Berge-Henegouwen and C. J. Mulder, "Pioneer in the Gluten-Free Diet: Willem-Karel Dicke 1905–1962, Over 50 Years of Gluten-Free Diet," *Gut* 34, 1993: 1473–75.

17   It is estimated that 4.5 million people: Henri A. van der Zee, *The Hunger Winter: Occupied Holland 1944–1945* (Lincoln University of Nebraska Press, 1998), 304–5.

17   Those caught in the famine: van der Zee, *Hunger Winter.*

18   claim that he had suspected: "Pioneer in the Gluten-Free Diet."

22   four to ten years in the United States: University of Chicago Celiac
      Disease Center, "Celiac Disease Facts and Figures," http://www
      .uchospitals.edu/pdf/uch_007937.pdf.

22   only recently learned to screen: *Celiac Central,* "Celiac Disease Featured
      in Peer-Reviewed Medical Journal for Primary Care and Family
      Physicians," http://www.celiaccentral.org/research-news/Celiac
      -Disease-Research/134/researchers—gluten-challenge—modified
      /vobid—9037/.

22   more than three hundred symptoms: University of Chicago Celiac Disease
      Center, "Celiac Disease Facts and Figures."

22   average around four thousand dollars: Ibid.

23   The biopsies of my intestinal tissue: Cleo Libonati, *Recognizing Celiac
      Disease: Signs, Symptoms, and Associated Disorders and Complications*
      (Fort Washington, PA: Gluten-Free Works Publishing, 2007), 14, 31.

25   "breads of poverty": William Rubel, *Bread: A Global History* (London:
      Reaktion Books, 2011).

3. Wheat Exile

33   about half the American population: http://www.cureceliacdisease.org
      /living-with-celiac/guide/fact-sheets.

33   one-in-twenty chance: http://www.cureceliacdisease.org/living-with
      -celiac/guide/fact-sheets.

33   most common autoimmune disorder in the world: http://www.cureceliac
      disease.org/faqs.

34   A recent study by the Mayo Clinic: "Celiac Disease: On the Rise," July
      2010, http://www.mayo.edu/research/discoverys-edge/celiac-disease
      -rise.

34   For decades: A. Fasano et al., "Prevalence of Celiac Disease in At-Risk
      and Not-at-Risk Groups"; Carlos Catassi, "Why Is Celiac Disease Endemic
      in People of the Sahara?" Letter. *Lancet* 354, 1999; L. Gandolfi et al.,
      "Prevalence of Celiac Disease Among Blood Donors in Brazil," *American
      Journal of Gastroenterology,* 2000: 95689–92.

34   more than half (58 percent): http://www.celiaccentral.org/celiac-disease
      /facts-and-figures/.

34 most likely to be a carrier: http://www.celiaccentral.org/riskfactors/. According to the National Foundation for Celiac Awareness, "About 95% of people with celiac disease have the HLA-DQ2 gene and most of the remaining 5% have the HLA-DQ8 gene." Not everyone with the gene develops the disease.

34 a first-degree blood relative: The estimates for the potential for developing the disease vary. According to the National Foundation for Celiac Awareness (www.celiaccentral.org/riskfactors/ "Celiac Disease: Who Is At Risk?"), the risk factor is a conservative 5–10 percent.

35 unchecked, celiac disease can lead: In recent years, the chances of undiagnosed celiacs developing intestinal cancers have been revised down. According to the National Foundation for Celiac Awareness, "Those with celiac disease are especially more likely to develop lymphomas in the small intestine because of their compromised immune system. In the past the increased risk of celiacs developing lymphomas was quite high, 40–100% more likely. However, more recent studies have shown that the risk of lymphoma is slightly higher than the normal population—much less than previously believed—and that this risk reaches unity with the normal population after a gluten-free diet has been maintained for several years."

35 400-percent greater chance: Rubio-Tapia et al., "Increased Prevalence and Mortality in Undiagnosed Celiac Disease," *Gastroenterology* 137 (1), July 2009: 88–93.

35 Other complications: University of Celiac Disease Center.

35 some recent investigations: http://www.sciencedaily.com/releases /2014/12/141202093805.htm?utm_source=feedburner&utm_medium =email&utm_campaign=Feed%3A+sciencedaily+%28Latest+Science +News+—+ScienceDaily%29.

36 90 percent of people with celiac: Carol Semrad, "Refractory Celiac Disease: What Is It? What to Do?" University of Chicago Celiac Disease Center, *Impact* 1 (3), 2008: 1.

39 "Tell me what you eat": Jean Anthelme Brillat-Savarin, *The Physiology of Taste*, trans. Anne Drayton (New York: Penguin Books, 1970), 13.

4. Cleaning House

45 This was why the Chinese: Harold McGee, *On Food and Cooking: The Science and Lore of the Kitchen* (New York: Scribner, 2004), 468.

49 Marcel Proust's "madeleine moment": Marcel Proust, *In Search of Lost*

Time: Volume 1: Swann's Way, trans. C. K. Scott Moncrief (New York: Modern Library, 2003), 58–64.

5. Guy Fieri and Me

51   It might be more accurate: Thomas and Carol Sinclair, *Bread, Beer, and the Seeds of Change: Agriculture's Imprint on World History* (Oxford and Cambridge, UK: CABI, 2010), 11. Sinclair and Sinclair use the phrase "genetic nudge" to describe the inherent appeal of grains. Rachel Laudan writes, "Throughout history, most societies have selected a few staple grains and have depended upon them for the entirety of history since. Only sugarcane has emerged to join those grains as an important source of food" (*Cuisine and Empire: Cooking in World History* [Berkeley: University of California Press, 2015], 31).

51   one that is around 10,000 to 12,000 years old: Joan P. Alcock, *Food in the Ancient World* (London: Greenwood Press, 2006), xvii–xviii, 31–34.

51   which includes modern-day Iraq, Turkey, and Syria: See, for example, Patrick McGovern, *Uncorking the Past: The Quest for Wine, Beer, and Other Alcoholic Beverages* (Berkeley: University of California Press, 2009), 85; and Reay Tannahill, *Food in History* (New York: Broadway Books, 1995), 32. It should be pointed out that the birthplace of the earliest forerunners to bread, as well as the locations of the earliest gathering and cultivation of wheat, is a subject of lively debate that changes as archaeologists uncover remains of ancient settlements. For instance, compared to mid-twentieth-century research that surveyed grain-finds and fixed the dates at about 7500 BC, Joan Alcock writes that einkorn was gathered in Syria around 12,000 BC, and was later supplanted by emmer, which grew wild, by 9000 BC. Alcock notes that wild barley appeared throughout the Jordan Valley and the Levant, and by 11,000 BC had made its way to modern Greece (*Food in the Ancient World,* xvii). Meanwhile, Michael Symons has written that the Natufians, who were established in modern-day Palestine by 10,000 BC, were cultivating wheat by about that date, qualifying them as "incipient agriculturalists" (Michael Symons, *A History of Cooks and Cooking* [Urbana: University of Illinois Press, 1998], 226). Most recently, in 2015, Rachel Laudan wrote that gathering and cooking of the seeds of herbaceous plants—which would include wheat and barley—began as long as 19,000 years ago, nearly 10,000 years before the Neolithic Revolution (*Cuisine and Empire,* 13). Recent finds on grindstones in Europe suggest that primitive flours may have been ground from wild grains (not wheat) some 25,000 years BP (Anna Revedin et al., "Thirty-Thousand-Year Old Evidence of Plant Food Processing,"

Proceedings of the National Academy of Sciences of the United States 107 [44], November 2, 2010: 18815–19).

51   in the Jordan Valley about a millennium later: *A History of Cooks and Cooking*, 226; Maguelonne Toussaint-Samat, *A History of Food*, trans. Anthea Bell (Cambridge, MA: Blackwell, 1992), 224.

51   In a famous and telling 1960 experiment: Tannahill, *Food in History*, 32.

52   responds well to dry (no irrigation) farming: N. W. Simmonds, *Evolution of Crop Plants* (London: Longman, 1976), 124.

52   3,000 to 4,000 years in the future: See, for example, William Alexander, *52 Loaves: A Half-Baked Adventure* (Chapel Hill, NC: Algonquin, 2011), 20.

52   edible part of the wheat grains: The description of ancient harvesting, threshing, winnowing, and grinding processes comes from Tannahill, *Food in History*.

52   While the Chinese had been making: McGovern, *Uncorking the Past*, 73. For a longer description of ancient cooking practices, see Bee Wilson's *Consider the Fork: A History of How We Eat and Cook* and Tannahill's *Food in History*.

53   flatbread or beer: Tom Standage, *A History of the World in Six Glasses* (London: Walker and Company, 2006), 3, 22–24. See also Carrie Lock, "Original Microbrews," *Science News* 166 (14), October 2, 2004: 216–18.

53   India by 6,500 BC, and to Egypt by 6,000 BC: Mark Kurlansky, *Salt: A World History* (New York: Penguin, 2002), 11.

54   no later than 4,000 BC: H. E. Jacob, *Six Thousand Years of Bread: Its Holy and Unholy History* (New York: Lyons Press, 1944), 13–15.

55   an executioner: Bernard Dupaigne, *The History of Bread* (New York: Harry N. Abrams, 1999), 78.

55   By the late Middle Ages: Alfio Cortonesi, "Self-Sufficiency and the Market: Rural and Urban Diet in the Middle Ages," *Food: A Culinary History from Antiquity to the Present*, ed. Jean-Louis Flandrin and Massimo Montanari, trans. Clarissa Botsford et al. (New York: Columbia University Press, 1999), 268.

55   1.3 to 2.0 kilograms of wheat bread per day: Dupaigne, *History of Bread*, 43.

55   two to four pounds of wheat bread: John Marchant et al., *Bread: A Slice of History* (Stroud, Gloucestershire, UK: The History Press, 2008), 47.

55   By 1870, this figure had dropped: Figures on bread consumption are from Marchant et al., *Bread: A Slice of History*, 47, 73–74, 213.

55   114 pounds of wheat: Michael Pollan, *The Omnivore's Dilemma: A Natural History of Four Meals* (New York: Penguin, 2007), 22.

57 sales of $10.5 billion: Stephanie Strom, "A Big Bet on Gluten-Free," *The New York Times*, February 17, 2014, http://www.nytimes.com /2014/02/18/business/food-industry-wagers-big-on-gluten-free .html?_r=0.

57 252 percent higher: L. Stevens and M. Rashid, "Gluten-Free and Regular Foods: A Cost Comparison," *Canadian Journal of Dietetic Practice and Research* 69 (3), Fall 2008: 147–50. Although the data are not current, the same figures for price differences between GF and conventional foods continue to circulate in other media.

58 the FDA does not require: U.S. Food and Drug Administration, "Gluten and Food Labeling," http://www.fda.gov/Food/GuidanceRegulation /GuidanceDocumentsRegulatoryInformation/Allergens/ucm367654 .htm.

58 The IRS allows: National Foundation for Celiac Awareness, "Tax Deduction Guide for Gluten-Free Products," http://www.celiaccentral .org/shopping/tax-deduction-guide-for-gluten-free-products/.

58 second poorest in New York State: New York State Community Action Association, "New York State Poverty Report March 2015, 54, http:// nyscommunityaction.org/wp-content/uploads/2014/03/2015-Poverty -Report-w-50th-logos-for-online.pdf.

6. In Memory of Beer

64 Beer Purity Laws: For more on the Beer Purity Laws, see Ian S. Hornsey, *A History of Beer and Brewing* (Cambridge, UK: Royal Society of Chemistry Press, 2003).

68 "dark purgative": Joan P. Alcock, *Food in the Ancient World* (London: Greenwood Press, 2006), 90.

68 unfiltered, uncarbonated, and unhopped: Hornsey, *History of Beer and Brewing*, 8.

68 served as potable drinking water: Peter Kaiser et al., "Healthy or Detrimental? Physiological, Psychiatric, and Evolutionary Aspects of Drinking Beer," in *Liquid Bread*, eds. Wulf Schiefenhovel and Helen MacBeth (New York: Berghahn Books, 2011), 21.

68 Some views hold that writing: Tom Standage, *A History of the World in Six Glasses* (London: Walker and Co., 2005), 35–39.

68 reached Europe around 5,000 BC: F. Xavier Medina, "Europe North and South, Beer and Wine: Some Reflections About Beer and Mediterranean Food," in *Liquid Bread*, 71.

68   north to the Hebrides: Hornsey, *History of Beer and Brewing*, 194.

68   strong and weak ale *per day*: Ibid., 290.

68   3.2 million of today's twelve-ounce bottles: Ibid., 346.

68   "fermenting sugar-rich extracts": Wulf Schiefenhovel and Helen MacBeth, "Introduction: Assembling Perspectives on Beer," in *Liquid Bread*, 3.

69   where palm sugar and dates were fermented: Hornsey, *History of Beer and Brewing*, 8.

69   The Chinese may have brewed: Patrick McGovern, *Uncorking the Past: The Quest for Wine, Beer, and Other Alcoholic Beverages* (Berkeley: University of California Press, 2009), 51.

69   called *chichi*: Schiefenhovel and MacBeth, "Introduction," *Liquid Bread*, 3.

70   Sorghum is the essential: McGovern, *Uncorking the Past*, 253, 257.

70   usually through a long straw: Ibid.

71   "a wholesome drink": Quoted in Hornsey, *History of Beer and Brewing*, 387–89.

7. What's Wrong with the Wheat?

———

75   can be reactive and harmful: For the differences between celiac disease, wheat allergy, and gluten sensitivity (sometimes also called non-celiac gluten sensitivity), see Anna Sapone et al., "Spectrum of Gluten-Related Disorders: Consensus on New Nomenclature and Classification," *BMC Medicine* 10 (13), 2012.

76   Some basic immunology is required: My thanks to Dr. Karin Heckman in the Biology Department at St. Lawrence University for help with the description in this paragraph.

76   Since the early 2000s, this peptide: Umberto Volta et al., "Non-Celiac Gluten-Sensitivity: Questions Still to Be Answered Despite Increasing Awareness," *Cellular & Molecular Immunology* 10, 2013: 383–92; B. Belderok, "Developments in Bread-Making Processes," *Plants, Food, and Human Nutrition* 55 (1), 2000: 86; O. Molberg et al., "Mapping of T-Cell Epitopes in Bread Wheat Ancestors: Implications for Celiac Disease," *Gastroenterology* 128 (2), February 2005: 393–401.

76   Numerous studies overlap: Hugh Freeman, "Celiac Disease: A Disorder Emerging from Antiquity, Its Evolving Classification and Risk, and

Potential New Treatment Paradigms," *Gut and Liver* 9, January 1, 2015: 28–37; Volta et al., "Non-Celiac Gluten-Sensitivity"; Hetty C. van den Broeck, "Presence of Celiac Disease Epitopes in Modern and Old Hexaploid Wheat Varieties: Wheat Breading May Have Contributed to Increasing Prevalence of Celiac Disease," *Theoretical Applied Genetics* 121, 2010: 1527–39; Francesco Tovoli et al., "Clinical and Diagnostic Aspects of Gluten-Related Disorders," *World Journal of Clinical Cases* 3 (3), March 16, 2015: 275–84.

77   even as celiac-causing peptides are expressed: Freeman, "Celiac Disease."

77   Possible factors include: Volta et al., "Non-Celiac Gluten-Sensitivity."

77   presumed safe: M. de Lorgeril and P. Salen, "Gluten and Wheat Intolerance Today: Are Modern Wheat Strains Involved?" *International Journal of Food Science and Nutrition* 65 (5), August 2014: 577–81.

77   the time frame in which the changes: Sapone et al., "Spectrum of Gluten-Related Disorders."

77   25,000 cultivars: Ibid. However, other studies assert only 10,000 cultivars (Frits Koning, "Gluten: A Two-Edged Sword," *Springer Seminars in Immunopathology* 27, 2005: 217–32).

77   provides up to 50 percent of the calories: Tovoli et al., "Clinical and Diagnostic Aspects."

77   industrialized bread-making has fallen: Volta et al., "Non-Celiac Gluten-Sensitivity."

77   Fermentation times in modern: M. Gobetti et al., "Sourdough Lactobacilli and Celiac Disease," *Food Microbiology* 2, April 24, 2007: 187–96.

77   those with less severe: Ibid. Also see R. Di Cagno, "Gluten-Free Sourdough Wheat Baked Goods Appear Safe for Young Celiac Patients: A Pilot Study," *Journal of Pediatric Gastroenterology and Nutrition* 51 (6), December 2010: 777–83.

78   driven by the availability: Volta et al., "Non-Celiac Gluten-Sensitivity."

78   beyond the glutenin and gliadin: Yvonne Junker et al., "Wheat Amylase Trypsin Inhibitors Drive Intestinal Inflammation via Activation of Toll-like Receptor 4," *The Journal of Experimental Medicine* 209 (13), 2012: 2395–408.

78   modern eaters consume: Volta et al., "Non-Celiac Gluten-Sensitivity"; Freeman, "Celiac Disease."

78   about 4.8 grams of gluten: Scott Adams, *Celiac.com,* July 26, 1996, http://www.celiac.com/articles/38/1/How-much-gluten-is-in-a-normal-diet-and-how-much-does-it-take-to-cause-damage-in-a-celiac/Page1.html. (All data in this paragraph are from *Celiac.com.*)

80   despite a strict elimination diet: Z. Mermon et al., "An Orthodontic
      Retainer Preventing Remission in Celiac Disease," *Clinical Pediatrics* 52
      (11), November 2013: 1034–37.

80   is *not* the cause of gluten-related disorders: Emily Eaton, *Growing
      Resistance: Canadian Farmers and the Politics of Genetically-Modified
      Wheat* (Winnipeg: University of Manitoba Press, 2013), 69–73. The
      entire summary of the Canadian response to GM wheat is informed
      by Chapter 4, "Make Their Case Against GM Wheat: Articulating the
      Politics of Production Through Discourses of Consumption," in *Growing
      Resistance,* 90–116.

81   may not be as benign as initially believed: Anthony Samsel and Stephanie
      Seneff, "Glyphosate, Pathways to Modern Diseases II: Celiac Sprue and
      Gluten Intolerance," *Interdisciplinary Toxicology,* 2013. Responses to
      "Samsel and Seneff," as the article has come to be known, can be found
      online: http://www.huffingtonpost.com/tamar-haspel/condemning
      -monsanto-with-_b_3162694.html; and http://www.science20.com
      /agricultural_realism/a_fishy_attempt_to_link_glyphosate_and_celiac
      _disease-132928.

82   genetically modify wheat: Freeman, "Celiac Disease."

83   statements about strategic breeding: Donald Kasarda, "Can an Increase
      in Celiac Disease Be Attributed to an Increase in the Gluten Content of
      Wheat as a Consequence of Wheat Breeding?" *Journal of Agricultural
      and Food Chemistry* 61, 2013: 1155–59; Alison Aubrey, "Doctors
      Say Changes in Wheat Do Not Explain Rise of Celiac Disease," *The
      Salt,* December 26, 2013, http://www.npr.org/sections/thesalt/2013
      /09/26/226510988/doctors-say-changes-in-wheat-do-not-explain
      -rise-of-celiac-disease; "Dr. FAQ: Stefano Guandalini on the Rise
      of Celiac Disease," *ScienceLife,* February 5, 2014, http://sciencelife
      .uchospitals.edu/2014/02/05/dr-faq-stefano-guandalini-on-the-rise-of
      -celiac-disease/.

85   does not always support: Moises Velasquez-Manoff, "Who Has the Guts
      for Gluten?" *The New York Times,* February 23, 2013, http://www
      .nytimes.com/2013/02/24/opinion/sunday/what-really-causes-celiac
      -disease.html.

85   explorations of the human microbiome: Martin J. Blaser, *Missing
      Microbes: How the Overuse of Antibiotics Is Fueling Our Modern Plagues*
      (New York: Henry Holt, 2014), 5–11. See also Maria Sellitto et al., "Proof
      of Concept of Microbiome-Metabolome Analysis and Delayed Gluten
      Exposure on Celiac Disease Autoimmunity in Genetically At-Risk
      Infants," *PLOS One* 7 (3), 2012, http://www.ncbi.nlm.nih.gov/pmc
      /articles/PMC3303818/.

85   precedes a celiac-disease diagnosis: C. Cicerone et al., "Th17, Intestinal

Microbiota and the Abnormal Immune Response in the Pathogenesis of Celiac Disease," *Gastroenterology Hepatology (Bed and Bench)* 8 (2), 2015: 117–22.

85   In 2013, the *New York Times* reported: Velasquez-Manoff, "Who Has the Guts for Gluten?"

87   "celiac iceberg": Freeman, "Celiac Disease."

88   there's been a fourfold increase: University of Nottingham, "Fourfold Increase in Rate of Diagnosed Cases of Celiac Disease in the UK," *ScienceDaily*, May 11, 2014, www.sciencedaily.com/releases /2014/05/140511214807.htm (accessed June 5, 2015).

88   For every one person: Tovoli et al., "Clinical and Diagnostic Aspects."

88   Africa, Asia, and South America: N. Gujral et al., "Celiac Disease: Prevalence, Diagnosis, Pathogenesis and Treatment," *World Journal of Gastroenterology* 18 (42), November 14, 2012.

88   In Asia in particular: Sapone et al., "Spectrum of Gluten-Related Disorders."

88   recover more quickly: Andrew Pollack, "As Celiac and Gluten Sensitivities Gain Prominence, Drug Companies Race to Find Treatments," *The New York Times,* April 28, 2015, http://www.nytimes.com/2015/04/29 /business/celiac-diseases-prominence-has-drug-companies-racing-to -find-treatments.html?smprod=nytcore-iphone&smid=nytcore-iphone -share&_r=0.

8. Strange Grains

———

96   dermatitis herpetiformis: Also known as DH, dermatitis herpetiformis is often an early sign of celiac disease, and is frequently mentioned as a symptom in online information about celiac disease. Eugenia Lauret and Luis Rodrigo, "Celiac Disease and Autoimmune-Associated Conditions," *BioMed Research International*: Article ID 127589. Published online July 24, 2013.

97   "beany": *The How Can It Be Gluten Free Cookbook* (America's Test Kitchen, 2014), 11, 18.

97   "tree bread": H. E. Jacob, *Six Thousand Years of Bread: Its Holy and Unholy History* (New York: Lyons Press, 1944), 38.

97   *castagne e legumi*: Ibid.

97   In especially ghastly times: Ibid.

98   the Scandinavians used: Ibid.

98   And when the Puritans reached: Michael Pollan, *The Omnivore's Dilemma: A Natural History of Four Meals* (New York: Penguin, 2007), 25.

9. The Fearful Gourmand

105   dine out 90-percent less: Scott Adams, *Celiac.com*, April 9, 2010, http://www.celiac.com/articles/22077/1/Take-Charge-of-Your-Meal-When-Eating-Out/Page1.html.

108   "roving gourmand": See "One Foot in the Grave," in Jim Harrison, *The Raw and the Cooked: Adventures of a Roving Gourmand* (Boston: Grove, 2002).

10. The Less-Traveled GF Road

119   I began to root around: My sources consisted of food and culinary encyclopedias: *The Oxford Companion to Food, The Cambridge Companion to Food, On Food and Cooking: The Science and Lore of the Kitchen, Food Lover's Companion.*

119   a case for calling flatbread: William Rubel, *Bread: A Global History* (London: Reaktion Books, 2011), 100.

119   "bread" was most likely synonymous: Ibid.

121   as America's Test Kitchen suggests: *The How Can It Be Gluten Free Cookbook* (America's Test Kitchen, 2014), 201.

122   *papadums* or *papads*: Alan Davidson and Tom Jain, *The Oxford Companion to Food* (New York: Oxford University Press, 2006), 622.

122   domesticated in China around 3,000 BC: The dates given for buckwheat domestication are various, with the most conservative at 1000 BC and the earliest at 6000 BC. Andrea Pieroni, "Gathering Food from the Wild," in *The Cultivation of Plants*, eds. Sir Ghillean Prance and Mark Nesbitt (New York: Routledge, 2005), 58.

11. Spring at the Market

128   raw beet juice: The discussion about the benefits of nitrates in beetroot juice has since become more complex. Studies investigating the benefits

of beetroot juice include F. J. Larsen et al., "Dietary Inorganic Nitrate Improves Mitochondrial Efficiency in Humans," *Cellular Metabolism* 13 (2), February 2, 2011:149–59. More general-interest articles can be found on the *Sweat Science* blogs: http://sweatscience.com/the-beet -goes-on-nitrates-improve-cycling-time-trial-performance/. Recent, more critical inquiries can be found at: http://www.runnersworld.com/drinks -hydration/dose-reality-beet-juice.

129   "Gluten Contamination Elimination Diet": Justin Hollon et al., "Trace Gluten Contamination May Play a Role in Mucosal and Clinical Recovery in a Subgroup of Diet-Adherent Non-Responsive Celiac Disease Patients," *BMC Gastroenterology* 13 (40), 2013.

131   nixtamalization: See, for example, Alan Davidson and Tom Jain, *The Oxford Companion to Food* (New York: Oxford University Press, 2006), 534.

12. The God Enzyme

141   But Omission thrust questions: Critics of the Craft Brewing Alliance's Omission beer include the *Gluten Free Dietician*: http://www .glutenfreedietitian.com/omission-beer-the-controversy-over-gluten -free-labeling-of-malt-based-beverages-continues/.

142   have approved Omission: CSA Recognition Seal and explanation: http:// www.csaceliacs.org/labeling_beer_with_gluten_content_statements.jsp.

142   R-5 ELISA: M. L. Colgrave et al., "Using Mass Spectrometry to Detect Hydrolysed Gluten in Beer That Is Responsible for False Negatives by ELISA," *Journal of Chromatography* 1370, November 28, 2014: 105–14. See also P. Koehler et al., "AACI Approved Methods Technical Committee Report: Collaborative Study on the Immunochemical Determination of Partially Hydrolyzed Gluten Using an R5 Competitive ELISA," *Cereal Foods World* 58 (3), 2013: 154–158. The abstract can be found at the NFCA website, http://www.celiaccentral.org/research-news/Celiac -Disease-Research/134/vobid—10134/.

142   "quite safe": Gilbert Kruizinga, et al., "Threshold for Gluten-Induced Mucosal Damage," *American Journal of Clinical Nutrition*, November 28, 2012.

142   not designed to measure: B. Gessendorfer et al., "Preparation and Characterization of Enzymatically Hydrolyzed Prolamins from Wheat, Rye, and Barley as References for the Immunochemical Quantitation of Partially Hydrolyzed Gluten," *Analytical and Bioanalytical Chemistry* 395 (6), November 2009: 1721–28; Colgrave et al., "Using

Mass Spectrometry"; National Foundation for Celiac Awareness, "Study Validates the R5 Competitive ELISA," August 1, 2013, http://www.celiaccentral.org/research-news/study-validates-r5-competitive -elisa-10134/pg—1/.

143   Derived from a mold: Information on the brewing process and history of Omission Beer are from the author's interview with Amy Jeuck, December 21, 2014.

143   autoimmune reaction in a person: "Beer from Barley Malt Made Gluten -Free with Brewers Clarex" (DSM Food Specialties BV), 1–2.

144   According to Omission's brewmaster: Phone interview with Joe Casey, January 2015.

145   Swedish study: "Gluten Content in Beer," SLV, 2005, trans. Theresa Simoni, "Gluteninnehall i de ol som analsyerats vid Livsmedelsverket." *Livsmedelsverket*, Oktober 2005.

13. Summer Rituals

———

157   David Buchanan: David Buchanan, *Taste, Memory: Forgotten Foods, Lost Flavors, and Why They Matter* (White River Junction, VT: Chelsea Green Publishing, 2012), 200.

14. GF by Choice

———

161   *The Gluten-Free Edge* was published: See Peter Bronski and Melissa McLean Jory, *The Gluten-Free Edge* (New York: The Experiment, 2012).

162   Some studies suggest: Runners' forums on the internet are full of conversations on this question, but an interesting scientific study emerged in 1987: "Acute Ischaemic Colitis in a Female Long Distance Runner," *Gut* 28, 1987: 296–99.

164   it is derived from the Latin: *Oxford English Dictionary*.

16. Avoiding the Doctor

———

182   "dispatching a lunch": A. J. Liebling, "A Good Appetite." Reprinted in *Secret Ingredients: The New Yorker Book of Food and Drink*, ed. David Remnick (New York: Modern Library, 2008), 30–45.

17. Getting GF with America's Test Kitchen

———

186   popular online recipe: http://food52.com/recipes/28886-my-new-roots
-life-changing-loaf-of-bread.

190   Technically an herb: According to the University of Maryland Medical
Center, "Psyllium is a soluble fiber used primarily as a gentle bulk
forming laxative in products such as Metamucil. It comes from a shrub
-like herb called *Plantago ovata* that grows worldwide but is most
common in India. Each plant can produce up to 15,000 tiny, gel coated
seeds, from which psyllium husk is derived." http://umm.edu/health
/medical/altmed/supplement/psyllium.

191   Thus the dough can trap: *The How Can It Be Gluten Free Cookbook*
(America's Test Kitchen, 2014), 21.

191   led M. F. K. Fisher to liken: M. F. K. Fisher, "How to Rise Up Like New
Bread," *The Art of Eating* (Houghton Mifflin Harcourt, 2004), 246–47.

193   When I finally spoke to Jack Bishop: Phone interview, July 12, 2014.

18. Rising Hopes

———

203   Celiac Disease Foundation Conference: June 7–8, 2014, Pasadena, CA.
Speakers included Alessio Fasano, MD, founder of the Boston Center
for Celiac Research; and Dr. John Zone, professor and chair of the
Department of Dermatology at the University of Utah.

204   When we met them: June 9, 2014, Whisk Gluten-Free Bakery, Pasadena,
CA.

206   almost the same process as Omission: For all of my misgivings about
drinking a GR beer that is not made in a dedicated GR facility, the
process, according to the Stone Delicious IPA website, is much the same.
Instead of using Brewers Clarex, Stone uses Clarity Ferm, a clarifying
product introduced during the fermentation stage that also disrupts the
formation of epitopes. Like Omission, the GR/GF certifier White Labs
uses the R-5 Competitive ELISA Gliadin assay, which according to White
Labs' website is able to detect gluten down to 10 PPM.

210   track down Eliza Hale: September 15, 2015.

19. Harvest Time

———

217   One day closer to the winter: December 17, 2015, Heuvelton, NY.

20. A Bakery of Our Own

———

223   North Country's first gluten-free bakery: I spoke several times with Chris Durand, most extensively on March 18, 2015. Durand and his staff were trained by the America's Test Kitchen staff at the King Arthur Flour offices in Norwich, Vermont. Still in the process of establishing his business, he had some stark numbers to share: $147,000 to prep the bakery for opening, and an estimated $1,000 gross per day to break even—which is *five hundred* $2.00 cupcakes. Like the costs that eaters with celiac disease face at the checkout, Durand's costs were largely driven by materials: a forty-bag pallet of King Arthur GF flour—"the Cadillac of flours," in his words—costs $29,000 and has a one-year shelf life. If there was a silver lining, it was that all of that flour had, by his estimate, led to a 69-percent repeat business after the first six weeks.

BIBLIOGRAPHY

Alcock, Joan P. *Food in the Ancient World.* London: Greenwood Press, 2006.

Alexander, William. *52 Loaves: One Man's Relentless Pursuit of Truth, Meaning, and a Perfect Crust.* Chapel Hill, NC: Algonquin, 2011.

Aretaeus. *The Extant Works of Aretaeus the Cappadocian.* Edited and translated by Francis Adams. London, 1856. Available on Google Books.

Aubrey, Alison. "Doctors Say Changes in Wheat Do Not Explain Rise of Celiac Disease." *The Salt,* September 26, 2013.

Belderok, B. "Developments in Bread-Making Processes." *Plants, Food, and Human Nutrition* 55 (1), 2000.

Blaser, Martin J. *Missing Microbes: How the Overuse of Antibiotics Is Fueling Our Modern Plagues.* New York: Henry Holt, 2014.

Bobrow-Strain, Anthony. *White Bread: A Social History of the Store-Bought Loaf.* Boston: Beacon Press, 2012.

Brillat-Savarin, Jean Anthelme. *The Physiology of Taste.* Translated by Ann Drayton. New York: Penguin, 1970.

Bronski, Peter, and Melissa McLean Jory. *The Gluten-Free Edge.* New York: The Experiment, 2012.

Brussow, Harald. *The Quest for Food: A Natural History of Eating.* New York: Springer, 2007.

Buchanan, David. *Taste, Memory: Forgotten Foods, Lost Flavors, and Why They Matter.* White River Junction, VT: Chelsea Green Publishing, 2012.

Catassi, Carlo. "Why Is Celiac Disease Endemic in People of the Sahara?" Letter. *Lancet* 354, 1999.

Child, Julia. *My Life in France.* New York: Anchor Reprint Edition, 2006.

Cicerone, C., et al. "Th17, Intestinal Microbiota and the Abnormal Immune Response in the Pathogenesis of Celiac Disease." *Gastroenterology Hepatology (Bed and Bench)* 8 (2), 2015.

Cortonesi, Alfio. "Self-Sufficiency and the Market: Rural and Urban Diet in the Middle Ages." *Food: A Culinary History from Antiquity to the Present.* Edited by Jean-Louis Flandrin and Massimo Montanari. Translated by Clarissa Botsford et al. New York: Columbia University Press, 1999.

Davidson, Alan, and Tom Jain. *The Oxford Companion to Food.* New York: Oxford University Press, 2006.

de Lorgeril, Mike, and P. Salen. "Gluten and Wheat Intolerance Today: Are Modern Wheat Strains Involved?" *International Journal of Food Science and Nutrition* 65 (5), August 2014.

Di Cagno, R. "Gluten-Free Sourdough Wheat Baked Goods Appear Safe for Young Celiac Patients: A Pilot Study." *Journal of Pediatric Gastroenterology and Nutrition* 51 (6), December 2010.

Dudley, Robert. *The Drunken Monkey: Why We Drink and Abuse Alcohol.* Berkeley: University of California Press, 2014.

Dupaigne, Bernard. *The History of Bread.* New York: Harry N. Abrams, 1999.

Eaton, Emily. *Growing Resistance: Canadian Farmers and the Politics of Genetically-Modified Wheat.* Winnipeg: University of Manitoba Press, 2013.

Fasano, A., et al. "Prevalence of Celiac Disease in At-Risk and Not-At-Risk Groups." *Frontiers in Celiac Disease.* Basel: Karger, 2008.

Federoff, Nina, and Nancy Marie Brown. *Mendel in the Kitchen.* Washington, DC: Joseph Henry, 2006.

Fernandez-Armesto, Felipe. *Near a Thousand Tables: A History of Food.* New York: The Free Press, 2002.

Fisher, M. F. K. *The Art of Eating.* New York: Wiley, 2004.

Freeman, Hugh. "Celiac Disease: A Disorder Emerging from Antiquity, Its Evolving Classification and Risk, and New Potential Treatment Paradigms." *Gut and Liver* 9 (1), January 2015.

Gandolfi, L., et al. "Prevalence of Celiac Disease Among Blood Donors in Brazil." *American Journal of Gastroenterology,* 2000.

Garnsey, Peter. *Cities, Peasants and Food in Classical Antiquity: Essays in Social and Economic History.* Edited by Walter Scheidel. Cambridge, UK: Cambridge University Press, 1998.

Gessendorfer, B., et al. "Preparation and Characterization of Enzymatically Hydrolyzed Prolamins from Wheat, Rye, and Barley as References for the Immunochemical Quantitation of Partially Hydrolyzed Gluten." *Analytical and Bioanalytical Chemistry* 395 (6), November 2009.

Gobetti, M., et al. "Sourdough Lactobacilli and Celiac Disease." *Food Microbiology* 2, April 24, 2007.

Green, Peter H. R. *Celiac Disease: A Hidden Epidemic.* New York: William Morrow, 2006.

Grigg, D. B. *The Agricultural Systems of the World: An Evolutionary Approach.* London: Cambridge University Press, 1974.

Gujral, N., et al. "Celiac Disease: Prevalence, Diagnosis, Pathogenesis and Treatment." *World Journal of Gastroenterology* 18 (42), November 14, 2012.

Harrison, Jim. *The Raw and the Cooked: Adventures of a Roving Gourmand.* Boston: Grove, 2002.

Harrison, Mark. *Disease and the Modern World: 1500 to the Present Day.* Cambridge, UK: Polity, 2004.

Herbst, Ron, and Sharon Herbst. *The Deluxe Food Lover's Companion.* New York: Barron's, 2015.

Hollon, Justin, et al., "Trace Gluten Contamination May Play a Role in Mucosal and Clinical Recovery in a Subgroup of Diet-Adherent Non-Responsive Celiac Disease Patients." *BMC Gastroenterology* 13 (40), 2013.

Hornsey, Ian S. *A History of Beer and Brewing.* Cambridge, UK: Royal Society of Chemistry Press, 2003.

How Can It Be Gluten Free Cookbook, The. America's Test Kitchen, 2014.

Jacob, H. E. *Six Thousand Years of Bread: Its Holy and Unholy History.* Translated by Richard and Clara Winston. New York: Lyons Press, 1997.

Junker, Yvonne, et al. "Wheat Amylase Trypsin Inhibitors Drive Intestinal Inflammation via Activation of Toll-like Receptor 4." *The Journal of Experimental Medicine* 209 (13), 2012.

Kaiser, Peter, et al. "Healthy or Detrimental? Physiological, Psychiatric, and Evolutionary Aspects of Beer Drinking." *Liquid Bread: Beer and Brewing in Cross-Cultural Perspective.* Oxford, NY: Berghahn Books, 2011.

Kaplan, Steven L. *The Bakers of Paris and the Bread Question 1700–1775.* Durham, NC: Duke University Press, 1996.

———. *The Famine Plot Persuasion in Eighteenth-Century France.* Transactions of the American Philosophical Society 72 (3), 1982. The American Philosophical Society: Independence Square, Philadelphia.

Kasarda, Donald. "Can an Increase in Celiac Disease Be Attributed to an Increase in the Gluten Content of Wheat as a Consequence of Wheat Breeding?" *Journal of Agricultural and Food Chemistry* 61, 2013.

Kiple, Kenneth. *The Cambridge World History of Food.* Cambridge, UK: Cambridge University Press, 2000.

Klintzman, Robert. *Am I My Genes? Confronting Fate and Family Secrets in an Age of Genetic Testing.* New York: Oxford University Press, 2012.

Koning, Fris, et al. "Gluten: A Two-Edged Sword." *Springer Seminars in Immunopathology* 27, 2005.

Kruizinga, Gilbert, et al. "Threshold for Gluten-Induced Mucosal Damage." *American Journal of Clinical Nutrition,* November 28, 2012.

Kurlansky, Mark. *Salt: A World History.* New York: Penguin, 2002.

Larsen, F. J., et al. "Dietary Inorganic Nitrate Improves Mitochondrial Efficiency in Humans." *Cellular Metabolism* 13 (2), February 2, 2011.

Laudan, Rachel. *Cuisine and Empire: Cooking in World History*. Berkeley: University of California Press, 2015.

Lauret, Eugenia, and Luis Rodrigo. "Celiac Disease and Autoimmune-Associated Conditions," *BioMed Research International:* Article ID 127589. Published online July 24, 2013.

Levi, Darline Gay. *The Ideas and Careers of Simon-Nicolas-Henri Linguet*. Carbondale: University of Illinois Press, 1980.

Libonati, Cleo. *Recognizing Celiac Disease: Signs, Symptoms, and Associated Disorders and Complications*. Fort Washington, PA: Gluten-Free Works Publishing, 2007.

Lieberman, Daniel E. *The Story of the Human Body: Evolution, Health, and Disease*. New York: Pantheon, 2013.

Liebling, A. J. "A Good Appetite." *Secret Ingredients: The New Yorker Book of Food and Drink*. Edited by David Remnick. New York: Modern Library, 2008.

Lock, Carrie. "Original Microbrews." *Science News*, October 2, 2004.

Mager, Anne Kelk. *Beer, Sociability, and Masculinity in South Africa*. Bloomington: Indiana University Press, 2010.

Marchant, John, et al. *Bread: A Slice of History*. Gloucester, UK: The History Press, 2007.

Matossian, Mary Kilbourne. *Poisons of the Past: Molds, Epidemics, and History*. New Haven: Yale University Press, 1989.

McGee, Harold. *On Food and Cooking: The Science and Lore of the Kitchen*. New York: Simon & Schuster, 2004.

McGovern, Patrick. *Uncorking the Past: The Quest for Wine, Beer, and Other Alcoholic Beverages*. Berkeley: University of California Press, 2009.

McGrew, M. C. "Ethanol Ingestion by Animals." *Liquid Bread: Beer and Brewing in Cross-Cultural Perspective*. Edited by Wulf Schiefenhovel and Helen MacBeth. New York: Berghahn Books, 2011.

Mermon, Z., et al. "An Orthodontic Retainer Preventing Remission in Celiac Disease." *Clinical Pediatrics* 52 (11), November 2013.

Molberg, O., et al. "Mapping of T-Cell Epitopes in Bread Wheat Ancestors: Implications for Celiac Disease." *Gastroenterology* 128 (2), February 2005.

Perkins, John. *Geopolitics and the Green Revolution: Wheat, Genes, and the Cold War*. Oxford, UK: Oxford University Press, 1997.

Perlmutter, David. *Grain Brain: The Surprising Truth About Wheat, Carbs, and Sugar—Your Brain's Silent Killers*. New York: Little, Brown, 2013.

"Pioneer in the Gluten-Free Diet: Willem-Karel Dicke 1905–1962, Over 50 Years of Gluten-Free Diet." *Gut* 34, 1993.

Pollack, Andrew. "As Celiac and Gluten Sensitivities Gain Prominence, Drug Companies Race to Find Treatments." *The New York Times*, April 28, 2015.

Pollan, Michael. *The Omnivore's Dilemma: A Natural History of Four Meals.* New York: Penguin, 2007.

Prance, Sir Ghillean, and Mark Nesbitt, eds. *The Cultivation of Plants.* New York: Routledge, 2005. Available on Google Books.

Proust, Marcel. *In Search of Lost Time, Volume 1: Swann's Way.* Translated by C. K. Scott Moncrief. New York: Modern Library, 2003.

Renfrew, J. M. "The Archeological Evidence for the Domestication of Plants: Methods and Problems." *The Domestication and Exploitation of Plants and Animals.* Edited by Peter J. Ucko and G. W. Dimbleby. New Brunswick, NJ: Aldine Transaction, 2007.

Rividen, Anna, et al. "Thirty Thousand Year Old Evidence of Plant Food Processing." *Proceedings of the National Academy of Sciences of the United States* 107 (44), November 2, 2010.

Rubel, William. *Bread: A Global History.* London: Reaktion Books, 2011.

Rubio-Tapia, et al. "Increased Prevalence and Mortality in Undiagnosed Celiac Disease." *Gastroenterology* 137 (1), July 2009.

Safran Foer, Jonathan. *Eating Animals.* New York: Little, Brown, 2009.

Samsel, Anthony, and Stephanie Seneff. "Glyphosate, Pathways to Modern Diseases II: Celiac Sprue and Gluten Intolerance." *Interdisciplinary Toxicology,* 2013.

Sapone, Anna, et al. "Spectrum of Gluten-Related Disorders: Consensus on New Nomenclature and Classification." *BMC Medicine* 10 (13), 2012.

Schiefenhovel, Wolf, and Helen MacBeth. "Introduction: Assembling Perspectives on Beer." *Liquid Bread: Beer and Brewing in Cross-Cultural Perspective.* Edited by Wulf Schiefenhovel and Helen MacBeth. New York: Berghahn Books, 2011.

Scott-Mumby, Keith. *Fire in the Belly: The Surprising Cause of Most Diseases, States of Mind, and Aging Processes.* Reno, NV: Mother Whale Publishing, 2012.

Semrad, Carol. "Refractory Celiac Disease: What Is It? What to Do?" University of Chicago Celiac Disease Center, *Impact* 1 (3), 2008.

Serventi, Silvano, and Francoise Sabban. *Pasta: The Story of a Universal Food.* New York: Columbia University Press, 2000.

Simmonds, N. W. *Evolution of Crop Plants.* London: Longman, 1976.

Simoni, Theresa, trans. "Gluten Content in Beer." SLV, 2005.

Sinclair, Thomas, and Carol Sinclair. *Bread, Beer, and the Seeds of Change: Agriculture's Imprint on World History.* Oxford and Cambridge, UK: CABI, 2010.

Standage, Tom. *An Edible History of Humanity.* London: Walker and Co., 2007.

_____. *A History of the World in 6 Glasses.* London: Walker and Co., 2005.

Stevens, L., and M. Rashid. "Gluten-Free and Regular Foods: A Cost Comparison." *Canadian Journal of Dietetic Practice and Research* 69 (3), Fall 2008.

Stika, Hans-Peter. "Beer in Prehistoric Europe." *Liquid Bread: Beer and Brewing in Cross-Cultural Perspective.* Edited by Wulf Schiefenhovel and Helen MacBeth. New York: Berghahn Books, 2011.

Symons, Michael. *A History of Cooks and Cooking.* Champaign: University of Illinois Press, 1998.

Tannahill, Reay. *Food in History.* New York: Broadway Books, 1995.

This, Herve. *Molecular Gastronomy: Exploring the Science of Flavor.* New York: Columbia University Press, 2006.

Thomson, Jennifer A. *Seeds for the Future: The Impact of Genetically Modified Crops on the Environment.* Ithaca, NY: Comstock Publishing Associates, 2006.

Tommasini, Alberto, et al. "Ages of Celiac Disease: From Changing Environment to Improved Diagnostics." *World Journal of Gastroenterology* 17 (32), 2011.

Toussaint-Samat, Maguelonne. *A History of Food.* Translated by Anthea Bell. Cambridge, MA: Blackwell, 1992.

Tovoli, F., et al. "Clinical and Diagnostic Aspects of Gluten-Related Disorders." *World Journal of Clinical Cases* 3 (3), March 16, 2015.

van Berge-Henegouwen, G. P., and C. J. Mulder. "Pioneer in the Gluten-Free Diet: Willem-Karel Dicke 1905–1962, Over 50 Years of Gluten-Free Diet." *Gut* 34 (11), November 1993.

van den Broeck, Hetty C. "Presence of Celiac Disease Epitopes in Modern and Old Hexaploid Wheat Varieties: Wheat Breading May Have Contributed to Increasing Prevalence of Celiac Disease." *Theoretical Applied Genetics* 121, 2010.

van der Zee, Henri. *The Hunger Winter: Occupied Holland 1944–1945.* Lincoln: University of Nebraska Press, 1998.

Velasquez-Manoff, Moises. "Who Has the Guts for Gluten?" *The New York Times,* February 23, 2013.

Volta, U., et al. "Non-Celiac Gluten-Sensitivity: Questions Still to Be Answered Despite Increasing Awareness." *Cellular & Molecular Immunology* 10, 2013.

Wilson, Bee. *Consider the Fork: A History of How We Cook and Eat.* New York: Basic Books, 2012.

INDEX

bread (*cont'd*):
from peas, beans, acorns, 97
purity of, 82, 82n
"tree bread," 97
yeast, origin of, 54
breakfast cereals, 38, 79
Brewers Clarex, 143, 147
Brewery Brunehaut ale, 65, 66
Brillat-Savarin, Jean Anthelme, 39, 40
Bronski, Peter, 161–162
brown rice flour, 131
Buchanan, David, 157
buckwheat, 122, 132, 246n
buckwheat crêpes, 122
buckwheat flour, 95n, 120–123, 123n
buckwheat pancakes, 123, 124
Butler's (restaurant), 110–111

Cain, Nancy, 187n
cake, 171–175, 224
Canada, wheat and herbicides, 81–82
canola oil, 92
caramel coloring, 38
Carlsberg beer, 146, 147
cassava, 94, 124
Celia Saison ale, 137, 139, 207
"celiac," use of term, 163–164
celiac disease, 7, 8, 13, 236n–237n, 242n
in Amish household, 217–220
antibody results, 36, 36n
author's first bout with, 7–10
bacteria in the gut, 85, 86, 118n, 244n
cancer risk and, 35, 238n
causes, 75–80, 83n, 85
chemical and emotional withdrawal, 37, 46–47
in children, 35, 217–220
cross-contamination, 37, 106, 153
detoxification, 35–36
diagnosis, 11, 18–23
endoscopies in asymptomatic patients, 180
epidemiology of, 34, 34n, 85–86, 88
family history, 32
genetic predisposition to, 33, 34, 238n
genetic test for, 34–35

history of, 14n, 15–16
hygiene theory, 85–87
intolerances to other foods and, 37–38
leaky gut syndrome, 214
Marsh scale, 23
nutritional deficiencies from malabsorption, 37
pondering extreme scenarios, 36–37
"refractory" disease, 36
risk factors, 33
toxicity threshold, 8, 235n
villous atrophy, 12
Celiac Disease Foundation Conference, 203–204, 249n
"celiac iceberg," 87–88, 245n
cereals, 38, 79
chapati, 123
Charlemagne, 207–208
chestnuts, 97, 98
chickpea (garbanzo bean) flour, 95n, 97, 98, 121
chickpeas, 122
Child, Julia, 100, 107
Chinese cuisine, 114
Chopped (TV show), 61n
cider, 67, 117–118, 139, 159
citric acid, 38
Clarex, 143, 147
commercial farm share (CSA), 49, 59–60, 127, 128, 135, 215
Complete Italian Vegetarian Cookbook (Bishop), 99, 187
cookbooks, 91, 102, 121, 186–188, 193, 194, 218. *See also The How Can It Be Gluten Free Cookbook*
cookies, 101, 196–197
cooking gluten-free, 45, 60, 91–103, 133, 135, 231–232. *See also* gluten-free diet; gluten-free foods
Cook's Country (television show), 186
Cook's Illustrated (magazine), 186
corn, 120, 131, 131n, 247n
cornmeal, 98
Craft Brew Alliance, 143, 144
crêpes, 100, 101, 122, 125, 198, 199
croissants, 197
cross-contamination, 37, 106, 153